MW00748396

MEDIA IN THE AGE
OF MARKETIZATION

THE HAMPTON PRESS COMMUNICATION SERIES

Popular Culture
John A. Lent, *series editor*

Jewish Jesters: A Study in American Popular Comedy
Arthur Asa Berger

Media in the Age of Marketization
Graham Murdock & Janet Wasko (editors)

Indian Popular Cinema: Industry, Ideology and Consciousness
Manjunath Pendakur

MEDIA IN THE AGE OF MARKETIZATION

edited by

Graham Murdock
Loughborough University, UK

Janet Wasko
University of Oregon

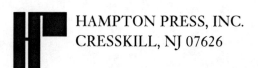

HAMPTON PRESS, INC.
CRESSKILL, NJ 07626

Copyright © 2007 by Hampton Press, Inc.

All rights reserved. No part of this publication may be reproduced, stored in a retrieval system, or transmitted in any form or by any means, electronic, mechanical, photocopying, microfilming, recording, or otherwise, without permission of the publisher.

Printed in the United States of America
Library of Congress Cataloging-in-Publication Data

Media in the age of marketization / edited by Graham Murdock, Janet Wasko
    p. cm. -- (The Hampton Press communication series : popular culture)
  Includes index.
  ISBN 1-57273-730-1 (hardbound) -- ISBN 1-57273-731-X (paperbound)
1. Communication in marketing. 2. Communication and culture. 3. Communication policy. 4. Communication--Economic aspects. 5. Free enterprise--Social aspects. I. Murdock, Graham. II. Wasko, Janet.

  HF5415.123.M43 2007
  302.3--dc22
                              2007017277

Hampton Press, Inc.
23 Broadway
Cresskill, NJ 07626

CONTENTS

Section Four—Resistances:
Rebuilding The Commons

ACKNOWLEDGEMENTS

The editors would like to thank Yeong Doo Moon, University of Oregon, for his work on the subject index for this volume. Our gratitude also goes to Barbara Bernstein and John Lent for their support of the project.

INTRODUCTION

With the Hopes that our World is built on they were utterly out of touch. They denied that the moon was Stilton, they denied she was even Dutch. They denied that Wishes were Horses; they denied that a Pig had Wings. So we worshipped the Gods of the Market who promised these beautiful things.

Rudyard Kipling

In 1919, Rudyard Kipling, remembered now as a apologist of empire, was grieving for his son who had been declared missing in action on the Western Front, one more casualty of the world's first mechanized and global war. His poem, "The Gods of the Copybook Headings," from which the lines quoted above are taken, was a bitter attack on the constellations of power that had precipitated the carnage and the lies and delusions they had mobilized to recruit volunteers to their cause. It is the anguished cry of a disappointed conservative.

Confronting the same devastated landscape, those with more radical convictions looked for ways of curbing capital. Against the odds and in the face of concerted armed opposition, including troops sent by the major Western powers, the Bolsheviks seized power in Russia and set about creating a modern industrial economy without capitalism. Elsewhere socialist insurgencies and insurrections were quickly crushed, and critics of capital settled for carving out an enlarged public sphere through varying combinations of public ownership and public interest regulation. Across Europe, public service institutions, funded out of the public purse and charged with providing the cultural resources for full citizenship, dominated the operation of the crucial new medium of broadcasting. Telecommunications facilities were incorporated into state monopolies. In the United States, although the concerted battle to establish a viable noncommercial broadcasting sector was ultimately unsuccessful, advertising-financed stations found themselves faced with a series of public interest requirements designed to ensure a more level playing field in the competition for ideas. The monopoly private telephone operator was obliged to abide by the principle of universal service, delivering affordable facilities to anyone who wanted them rather than cherry-picking the most profitable markets.

These initiatives, though continually threatened, survived into the last quarter of the twentieth century, and despite their limitations, they did provide a significant counter to the ever-upwards march of private ownership, market relations, and commodification in other key areas of communication and culture—book publishing, the press, the film industry, and the movie industry. They provided a working alternative to the untrammeled institutional power of capital and promoted a counter view of central purposes of public communication. In place of capital's incessant celebration of the sanctity of individual choice and of markets as the primary sphere of personal freedom and self-actualization, they insisted that the ideals of democracy required people to acknowledge their common membership of political and moral communities and defend initiatives that contributed to the common good, even when they entailed a reduction of choices in the realm of private consumption.

It is this always fragile social contract that has been progressively undercut and dismantled by the worldwide pursuit of marketization over the last two-and-a-half decades. This movement has involved a concerted institutional and ideological attack on the established organization of public culture. Institutionally, it has been pursued through four major interventions employed in varying combinations: privatization (the sale of public assets to private investors); liberalization (opening previously monopoly or restricted markets to new entrants); the re-gearing of regulation (away from the defense of the public interest, however defined, to the promotion of "fair" competition); and corporatization (urging or obliging publicly financed organizations to seek additional sources of income and to maximize the market value of their holdings). Ideologically, it has been underpinned by an elaborated consumerism celebrating the pleasures of personalized lifestyles and aggressively promoted by an advertising and marketing system that has employed deep sponsorship, product placement, and viral marketing to penetrate every available social and cultural space, from school corridors to art exhibitions and video games.

Marketization is a global movement. It has taken full advantage of the growing disillusion with state management and public ownership marked by the collapse of the Soviet Union and the decisions by the Indian and Chinese governments to re-open relations with the capitalist world system. Elsewhere, countries have been given little choice as major lenders have placed marketization at the heart of the structural readjustment programs required as a condition of obtaining loans and aid.

It is also a movement that coincides with the accelerating shift in the center of productive gravity in capitalism's core regions, away from industrial manufacture and towards command over the creation, ownership, and deployment of strategic informational and symbolic resources. "Information capitalism" is too narrow a term to cover the full scope of what is involved in this shift. Consequently, we prefer to describe this emerging system as "cultural capitalism," using "culture" here in its most general sense to cover both the meanings systems that societies deploy to define, explain, and control all the various artifacts, performance, and rituals through which these understandings are expressed and put to work. As the central site on which collective meanings are constructed, communicated, and contested, media systems have been in the vanguard of marketization.

This book then sets out to explore the notion that marketization is the central force that is currently restructuring the communications landscape and to examine the consequences of this development for the constitution of public culture. The contributors analyze the core institutional processes of marketization and assess their impact on the structure and operations of media and communications systems around the world over the last two decades. The chapters are grouped into sections organized around four key themes; consolidation, incorporation, globalization, and resistance.

This collection is dedicated to Herbert I. Schiller, who inspired many of us with his relentless and dogged critique of capitalism's annexation of public communication and his unwavering commitment to highlighting the resources for hope provided by dissident cultural workers and popular resistance. The main focus of this volume—the marketization of media and information—was always at the heart of his work. Although marketization and its related trends have advanced considerably since his death in 2000, he would not have been surprised by many of the developments discussed in this volume.

CONSOLIDATIONS:
LIMITING PUBLIC EXPRESSION

The first section details three of the main ways in which corporations have cemented and extended their influence over contemporary communications and culture under marketization. In the first chapter, Eileen Meehan describes a significant example of media marketization by focusing on commercial television in the United States. The dismantling of media regulation and antitrust law since the 1970s has allowed an integration of previous oligopolies into five transindustrial conglomerates that control television as well as other media resources. The Big Five—Time Warner, Disney, General Electric, News Corporation, and Viacom—have been allowed to intertwine their interests in commercial television through programming contracts, affiliation contracts, and joint ventures, thus softening competition and rivalry and masking a functional integration of the oligopolists.

Meehan examines the Big Five's structures and alliances by looking at broadcast television's old oligopoly and dissecting the new configuration. The Big Five are described in terms of internal markets and corporate synergy, as well as external alliances. The discussion offers an analytic model to assess the overall effect of synergy, which is employed to recirculate, recycle, repackage, reversion, and redeploy the intellectual properties that a company already owns.

Rick Maxwell's chapter is inspired directly by Herb Schiller's work on marketing research and presents a "Schillerian" analysis of marketing. He draws on power structure analysis, which identifies and analyzes key players and dominant institutions; systemic analysis, which interprets the power structure as an inseparable part of the imperialist system and therein contextualizes the aims and actions of key players; and prospective analysis of democratic forces, which assesses challenges to the power structure that attempt to create nondominating forms of communication, including marketing research.

Finally, Jim McGuigan presents a multidimensional analysis of the Millennium Dome exposition, explaining the decisive role of corporate sponsorship. The study uses a combination of political economy, textual interpretation, and research on mediation and visitor experience, in effect, analyzing the interrelated dimensions of production, representation, and consumption. McGuigan's argument further substantiates Herb Schiller's thesis concerning "the corporate takeover of public expression," and how corporations not only have commandeered the communications and cultural industries, but also have invaded the public sector, McGuigan concludes that ". . . the New Millennium Experience represented a very limited and constrained space for critical reflection on time and place due to the overweening presence of a corporate agenda."

INCORPORATIONS:
CAPTURING PUBLIC CULTURE

The next section is directly related to McGuigan's concerns and examines how corporate strategies and rhetorics have restructured core arenas of public culture. In the first chapter of the section, Vincent Mosco draws on Herb Schiller's 1989 book, *Culture Inc.*, which demonstrated the value of a political economy approach to culture, as well as his notable scholarly versatility, by examining struggles over public space in New York City. Mosco's discussion builds on this work by taking up the political economy of one of the most significant spaces in the United States today, the site of the attacks on the World Trade Center or ground zero. Building on the view that a community's economic life cannot be separated from its symbolic content, Mosco turns to the case of New York's ground zero and what we can learn from the political, economic, and cultural struggles over who will control it. He traces the power politics that contributed to the construction of the Trade Center and details the redevelopment of the WTC district that was widely touted as a victory for free markets and private enterprise.

Dan Schiller extends the analysis of incorporations with an historical look at telecommunications policies and developments. For nearly a century, industrial, financial, and commercial telecommunications users have played a formative, and at key points, a determining, role in U.S. telecommunications system development. Schiller traces the history of telecommunications that has been written largely from the supply side and has stressed the role of the carriers that provide society with access to different network systems and services. However, the chapter also describes and documents the demand side of the telecommunications equation. In other words, business users have repeatedly made critical contributions to the structure and policy of telecommunications.

In the next chapter, Oscar Gandy focuses on the ways in which corporate control of media and other cultural institutions helps to reproduce inequality through the formation of an isolated racial class. He employs a political economy of communication that is sensitive to the role that identity plays in both production and consumption. Gandy observes that this racial class, composed largely of African Americans, is likely to take shape within the confines of a hermetically sealed and hopelessly "corrupted" public sphere that is defined to a great extent by advertising. The chapter discusses consumption and identity formation, tastes and preferences, the role of advertising, segmentation, and segregation, and the black public sphere. Gandy urges us to challenge the dominant paradigm of media policy research that sees no alternative to a marketplace logic in the sphere of information.

GLOBALIZATIONS:
BREACHING THE WALLS

This section begins with two chapters examining important aspects of the emerging global marketplace for culture and information and concludes with a case study of China as a key nation in the emerging global political economy. John Sinclair reviews the cultural imperialism perspective and examines the reasons why "cultural globalization" emerged as a more valid way of conceptualizing how cultural influence works. He also takes into account how certain key assumptions and concerns of the cultural imperialism approach nevertheless have persisted into the present, including the belief that cultural globalization is really a process of "Americanization." Finally, by way of a case study, the chapter provides an assessment of the impact of marketization upon the television industry of Latin America, a major world region long subject to the hegemony of the United States. Sinclair calls for revisiting the world in which cultural imperialism was a plausible paradigm, so that a baseline might be established that can assess both the real-world changes of the last few decades as well as the theoretical responses that have been made to them.

Meanwhile, Jane Kelsey examines the globalization of cultural policy-making and the difficulties of defending cultural space against the offensive policies of neoliberal globalization. The chapter carefully details the problems of subordinating cultural policy to international trade agreements. Kelsey challenges ". . . the seductive belief that contradictions between culture and globalized capitalism can be resolved through technical exclusions and exceptions or a competition of legal texts." She concludes that a more sophisticated strategy is needed to confront neoliberal globalization—one in which resistance to trade agreements is just one tactic in a much broader struggle.

This section concludes with an important case study of changes in the public media sector of the world's most populous nation. Yuezhi Zhao presents an overview of the implications of marketization in China, where the media continue to herald informatization and digitalization and embrace the information society utopia with almost the same enthusiasm as it once did with the communist utopia. However, the actual political and social dimensions of the Chinese "information revolution" are much darker. Zhao argues that China's information revolution in the age of marketization and globalization is profoundly antidemocratic. She notes that this state-controlled and market-driven revolution is inspired by a deep-rooted technocratic rationality and driven primarily by the convergent interests of domestic bureaucratic and international corporate capital, along with the consumption priorities of China's urban middle classes. Although this "revolution" has empowered a super-wired elite, it has been premised upon the exclusion of the majority of the population from meaningful political participation in shaping the direction of the country's reform process and is intrinsically connected to the deepening economic inequality and pervasive social injustice facing millions across China. Zhao concludes that "The resulting explosive social tensions, rather than the continued aggregation of television sets, mobile phones, and Internet accounts, are likely to shape the course of Chinese history in the twenty-first century."

RESISTANCES:
REBUILDING THE COMMONS

The volume concludes by looking at developments promoting alternatives to greater marketization, specifically focusing on new social movements and new communication networks. In the final chapter, Sasha Costanza-Chock considers progressive efforts to resist marketization and outlines the continuous and seemingly unstoppable growth in progressive tendencies that are challenging further marketization of cultural production. Costanza-Chock discusses the globalizing tendencies of these developments, including the worldwide distribution of audiovisual materials and software, which attempts to undermine the so-called "intellectual property rights" regime; the linkage of mass movements that resist the enclosure of the knowledge commons; the progressive and international stance of workers and unions in communications industries, as well as various reformist organizations that aim to change state or corporate communications practice or policy; and, finally, the growth of local autonomous media production that is increasingly linked in global networks. Despite threats from various sources, he argues that a transnational movement around popular control of communication must be nurtured as a key element in the struggle to establish alternatives to the ongoing marketization of media and cultural production.

Both marketization and the resistances to it are growing every day. This volume offers a provisional inventory of key processes and exemplars during the formative period of this process. Its intention is to offer a map of the field of engagement, to detail the main forces in play, to make clear what the stakes in this struggle are, and to invite intellectuals and activists who care about the future of public culture and democratic communication to push the debate forward by contributing new evidence, case studies, and proposals for intervention and change.

SECTION ONE

CONSOLIDATIONS

Limiting Public Expression

CHAPTER ONE

DEREGULATION AND INTEGRATED OLIGOPOLIES

Television at the Turn of the Century

Eileen R. Meehan

Whether termed neoconservative or neoliberal, deregulationist policies in capitalist nations have increased economic centralization over the last twenty years in terms of both national and global markets (Gerbner et al., 1996; Schiller, 2000; Streeter, 1996). Arguing that deregulation would "let the market decide," neoconservatives removed the restraints that once separated oligopolized markets, allowing the oligopolists to decide for themselves what they wanted to do. The companies in question have typically expanded their holdings across industries, thus collapsing multiple oligopolies controlling distinct industries into a few oligopolies spanning integrated industries. With no constraints keeping oligopolists separated, firms have joined forces in contractual relationships and joint ventures, softening rivalries among them as their vested interests intertwine. In effect, such marketization fosters concentration in ownership and coordination among owners, thereby insulating owners against demand. This outcome is the precise opposite of a fully free, competitive market. Whereas neoconservative rhetoric glorifies the free market, neo-conservative policies favor transindustrial conglomerates using their corporate structure, market share, and alliances to centralize industries in a mega-oligopoly (Bagdikian, 2000; Bettig and Hall, 2003; McChesney, 1999).

This chapter examines that through a case study of neoconservatives' dismantling of broadcast regulation, antitrust law, and cable regulation for commercial television in the United States. In the late 1940s through the 1970s, liberal regulation organized separate oligopolies in broadcast networking, cable delivery, cable channels, and television production. From 1980 on, neoconservative deregulation has fostered the integration of these oligopolies under the aegis of five transindustrial conglomerates: AOL Time Warner, Disney Company, General Electric (GE), News Corporation, and Viacom.[1] Further, policies allowing the Big Five to intertwine their interests through programming contracts, affiliation contracts, and joint ventures has softened rivalry, suggesting that the appearance of oligopoly may mask a functional integration of the oligopolists. By examining television's Big Five's structures and alliances, we will see how this works. But to understand the current status quo, however, we begin with a consideration of broadcast television's old oligopoly, then trace the new oligopoly, next present brief profiles of each of the Big Five in terms of internal markets and corporate synergy, and finally discuss external alliances among the Big Five.

WITHOUT NOSTALGIA:
THE OLD BROADCAST OLIGOPOLY

By 1929, advertisers, advertising agencies, and national radio networks had worked out the fundamental relations and markets that would constitute the broadcasting industry until deregulation in the 1980s.[2] During that period, two companies—the Radio Corporation of America (RCA) and the Columbia Broadcasting System (CBS)—dominated national broadcasting. Primarily owned by General Electric (GE), Westinghouse, and American Telegraph & Telephone (AT&T), RCA operated two networks under auspices of its National Broadcasting Corporation (NBC). The third network was operated by the Columbia Broadcasting System owned by William Paley, heir to his father's fortune made in cigars. Between 1929 and 1936, internecine struggles between GE, Westinghouse, and AT&T combined with governmental investigations plus public concern over the "radio octopus" yielded an independent RCA running two networks to CBS' one.

This duopoly persisted until 1941 when the FCC ordered RCA to divest itself of one radio network. Even as RCA appealed that decision, it continued researching television. In 1943, RCA sold half of its stations and one of its networks to Edward J. Noble, who had made his fortune in Lifesaver candies. The new oligopoly gave one network each to three companies: RCA, CBS, and the new American Broadcasting Company (ABC). ABC got the less desirable radio station from each of NBC's market-by-market dyads but still mounted a profitable operation. This changed with the end of World War II, when both RCA and CBS innovated television— RCA with an all-electronic system of monochrome television operating on the very high frequencies, CBS with a partially mechanical system of color television using the ultra high frequencies. By the 1947-1948 television season, ABC was scrambling to gain some purchase in the new medium.

The radio oligopoly set the pattern for the television oligopoly, with television effectively dominated by RCA and CBS, which had schedules and advertisers in place as well as tremendous investments in the development of television technologies. For much of the 1950s and 1960s, industry pundits joked that television was a three-way race in which ABC came in fourth. Ironically, the fourth networks mounted first by Dumont and then by Kaiser never made it into the joke.

Initially, RCA, CBS, and ABC had been allowed to produce their own television programming (in-house). However, the Federal Communication Commission (FCC) worried that such an internal market would encourage networks to favor their own series over those produced by independent firms or by movie studios. Partly because television was believed to have decreased box office revenues for movies,[3] allowing film studios to contract for television series seemed an appropriate way to foster continued competition between television and film. (This notion that industries or technologies competed is worth noting, because it undergirded much of the FCC's later regulation of cable.) Treating the film studios as just another content producer, the FCC promulgated regulations to sever television production from television networking operations. This guaranteed that ABC, CBS, and NBC would not dominate the market for programs. However, the regulations did not produce a fully competitive market for television programming because networking was deadlocked by ABC, CBS, and NBC. As gatekeepers, the networks generally kept the number of program suppliers between seven and ten, including selected film studios, that controlled the production of made-for-television movies (Cantor, 1980; Gitlin, 1983).

In the 1970s, FCC decisions about cable television were driven by network lobbying, National Association of Broadcasters lobbying, concerns about competition between broadcasting and cable, and the local monopoly in cable service that each system operator enjoyed. As cable operators moved into cities and as more cable systems were owned by a single firm, the FCC worried about the possible threat that cable television might pose to "free TV." Network campaigns against cable focused on such putative horrors as Americans being forced to pay cable fees in order to watch World Series baseball games. In California, CBS mounted a successful ballot initiative to save free television.

But if cable was a threat to broadcast television, cable also faced a threat from telephony. Historically, AT&T had forced local telephone companies to join with it in order to gain access to long distance service and switching technologies. This policy gave the local firm a monopoly over its immediate area and forced its assimilation into the Bell System. With the system owning the poles upon which cable operators wanted to string their wires, the possibility of AT&T assimilating cable into its fold was truly a clear and present danger.

The upshot of all these concerns and regulations was the articulation of cable television as an industry distinct from broadcast television and telephony but with some similar functions. Like telephone companies, cable companies were common carriers relying on wired systems to carry signals. But where telephone companies carried individual calls from point to point, cable companies distributed channels, which carried programming, from a central location to every home on the cable. Because the companies operating cable systems neither owned channels nor produced content, they depended on other firms to do those tasks. This generated a separate market for cable channels, ensuring that cable system owners relied on an external market that they entered as buyers seeking channels to create a menu of channels for their systems. As cable systems across the nation increasingly came under the ownership of a relatively few owners, these multiple cable system operators (MSOs) tended to build a single menu for their multiple systems, thus achieving operational and cost efficiencies in terms of national distribution of cable channels. In this way, cable systems reproduced the appearance of localism in tandem with a focus on national distribution, thus following broadcasting's pattern.

FCC regulations positioned cable systems to compete with broadcast stations and networks. Broadcasters successfully lobbied the FCC for some protections, including the requirement that a local cable system must carry all local television stations. This ensured that stations affiliated with the networks would appear on cable, thus ensuring that cable systems would carry the three national networks. Regulations did not address the role of the film studios as program producers for either broadcast or cable television.

The cumulative effect of regulation was the articulation of three separate industries—telephony, broadcast television, and cable television—with delivery systems controlled by separate firms. Telephony was monopolized by AT&T, which used internal markets to supply all its needs. In contrast, the cable and broadcast television industries were comprised of multiple, external markets. In the market for television programming, studios and independent producers hawked their wares to networks and channels. In a separate market, cable system owners put together their menus by selecting from available channels. In yet another market, networks sold time slots and audiences to advertisers with prices based on ratings produced by the A. C. Neilsen Company (ACN). In the market for ratings, advertisers and networks shared a demand for measurements of "good" consumers, but given the link between numbers of good consumers and prices for ad slots, disagreed on how generous the estimates of numbers of viewers should be.

In cable's early years, these last two markets were problematic. Advertisers were reluctant to advertise on cable channels until cable systems reached at least 50 percent of broadcast networks' reach. Similarly reluctant to measure cable channels was ACN, until cable channel mogul Ted Turner paid for separate numbers showing TBS' performance with the ACN sample. As these problems resolved in the late 1970s, cable channels and MSOs were poised to fully integrate themselves into broadcast television. Only FCC regulation and antitrust laws stood in the way.

As we look back without nostalgia to these "glorious days of yesteryear,"[4] we can see how the state fostered the creation of external markets by requiring networks and channels to deal with program suppliers and by requiring firms that owned cable systems to deal with firms that owned cable channels. The result was by no means the full, free competition favored by Adam Smith, but rather a series of closed markets in which a few buyers traded with few sellers. Through regulation, the state maintained the separation of cable owners and network owners. This was naturalized in the rhetoric of the period as fostering competition between free television and cable television, thus ensuring that the American people got the programming that they truly wanted either for free or for a reasonable price.

THE NEW OLIGOPOLY
WITHOUT ROSE-COLORED GLASSES

The same rhetoric was redeployed to explain deregulation: the erasure of onerous rules that had once limited competition would magically produce a fully competitive marketplace filled with choices, that is, hundreds of channels and thousands of programs serving every taste possible. By breaching the separations between cable and broadcast television as well as between cable and telephony, the government would ensure that consumers would enjoy the widest selection at the lowest prices. It is worth noting that much of deregulatory legislation was written by lobbyists and other representatives of the companies and industries to be deregulated. With Congress passing deregulatory legislation and regulatory agencies adopting deregulatory agendae under the administrations of Ronald Reagan, George H. W. Bush, Bill Clinton, and George W. Bush, media corporations began transforming themselves into transindustrial conglomerates—in essence, into collections of internal markets that could be fed using intellectual properties already owned.

Over the last twenty years, deregulation has melded broadcast and cable television into a single industry in which the same companies can control program production, broadcast networks, cable channels, and cable systems as well as other media. Let's take a brief look at the five companies that control the major networks, which are, at this writing: Disney for ABC; Viacom for CBS and UPN; General Electric for NBC; News Corporation for FOX; and AOL Time Warner for WB.

THE WONDERFUL WORLD OF DISNEY TELEVISION[2]

Disney's operations in television center on ownership of one broadcast television network (ABC), four cable channels (ABC Family, The Disney Channel, SoapNet, and Toon Disney), and equity in nine joint ventures in cable that will be discussed later. Disney produces and distributes television programming under three labels: Buena Vista Productions, Touchstone Television, and Walt Disney Television. The last brand name is closely guarded by the company. Products with that imprimatur are generally limited to the Disney Channel, Toon Disney, and ABC. In 2002-2003, most dramatic or comedic series on ABC were produced in-house although Disney had agreements with and produced programming for Viacom and News Corporation.

These production agreements and joint ventures are particularly interesting given Disney's commitment to corporate synergy under the leadership of chief executive officer Michael Eisner. Since the mid-1980s, Eisner has rebuilt Disney to expand and integrate operations in film, television, radio, publishing (books, magazines, comic books, and music), audio products, home video, theatrical production, theme parks, resorts, licensing and merchandising, educational products, and so on. For Eisner, the goal is to use Disney's structure to promote each of its major projects across every level of operations. Disney particularly uses theatrically released animations as platforms from which to launch a plethora of events, media artifacts, and licensed merchandise.

How this works is demonstrated by Wasko's intensive discussion of Disney's activities for the 27 June 1997 release of *Hercules* (Wasko, 2002). She notes that 100 manufacturers held licenses to produce 6,000 to 7,000 distinct items, which were then stocked in Disney stores, available from Disney Online or Disney Catalog, and saturated throughout the retail system. While these items earn revenues for Disney prior to the film's release, they also encourage people to see the film. Disney itself crafted a multimedia show that toured twenty cities in five months, offering eleven attractions that promoted the film, its characters, the games created by Disney Interactive based on the film, the *Hercules* web site, and so forth. The company licensed the film to Field Enterprises as *Hercules on Ice*, the first of the eighteen Disney on Ice productions to proceed its film. Across the retail system, a plethora of picture books, coloring books, sticker books, and sing-a-long cassettes joined the official soundtrack, the official "art of" book costing fifty dollars, dolls, play sets, tee shirts, collectibles, backpacks, plastic cups, party gear, caps, and other licensed trinkets on the shelves — again, simultaneously earning revenues and promoting *Hercules*.

The film also provided fodder for Disney's television operations, with the Disney channel running *Movie Surfers Go Inside Disney's Hercules* and *Disney's Hercules Strikes Manhattan*. The latter included footage from Disney's Hercules Electrical Parade in New York City, which was also covered by the cable channel E!, co-owned by Disney and cable MSO Comcast. ABC ran a live-action special on *Hercules* in prime time, featuring the actors who voiced main roles and Michael Bolton who performed the film's theme song. A&E's signature program, *Biography*, offered a profile of the mythical Hercules.

Hercules continues to feed Disney operations as the company's Web site reveals. The film can be purchased in five versions: VHS, VHS Gold Collection, VHS Spanish, DVD, and DVD Gold Collection from the Disney Web site. Also available is a prequel, *Hercules from Zero to Hero* on VHS, a six inch doll of Hercules seated in his "mighty hero cycle," chunky action figures, 11.5-inch-tall action figures, and a CD-ROM animated storybook. The live stage show *Hercules — A Muse-ical Comedy*, which features songs from the film, is performed on Disney cruise ships. By using its intellectual properties to feed multiple operations over the years, Disney avoids the costs of having to create new ideas for each of its operations.

These patterns of corporate behavior — transindustrial conglomeration, synergistic reuse of intellectual properties, and alliances with other oligopolists — repeat with subtle differences across the rest of television's Big Five. Our discussion of the remaining four will focus on those individuated repetitions of the patterns.

GENERAL ELECTRIC: FROM FINANCE TO TECHNOLOGY WITH TELEVISION ON THE SIDE

GE's primary foci have been in finance and technology with close ties to the American military. Operations in these areas, which range from commercial insurance to civilian power systems to nuclear triggers, earn over half of GE's revenues. Given the size of the company and the scope of its operations, GE's entertainment holdings appear almost as an afterthought. However, GE is moving to expand them by buying the Universal Studios film and television productions currently owned by Vivendi, a transnational conglomerate with holdings in entertainment and utilities.

GE's television operations begin with it 31% stake in SES Global, the largest provider of satellite services in the world whose clients include ". . . the broadcast and cable TV industries, as well as broadcast radio . . . ,"[5] thus giving GE a vested interest in the harmonious integration of technologies once seen as competitive. Under the NBC umbrella, GE earns 5.4% of its revenues and owns the NBC Television Network, NBC Studios, the Spanish-language network Telemundo, and two Spanish-language cable channels, MUN2 and Telemundo Internacional. Other cable operations include the BET channels, Bravo, and six joint ventures in cable channels, discussed below. In programming, like the rest of the Big Five, GE requires that independent producers cede their copyrights as the price for running their shows (Compaine and Gomery 2000). Thus, the closing credits identify such programs as co-productions with NBC Studios.

GE's television operations serve the historical function that programming fulfilled in network radio: motivating corporations to buy equipment and services and motivating individuals to purchase home electronics. GE's networking, programming, and channel operations provide a reason for companies to buy the equipment necessary to run television stations, cable channels, and cable systems by giving these firms something to run on those operations. Second, GE's SES operations provide services to link stations to networks and cable channels to local systems. Third, networking, programming, and channel operations provide a reason for people to buy television sets and VCRs. For GE, then, the metaphorical software of programming drives the sale of hardware in both the professional and consumer markets. While exploitation of technology and entertainment intertwine, GE's interest in Universal suggests that GE is seeking new entertainment operations (in this case, theatrical film) as well as building synergy across operations in broadcasting, cable, and film.

VIACOM TAKES TWO

Viacom similarly interconnects film, broadcast television, and cable channels. Among other holdings, Viacom owns two broadcast networks (CBS and UPN), four film studios (Paramount Pictures, MTV Film, Nickelodeon Films, and Paramount Classics), five television production units (Paramount Television, Big Ticket Television, Spelling Television, Viacom Productions, NickToons, and CBS Enterprises), two groups of cable channels (BET Network with four brands and MTV Networks with eleven), and a group of pay channels (Showtime Networks with various channels denoted as Showtime, FLIX, and The Movie Channel).

In programming, Viacom's production units work together. For the 2002-2003 broadcast year, CBS provided UPN with *Half and Half* and

Paramount Television provided CBS with *JAG*. CBS and UPN co-produced *Haunted*, which ran on UPN while UPN and Paramount co-produced *Bram and Alice* for CBS. For CBS and UPN, this intertwining of production gives them a vested interest in each other's success. Television series generally make their profits in syndication as reruns, not in their initial, network run. Keeping a show on as long as possible means having lots of episodes to strip across a network or cable channel. The connection of longevity and profits discourages CBS, for example, from scheduling a program against *Half and Half* that would appeal to *Half and Half*'s audience. Viacom further decreases the potential for rivalry between the two networks by positioning them to appeal to different segments of the A. C. Neilsen ratings sample: CBS attracts the largest share of the sample with heavy viewership among baby boomers while UPN attracts younger audiences and more specialized audiences. When we consider CBS and UPN as coordinated operations controlled by Viacom, it becomes clear that they are neither competitors nor rivals.

Viacom's use of synergy dates at least to its acquisition of Paramount and Paramount's *Star Trek* in 1993. Paramount had developed that failed television series into a franchise that reliably earned money in syndication around the globe, at the box office via a movie series, from book sales through original novels and film novelizations, and from licensing and merchandising. Paramount's operations were in-house so its acquisition by Viacom resulted in a vertical and horizontal expansion of Viacom's media holdings. Currently, Viacom owns five *Star Trek* television series: *Star Trek* with 79 episodes, the unaired pilot, and 6 movies; *Star Trek: The Next Generation* with 178 episodes and 4 movies; *Star Trek: Deep Space Nine* with 176 episodes; *Star Trek: Voyager* with 172 episodes; and *Enterprise* with 66 episodes completed between September 2001 and February 2004. I will briefly sketch a few of Viacom's uses for its *Trek* franchise to feed its UPN, SPIKE, Simon & Schuster, Pocket Books, Paramount Film, Paramount Television, licensing, and DVD and home video operations.

Viacom used its experience syndicating *The Next Generation* and *Deep Space Nine* to form UPN (Wasko, 1994) and then launched the network using reruns of *The Next Generation* (1987-1994) and *Deep Space Nine* (1993-1999) plus the new series *Voyager* (1995-2001). *Enterprise* currently airs on UPN and *The Next Generation* is being stripped on SPIKE as Viacom remakes that channel as television for men.

Individual episodes from each series are available on videotape and selected episodes are offered in boxed sets like *The Captains Collection* and *The Q Continuum*. For DVD, Viacom has repackaged *Star Trek* with two episodes per disk and is selling *The Next Generation* and *Deep Space Nine* only as boxed sets with each set covering a broadcast year. *Voyager*'s release on DVD is expected soon.

The films have also been variously repackaged on video and DVD in original theatrical versions, special editions, and directors' editions. In 2001, Viacom offered the boxed set *Star Trek: The Original Crew Movie Collection* with the theatrical versions of the six *Star Trek* films. In 2002, consumers could buy the theatrical versions of all nine *Trek* films in the boxed set *Star Trek: The Motion Picture Collection* as well as a new version of *The Original Crew Movie Collection* featuring the "directors' editions" of *Star Trek: The Motion Picture* and *The Wrath of Khan* and a "special edition" of *The Search for Spock*. This proliferation of versions allows Viacom to reap additional revenues with minimal cost from the "same" artifact. While differences between versions may be unimportant to most consumers, they are significant to ardent consumers ranging from *Star Trek* fans to professional collectors.

For Viacom's book publishing operations, *Trek* provides one ongoing paperback series for each television title as well as novelizations for each *Trek* film and selected episodes of *Deep Space Nine*, *Voyager*, and *Enterprise*. Book publishing for *Star Trek* alone includes a numbered paperback series, "giant" novel series, hardcover series,'crossover' books mixing characters from the various *Trek* series, and the "Shatnerverse" novels co-authored by William Shatner.[6] This is but the proverbial tip of the iceberg in terms of *Trek*'s ability to feed Viacom's Pocket Books and Simon & Schuster.[6]

Viacom's use of synergy with *Star Trek* contrasts with Disney's film-by-film approach to exploiting its animations. But in both cases, the ultimate owner seeks to exploit its intellectual properties across its media operations.

ALL THAT FITS IN THE NEWS CORPORATION

News Corporation's media interests in the United States include the FOX network, three nationally distributed cable channels (FX, Fox News, and Fox Movie Channels) and thirteen regional channels under the Fox Sports Networks brand.[7] News Corporation also participates in twelve joint ventures involving cable channels to be discussed below. In 1999, News Corporation sold its Fox Family cable channel and part of Fox Kids Europe to Disney in order to increase its bid for DirecTV, a satellite distributor of cable channels. With the success of that bid in 2003, News Corporation was positioned to ensure that its cable channels would be favored by the top satellite system in the United States. Along the way, it gained Disney as a partner in Fox Kids Europe.

News Corporation maintains a strong presence in the production and distribution of films and television programming. It owns six labels in film production (Blue Sky Studios, Twentieth Century Fox Films, Twentieth Century Fox, Twentieth Century Fox Animation, Fox Searchlight Pictures, and Fox 2000) and three labels in television production (Twentieth Century Fox Television, Fox Television Studios, and Twentieth Television). Like the rest of the Big Five, News Corporation controls the copyrights of series produced for it by small producers and enters contracts for programming with its "rival" networks.

News Corporation's use of synergy can seem rather subtle in comparison to Disney, with its regular flooding of the marketplace, or Viacom, with its control over the most intense ten years of *Star Trek*'s forty years of products. However, News Corporation has been quite adept at synergy as well, although not necessarily always successful, as a brief discussion of *The X-Files* (1993-2002) will show.

Created by Chris Carter and produced by his Ten Thirteen Productions, *The X-Files* went from cult hit to an anchor for FOX's schedule with old episodes being rerun as new episodes continued to appear. The series chronicled the adventures of Special Agents Mulder and Scully working in the Federal Bureau of Investigation's X-Files unit, from which they encountered monsters, paranormal phenomena, supernatural beings, conspiracy theorists, extraterrestrials, duplicitous bureaucrats, and, in a particularly tortuous story arc, conspiracies regarding extraterrestrials, UFO abductions, and alien-human hybrids. After it's first year, each season of the series was introduced by a special program in which Carter revealed the "secrets of *The X-Files*," thereby offering regular viewers a behind-the-scenes look at the series and orienting new viewers to the series' main story arcs. These specials recycled promotional materials circulated to media outlets and fans.[8]

During its first run, *The X-Files* provided fodder for a flood of authorized "behind-the-scenes" books, episode guides, and original novels as well as soundtracks, trading cards, and other paraphernalia. Episodes were sold individually on VHS tapes and in boxed sets, with the two episodes on each tape introduced by Carter. Seasons 1-9 are now available on DVD. The series provided the basis for a single film, *The X-Files: Fight the Future*, which was itself the basis for a novel and soundtrack. *Fight the Future* is available on VHS, DVD, and as a special collector's edition DVD. News Corporation subsequently syndicated *The X-Files* reruns to its FX cable channel.[9]

Of particular interest here is the redeployment of themes and characters in an apparent attempt to build a multi-series franchise based on *The X-Files*. In 1996, Carter and FOX redeployed elements and themes form *The X Files* to launch the new series *Millennium* (1996-1999). Like *The X Files*, *Millennium* manipulated darkness and light within shots to create a moody, brooding atmosphere in which things were not always as they first appeared.

The new show featured an ex-FBI agent, Frank Black, whose psychic abilities made him an adept, though deeply troubled, profiler. Although the series started with him with a family, wife and child were quickly eliminated from the series. Black was connected to a shadowy, conspiratorial group investigating mystic phenomena associated with the coming millennium and assisted them as well as law enforcement officials in investigations. More down-beat than *The X-Files*, *Millennium* lacked both the humorous by-play and sexual tension enacted by Mulder and Scully. FOX ran *Millennium* before *The X-Files*, clearly expecting that they would share an audience.

To foster that connection in 1997, FOX linked them together in the Fall of 1996 on the highly promoted Jose Chung Night. The network reran highly rated *The X File* episode "Jose Chung's *From Outer Space*" (originally aired in April) and premiered the *Millennium* episode "Jose Chung's Doomsday Machine." A famous and eccentric writer, Jose Chung had interviewed Scully regarding an alleged alien abduction and a subsequent alien autopsy for his book *From Outer Space*. That done, Chung moved on to research millennialist movements after enraging members of the Selfology movement. Chung and Black met at the apartment where a Selfologist has been murdered and each generates a profile of the killer. FOX's promotions emphasized that viewers would see a new side of Black, showing Black in a pastel trench coat telling crime scene investigators to "lighten up." But while the episode had considerable, wry humor, it lacked the complex writing and manipulation of conventions that characterized the original episode (Reeves, et al., 1996; Meehan, 1998). In the surprise ending, Black is unable to save Chung from murder, reinforcing the *Millennium's* dour outlook while eliminating the opportunity for further Chung-related hijinks—hence, a double surprise indeed!

Subsequently, Carter intermixed and redeployed elements of *The X Files* episodes "Nisei" (24 November 1995) and "Jose Chung's *From Outer Space*" in the *Millennium* episode "Somehow Satan Got Behind Me." In that episode, four devils met at a donut shop to trade stories about damnation. In a humorous tale, one devil explains how he damned the souls of a network censor and millions of television viewers. In the climactic scene, a television crew films a Scully-like actor pretending to autopsy a gray alien flanked by two actors dressed as gray aliens and armed with uzis. The censor bursts in and sprays the aliens with bullets reprising the scene in "Nisei" in heavily armed soldiers burst into a train car and pump hundreds of bullets into the scientists performing an autopsy on an extraterrestrial. All of this links back to FOX's highly promoted airing of Robert Kiviat's pseudo-documentary *Alien Autopsy: Fact or Fiction?* (28 August 1995, repeated September 4, 1995). In 2001, Carter and FOX undertook a less whimsical redeployment, spinning off *The X-Files* amateur conspiracy theorists in the short-lived program, *The Lone Gunmen* (March-June 2001).

Here we see a form of synergy in which creative people lift elements, themes, and characters from one product and rework them to form another. While Kiviat's redeployment of *Alien Autopsy* to *World's Greatest Hoaxes* may seem somewhat heavy-handed, Carter's redeployment of *Alien Autopsy* to "Jose Chung's *From Outer Space*" has a certain panache. Part of the fun derives from FOX's carriage of both *Alien Autopsy* and *The X-Files*. Another part rests on FOX's sustained use of UFOlogy, psychic phenomena, conspiracy theories, and other modern mythologies in its entertainment programming, specials, and tabloid magazine shows. This sustained use of some ideas, images, tropes, representations, stories, visions, claims, understandings, and assumptions creates a cultural fund of preferred elements that cohere to build identities or brands for specific operations. For News Corporation's FOX, pseudo-science and conspiracy theories have figured significantly in its hit program *The X-Files*, in lesser programs like *Millennium* and the tabloid magazine *Encounters,* and in specials like *UFOs: The Best Evidence Ever Caught on Tape* (1997) and *Conspiracy Theory: Did We Land on the Moon?* (2001). This form of synergy becomes important not simply as a form of branding but also as a commercial impetus to narrow the range of ideas presented via a specific operation. When content synergy and structural synergy combine, that further narrows the range of News Corporation's expression by recycling the ideas that brand FOX on FX, into television production units, into film production units, and so on.

AOL TIME WARNER: STILL TOGETHER

We turn finally to the last of the Big Five: AOL Time Warner. AOL's acquisition of Time Warner integrated America's largest internet service provider with its largest media conglomerate. In this way, AOL provided privileged access to AOL subscribers for Time Warner films, news, television programs, information products, recording starts, and so on. Besides being one of the top three cable MSOs, AOL Time Warner owners one broadcast network (WB), one regional cable channel (Turner South), seven basic cable channels (Boomerang, Cartoon Network, Cable News Network, CNN Headline News, Turner Broadcasting System, Turner Classic Movies, and TNT), and fourteen pay channels under the HBO and Cinemax brands. Similarly, the company has extended its CNN brand to include CNN en Espanol, CNNfn (financial news), CNN Newsource, CNN Airport Network, CNN Radio, and CNN Radio Noticias. Of course, AOL Time Warner's cable systems carry the company's channels and put it in a position to negotiate carriage of channels owned by the remainder of the Big Five.

AOL Time Warner owns ten brands under which it produces, licenses, and distributes films and television programming: Castle Rock, HBO Downtown Productions, HBO Independent Productions, New Line, Fine Line, Telepictures Productions, Warner Bros., Warner Bros. Animation, Hanna-Barbera, and Looney Tunes. Among the television programs that AOL Time Warner produced for the 2002-2003 television season were *Birds of Prey*, *Everwood*, *Gilmore Girls*, *Gilmore Girls: Beginnings*, and *Smallville*—all of which ran on WB. The company also supplies programming to other Big Five networks.

Like Viacom, AOL Time Warner has a long history of exploiting its intellectual properties and transindustrial structure—first as Warner Communications (WCI), then as Time Warner. A pivotal property has been the Batman character that WCI acquired as part of its purchase of DC Comics. Starting in the mid-1980s, WCI began the conscientious exploitation of the character, building it into franchise that spans multiple media operations and includes six versions of Batman, each with his own product line spanning multiple media operations. Here I will concentrate on the conglomerate's generation of versions of the same character.

AOL Time Warner currently deploys six versions of Batman. First is the cheery comic book figure from the 1960s,[10] who was featured in Saturday morning cartoon shows produced in the 1970s, that have been repackaged for the Cartoon Network and home videos. This Batman survives in comic book form and is still widely licensed for products targeting very young children. Next is Frank Miller's redesign of Batman as the Dark Knight. An older, bitter Batman, the Dark Knight was featured in two comic book series, both repackaged as graphic novels. Portions of those comics were recycled in the Warner-released documentary *Comic Book Confidential.* Third is the brooding but not-so-Dark Knight featured in four films: *Batman* (1989), *Batman Returns* (1992), *Batman Forever* (1995), and *Batman and Robin* (1997). Each of the films was adapted for video games and novels; each soundtrack was recycled into music CDs, published songs, and music videos; each story board was recycled into two comic books differentiated by the weight of their paper and price (collector's comic vs. regular comic); and each was promoted in a special magazine. In licensing, each film was connected to trading cards, toys, apparel, paper goods, plastic goods, jewelry, collector figurines, camping supplies, tooth brushes, school supplies, and so on. Fourth is the muscular, tough-talking Batman featured in two animated films, six cartoon series, and a complete line of related media and licensed goods. Fifth is Tim Burton's version of a muscular, tough-talking, but stylish and slightly retro Batman in his television cartoon series. And last is the new Batman motivating a recent series of Batman comic books and novels as well as the short-lived WB series *Birds of Prey* (2003-2004).

This last Batman is particularly interesting. In this continuing saga, Batman has mysteriously disappeared from Gotham City, leaving two women to continue the battle against crime: his protégé, Bat-Girl, who was shot by the Joker and uses a wheelchair, and his daughter, a mutant, whose mother was Catwoman. While straying from the story lines developed in the old DC comics and the newer movies, *Birds of Prey* capitalized on themes regarding mutant superheroes that had been developed by its rival Marvel Comics and on the "woman warrior" stereotype successfully used in the Lara Croft Tomb Raider franchise with its video games and films. It also brought Batman back into the discourse of the general commercial culture (as opposed to the specialist discourses of fans), while Frank Miller redesigns Batman yet again for another series of theatrically released films.

In this form of synergy, AOL Time Warner has tweaked and reinvented a single character over nearly two decades, using these versions to generate product lines that span the conglomerate's media and licensing operations. Here creativity is redefined as making more versions of the same thing to target age groups ranging from very young children to children to teens and adults. Old cartoons and recent cartoons become filler for the Cartoon Network; the live-action films become filler for AOL Time Warner's pay cable channels, cable channels, and the WB network. Using the comics and novels about the sixth version of Batman, AOL Time Warner filled a weekly slot on the WB with *Birds of Prey*, perhaps starting the promotional campaign for the next Batman film.

On AOL Time Warner's news side, announcements and new developments in the Batman franchise are featured in *Entertainment Weekly* magazine, *Time* magazine, *People* magazine, *People en Espanol*, CNN's "Hollywood Minute," and on AOL's opening page. While this encourages the manufacture of infotainment, it also encourages the treatment of information and news as just another set of intellectual properties to be run across all operations including the CNNs, *Sports Illustrated*, *Time*, *Entertainment Weekly*, *People*, *People en Espanol*, AOL's opening page, AOL's news pages, and so forth.

SYNERGY: THE SAME OLD STUFF

The overall effect of synergy, then, is to recirculate, recycle, repackage, reversion, and redeploy those intellectual properties that a company already owns. This redefines creativity as tweaking and re-tweaking the old to make it appear new. Creative people don't originate new ideas—they figure out how to reuse the old ones. With transindustrial conglomerates controlling so many venues, synergy blurs distinctions once based on technologies and industrial separation. The result is predictable: movies based on old television shows, television programs based on movies, books based on both, and so on—all designed with the intent of feeding transindustrial operations and with the hope of building a franchise that can span decades. While this may make 'good business sense,' it produces much that is uninspired and dull.

This is not what neo-conservatives promised when they undertook the deregulation of the information/entertainment sector of the economy. The deregulators swore that rewriting the rules would generate thousands of programs targeting highly variegated cultural tastes and made available through media venues that would compete fiercely to serve us. Instead, deregulation fostered such extensive corporate and industrial integration that the Big Five dominate broadcast networking and production as well as cable channels and production. If the European Union approves GE's acquisition of Universal, then all of television's Big Five plus Sony will oligopolize film production and distribution. To use the comedic form: the good news is that you have five TV networks; the bad news is that they run the same old stuff across the national networks, cable channels, and movie screens.

Now, for a Pollyanna moment: but even if there are only five companies owning six networks, that's still more than three—surely each one will compete vigorously with the other five to be number one. As we will see below, that hope is illusory at best.

INTERTWINED OPERATIONS: CONTRACT AND JOINT VENTURES

The Big Five are intertwined in joint ventures, programming contracts, and affiliate contracts, which give these conglomerates vested interests in the success of operations that would otherwise be rivals. First, we'll look at programming, ownership, and affiliation, then at joint ventures. The most obvious example of rivalry being short-circuited by ownership is Viacom's ownership of two networks that provide programming to each other. Viacom has a vested interest in the success of both CBS and UPN as networks and in the success of programs that CBS produces for UPN, or UPN produces for CBS, or that CBS and UPN produce together. Viacom also licenses programs from and to other members of the Big Five.

For example, the 2002-2003 season, programming contracts connected Viacom to AOL Time Warner's WB, GE's NBC, News Corporation's FOX. Viacom licensed *Greetings from Tucson* and *Do Over* to AOL Time Warner and produced *Frasier* for GE. Viacom subsidiaries joined with GE subsidiaries to produce *Ed* and *In-Laws*, which aired on NBC. Viacom and

News Corporation co-produced *Still Standing*, which ran on CBS. Finally, Viacom licensed *Buffy the Vampire Slayer* from News Corporation for UPN.

Perhaps the most interesting linkage between Viacom and News Corporation rests on a deregulatory anomaly. Under deregulation, companies can own more than one television station in a market. To form UPN in 1995, Viacom joined with Chris-Craft's BHC Communications, which owned a chain of ten television stations, giving Chris-Craft a stake in the new network. Although Viacom bought out that stake in 2000, Chris-Craft retained ownership of the ten UPN affiliates. When News Corporation bought Chris-Craft, it acquired the ten stations as well as an opportunity to place UPN in grave peril. Seven stations were located in cities where News Corporation already owned a station. Rather then disrupt UPN, News Corporation decided that its new stations would remain UPN affiliates. In seven markets, then, News Corporation's FOX station 'competes' with News Corporation's UPN station. Through its ownership of UPN affiliates, News Corporation gained an interest in Viacom's success with UPN.

Besides licensing *Buffy the Vampire Slayer* to Viacom's UPN and co-producing *Standing Still* with Viacom, News Corporation produced *Angel* and *Reba* for AOL Time Warner, produced *NYPD Blue* and *The Practice* to Disney, and licensed *Fastland* from AOL Time Warner. News Corporation has contracted to give Disney privileged access to programs under development. To raise capital to buy into DirecTV, News Corporation sold the cable Fox Family Channel and part of Fox Kids Europe to Disney. With its interest in DirecTV, News Corporation may be in a position to influence the menu offered by that satellite company to subscribers.

Besides Disney's programming contracts with Viacom and News Corporation, Disney licensed *The Drew Carey Show*, *George Lopez*, and *Whose Line Is It Anyway?* from AOL Time Warner. Disney also has an exclusive "first run" deal with Viacom's pay channel Showtime for films made under its Miramax, Touchstone, and Hollywood brands. Disney's "first look" contract with News Corporation was augmented by a similar contract with AOL Time Warner's HBO.

As noted, AOL Time Warner produced shows for Viacom, News Corporation, and Disney as well as licensing shows from News Corporation and Viacom. AOL Time Warner provided GE with the Emmy-award winners *Friends* and *West Wing* as well as *ER*, *Good Morning Miami*, and *Third Watch*. AOL Time Warner is further connected to GE's NBC through a programming agreement in which those companies share rights to televising races put on by the National Association For Stock Car Auto Racing (NASCAR). By sharing programming across their networks, the company that owns the program gains an interest in a rival network's ability to earn high ratings with that program and to do so for as long as possible in order for the program to recoup costs and earn profits via syndication.

That discourages the program owner's network from counterprogramming in a way that would steal the program's audience.

Another way that corporations interlock their interests is in joint ventures where companies co-own operations. For the Big Five, joint ventures create alliances between themselves as well as with cable MSOs. Let's review some current joint ventures, remembering that while particular relationships may change, the pattern of building alliances through joint ventures remains.

Mirroring entanglements in network programming are entanglements among the Big Five in cable channels. Disney, GE, and Viacom co-own History and History International. Disney and GE co-own A&E and A&E International. GE and News Corporation are major stake holders in National Geographic and National Geographic International. As noted above, Disney and News Corporation co-own Fox Kids Europe.

Also of interest is the intertwining of the Big Five's interests with those of companies that are primarily cable MSOs. Currently, the main participant in such relationships is Liberty Media, an MSO spun off from AT&T which, when independent, had been known as TCI. Liberty joins with Viacom to operate the BET/STARZ pay cable channel and with Disney, fellow MSO Comcast, and AT&T to operate E! Entertainment. Liberty owns 4% of AOL Time Warner,[11] 18% of News Corporation, and 3% of Vivendi Universal. Presumably, if the European Union approves Vivendi's sale of Universal to GE, Liberty will acquire a stake in GE. But Liberty already has a contractual connection to GE: NBC leases three hours of its Saturday morning schedule to cable's Discovery Channel, which is co-owned by Liberty and Discovery Communications. Liberty and AOL Time Warner share Court TV.

The intertwining of the Big Five through joint ventures gives each participant an interest in the success of the specific venture but also a concern for the metaphoric health of its partner. In fact, when conflicts occur between the Big Five, they tend to involve firms that are loosely connected as in the dispute over charges and carriage of Disney channels between Disney and AOL Time Warner. Similarly, the Big Five's ownership of cable channels, production of cable programming, and ties to MSOs (in our examples, Liberty Media) serve to integrate broadcast television with cable television.

CONCLUSION

This chapter has presented a snapshot showing how transindustrial structure merges industries, fosters synergy, and integrates oligopolies—all of which concentrates ownership and increases centralization in an economy. We have focused on commercial television in the United States, but the general effects are typical outcomes of marketization. This snapshot is necessarily static; it does not show the daily processes by which firms struggle to maintain themselves, repair damages, control their images, and so on. Over time, particular operations, joint ventures, and contracts will change, changing the data. But the pattern of relations and structures fostered by neo-conservatism will remain until that policy itself is replaced. To summarize, I will briefly resketch our findings and then comment on change as a socio-economic process.

The marketization of commercial television in the United States expanded the number of national networks from three to six, allowing the number of network owners to expand to six and then contract to five. At the same time, deregulation has allowed the Big Five in networking to control the production of network programming and to contract with each other for programs. The Big Five's lock on network distribution and its expansive ownership of cable channels gave it the market power to demand and get copyright ownership of programs created by independent firms. While the practice, appearing to be a form of corporate blackmail, raises ethical issues, deregulation allows it.

With the erasure of regulations separating cable and broadcast television, the relevant firms began merging those industries through companies' reorganization as transindustrial conglomerates. Neo-conservative policies favoring that form of conglomeration fostered the merging of media industries from film to broadcast/cable television to print publication and beyond, resulting in the expansion of each firm's internal markets, which need to be fed. Feeding those markets via synergy means transforming intellectual properties into "brand names" with product lines that can be consumed across media venues. Product lines are then bundled into franchises that the transindustrial moves through its many venues in a coordinated manner. Synergy redefines creativity as tweaking an old product to create a new one and then re-tweaking that to create another one—each one minimally different and entirely familiar. Synergy also redefines technologies once regulated to provide competition to networks into conduits controlled by the same transindustrials that control the networks.

Allowing the Big Five to contract with each other for broadcast programming, to undertake joint ventures in cable channels, and to own stations affiliated with a rival network short circuits competition. A company will not compete fully and freely against another firm, attempting to win the competition by forcing the other out of business, if the two companies rely on each other for revenues. Similarly, transindustrial conglomerates do not allow competition among divisions such that one division can push another out of business. To the degree that marketization allows transindustrialism and interlocking contracts between alleged rivals, economic concentration intensifies and persists.

This is a matter of grave concern. The transformation of individual oligopolies in networking, program production, cable channels, cable production, and cable system ownership into an oligopoly uniting networking, program production, cable channels, cable production, and sometimes cable system ownership—with connections to film and other media—is dramatic indeed.

For advocates of free markets, this outcome should illuminate the gap between the rhetoric and the results of marketization, deregulation, and neo-conservatism. For proponents of cultural diversity, this development bodes ill as synergy, branding, franchises, and corporate interlocks deliver the same old stuff through more venues using various technologies. For technological visionaries, this should be disheartening as transindustrial imperatives subsume technological capability. For anyone interested in a vibrant popular culture that speaks authentically to and of one's life, the implications should be clear: commercial culture can't do that given the constraints under which it is owned, manufactured, recirculated, repackaged, reversioned, recycled, and redeployed. For champions of free expression and democratic activism, the upshot of all this is obvious: whether termed neo-conservatism, neo-liberalism, deregulation, or marketisation, this ideological regimen reframes the search for news as a search for infotainment packages that can be recirculated, repackaged, reversioned, recycled, and redeployed in the interests of the owning transindustrial conglomerate.

For all such people, however, this chapter provides a reminder: economic systems are constructs, the outcomes of actions taken by individuals and institutions over time. Media oligopolies and transindustrial conglomerates are outcomes, not eternal verities. As the fall of post-war liberalism and the rise of neo-conservatism demonstrate, change is not only possible, but inevitable and dramatic. Throughout the ascendancy of both liberalism and neo-conservatism, people have organized to challenge assumptions, to reveal contradictions between promise and performance, and to struggle for progressive change. Within the American academy, scholars like Dallas Smythe, Herbert Schiller, and Thomas Guback did the same in the 1960s and 1970s. In the 1980s and 1990s, that tradition was carried forward by such researchers as Oscar Gandy, Vincent Mosco, Manjunath Pendakur, and Janet Wasko. In the new century, each of us—armed with the tools of critical research and active within progressive organizations—have a role to play in the struggle for change.

NOTES

1. Although Viacom is publicly traded, the controlling block of stock is owner by National Amusements. That company is privately held and controlled by Sumner Redstone

2. This account is drawn from Barnouw, 1990; Daniellian, 1939; Kellner, 1990; McChesney, 1993; Meehan, 1990; Streeter, 1996; and Tillinghast, 2000.
3. Other factors influencing the decline included suburbanization, societal emphasis on families and the baby boom, and the expansion in post-war leisure activities including motoring, shopping, do-it-yourself projects, etc. For a discussion of the post-war film industry in the United States, see Wasko (1982) pp. 103-106.
4. Introduction to the radio program *The Lone Ranger.*
5. General Electric. 10K Filing, Security Exchange Commission. EDGAR address. Accessed 6 June 2003.
6. The "Shatnerverse" novels are based on the premise that Captain Kirk didn't really die at the end of *Star Trek: Generations.*
7. This brand was originally a joint venture with Liberty Media. To buy-out the MSO, News Corporation ceded an 18% interest in itself to Liberty.
8. I would like to thank Denise Chaytor for her lectures to my Media Arts 431 Commercial Intertextuality class on these points.
9. This prompted a suit filed by star David Duchovney, which was eventually settled out-of court. Duchovney argued that this inhouse syndication depressed the show's earnings, hence his residuals. While details of the settlement are undisclosed, it apparently allowed Duchovney to limit his appearances on the show.
10. This character is distinct from the one created by Adam West in the 1966-68 television series Batman, produced by William Dozier under a license from Warner but without Warner's supervision or involvement in the actual series and subsequent film.
11. Under deregulation, Liberty/AT&T/TCI sat on AOL Time Warner/Time Warner's board, thus allowing one of the largest MSOs to sit on the board of a firm owning another of the largest MSOs

REFERENCES

Bagdikian, Ben (2000) *The Media Monopoly* (6th ed.). Boston: Beacon Press.
Barnouw, Erik (1990) *Tube of Plenty.* New York: Oxford University Press.
Bettig, Ronald V. and Jeanne Lynn Hall (2003) *Big Media, Big Money: Cultural Texts and Political Economics.* Lanham, MD: Rowman & Littlefield.
Cantor, Muriel (1980) *Prime-time Television.* Beverly Hills, CA: Sage.
Compaine, Benjamin and Douglas Gomery (2000) *Who Owns the Media?: Competition and Concentration in the Mass Media Industry.* Mahwah, NJ: Lawrence Erlbaum and Associates.
Danielian, N.R. (1939) *AT&T: The Story of Industrial Conquest.* New York: Vanguard Press.
Gerbner, George, Hamid Mowlana, and Herbert I. Schiller (Eds.) (1996) *Invisible Crises: What Conglomerate Control of Media Means for America and the World.* Boulder, CO: Westview Press.
Gitlin, Todd (1983) *Inside Prime Time.* New York: Pantheon Books.

Kellner, Douglas (1990) *Television and the Crisis of Democracy.* Boulder, CO: Westview Press.

McChesney, Robert W. (1993) *Telecommunications, Mass Media, and Democracy: The Battle for Control of U.S. Broadcasting, 1928-1935.* New York: Oxford University Press.

McChesney, Robert W. (1999) *Rich Media, Poor Democracy: Communication Politics in Dubious Times.* Urbana: University of Illinois Press.

Meehan, Eileen R. (1998) "Not your parents' FBI: *The X-Files.*" In A. A. Berger (Ed.), *The Postmodern Presence.* Walnut Creek, CA: Alta Mira Press.

Meehan, Eileen R. (1990) "Why we don't count." In Patricia Mellencamp (Ed.), *The Logics of Television.* Bloomington: Indiana University Press.

Reeves, Jimmie L., Mark C. Rodgers, and Michael Epstein (1996) "Rewriting the popular." In David Lavery, Angela Hague, and Marla Cartwright (Eds.), *"Deny All Knowledge": Reading the X-Files.* Syracuse, NY: Syracuse University Press.

Schiller, Dan (2000) *Digital Capitalism: Networking the Global Market System.* Cambridge, MA: MIT Press.

Smith, Adam (1776/2003) *The Wealth of Nations.* New York: Bantam.

Streeter, Thomas (1996) *Selling the Air: A Critique of the Policy of Commercial Broadcasting in the United States.* Chicago: University of Chicago Press.

Tillinghast, Charles (2000) *American Broadcast Regulation and the First Amendment: Another Look.* Ames: Iowa State University Press.

Wasko, Janet (2002) *Understanding Disney: The Manufacture of Fantasy.* Cambridge: Polity.

Wasko, Janet (1994) *Hollywood in the Information Age.* Austin: University of Texas Press.

Wasko, Janet (1982) *Movies and Money: Financing the American Film Industry,* Norwood, NJ: Ablex.

CHAPTER TWO

IMPERIOUS MEASURES

A Schillerian Approach to Global Marketing Research

Richard Maxwell

The October 26, 2003 issue of the *New York Times Magazine* announced the arrival of marketing research's latest devices. Joining the traditional tools of surveys, statistical indexing, and focus groups is the Magnetic Resonance Imaging (M.R.I.) machine. Marketing research—the branch of the marketing industry that tracks consumer habits, thoughts, desires, distastes, fantasies, and other personal attributes—has enlisted neuroscientists and their laboratories in the search for the truth about the inner life of consumers. You can't lie to the M.R.I., which measures the kind of brain activity that marketers have long dreamed could be rendered visible to them. By bypassing our rational filters that guide self-restraint in the face of a stimulating advertisement, marketers can know when we truly, secretly, madly fall for a sales pitch or product design. "To an M.R.I.," said the *Times'* reporter, "you cannot misrepresent your responses. Your medial prefrontal cortex will start firing when you see something you adore, even if you claim not to like it" (Thompson, 2003, p. 57). Although the reporter mildly derided neuromar-

---

*Portions of this essay draw directly from my book, *Herbert Schiller* (Rowman & Littlefield, 2003) and my contributions to Miller et al. (2001).

keting with a nod to the upscale reader's supposed disdain for the less noble chores of salesmanship, he nevertheless marveled at the science behind it. Imagine using technology to find out at long last which half of advertising investment is not wasted.

I have pulled this clipping out of my pocket as a little *homage* to Herbert Schiller, the inspiration for this essay on the consumer surveillance operations of marketing research. Although Schiller did not provide a sustained focus on the subject of marketing research, his commentaries on the subject were interspersed in a number of his books and essays over 50 years of work on the political economy of communication and culture. In general, Schiller's approach can be summarized as an analysis of the class system underlying the structure of production, distribution, and consumption of media messages and communication technology. It is not surprising, then, that Schiller perceived the state of marketing research as an index of how informational resources, mind management, and consumer surveillance support the class system of the contemporary political economy.

A "Schillerian" analysis of marketing can proceed from three points of departure: (a) power structure analysis, which identifies and analyzes key players and dominant institutions; (b) systemic analysis, which interprets the power structure as an inseparable part of the imperialist system and therein contextualizes the aims and actions of key players; and (c) prospective analysis of democratic forces, which assesses challenges to the power structure that attempt to create nondominating forms of communication, including marketing research.

POWER STRUCTURE
AND MARKETING RESEARCH

Power structure analysis offers a documentary look at the power elite that gives direction to the dominating institutions of a society. Like the radical sociologist C. Wright Mills, Schiller understood that the "higher circles" of decision makers, although a small minority, formed a group of common interests with sufficient power to determine a society's fate—in particular how and to what ends national resources are allocated (see Mills' *The Power Elite*, 1956). In determining how a society spends its technological resources, this elite's power far exceeds their numbers. Schiller called the intersecting institutional interests within the power structure a "complex." Schiller used the word "complex" to name the bureaucratic lineage and interrelationships of military, government, and communications-electronics-cultural businesses. Although Schiller identified a number of complexes, including the communications complex, the military-industrial complex, and the industrial-electronics complex, he used the idea of the complex consistently as a name for a real entity, "a bureaucratic colossus," as he and Joseph Phillips called it in their introduction to *Super–State: Readings in the Military Industrial Complex* (1970, p. 25). The marketing research complex is comprised by a government-academic-corporate power structure in which parallel imperatives to cultivate, organize, and manage public consciousness (or "knowledgeability" as Schiller sometimes said) determine development, function, and application of communication technique and technology.

A complex may be formed by system-serving bureaucratic roles and motivations that remain largely the same even as actors change over time. In that sense, a description of a complex can capture the contemporary features of a particular power structure. For example, an examination of the nascent marketing research of the late nineteenth century shows the complex of advertising and academic social science coming into being to improve tabulations of press circulation, the sign of commercial press value since the mid-1800s (Hurwitz, 1983, pp. 53-60). Soon after, academics like Walter Dill Scott and Harlow Gale convinced advertising agencies to use statistical projection mixed with behavioral analysis to predict habits of media consumption (Strasser, 1989, pp. 148-149). By 1910, when use of official statistical tabulation of populations—a foundation of modern forms of governance and citizenship—had been firmly established, academic psychologists advocated a form of marketing research that was based on the idea that consumers were irrational people. This view suited major advertisers well. As Strasser puts it, "The makers of branded products were particularly interested in combating consumers' rational interest in purchasing at the best price" (Strasser, 1989, p. 158). The irrational consumer cannot be trusted to know what truly motivates him or her to buy, but moreover this irrational soul was the sort of vulnerable subject marketers were seeking to manipulate. The years following the war were also significant for the rapidly rising standard of living in the United States and Europe, epitomized in an "ever widening range of consumer durables" (Kenwood and Lougheed, 1992, p. 245). The combination of growing material abundance, spreading credit availability, the social-psychological orthodoxy of irrational and malleable masses, and confidence in job growth and security created new importance for a merger of advertising, academia, and industry into a marketing research complex.

This particular complex shares features with present day arrangements, though there are superficial differences. Taken separately, they might appear to result from unplanned coincidence of interests of the various institutions. However if we understand their overall development historically, the attempt to manage the minds of consumers can be linked to the processes within the wider political economy of the twentieth century. In the early years, corporate leaders such as Henry Ford were interested in methods of regulating the activities of workers during nonwork times. The academic work of psychologists and social scientists during the 1910s and 1920s "began to create a general understanding that the social control of workers must stretch beyond the realm of the factory and into the very communities and structures within which they lived" (Ewen, 1976, pp. 15-16). The marketing research complex matured after World War II when an avalanche of psy-studies (psychoanalytic, behavioral, cognitive) of soldiers (Piirto, 1991, pp. 9-12) and university students animated new military-informational partnerships, including mass communication researchers with close ties to domestic, global, and military intelligence (Simpson, 1994), imperialist application of communication theory (Schiller, 1989, pp. 135-156; 2000, pp. 105-128), and the Cold War ideological fronts of American businesses supported by international advertising and marketing. In the new century, market research techniques have continued to be guided by this complex of ruling elites: in the case of neuromarketing, for example, the power structure is composed of major advertisers (the consumer goods manufacturers), research universities with clinical neuroscience labs, and the federal government that funds the university labs. So at Harvard's apposite "Mind of the Market Laboratory" we find academic psychology and marketing firms in partnership to explore how "technologies from cognitive neuroscience" can map "subconscious decision making patterns of consumers" (www.hbs.edu/mml/about.html). At Emory University Hospital there's BrightHouse, a marketing research firm, scanning "the brains of a representative sample of its client's prospective customers" (Thompson, 2003, p. 56).

Use of the M.R.I. to picture the mind of the consumer signals a new stage of visualization techniques developed within the marketing research complex. Visualization techniques, secondary to the statistics, form a unique aesthetic—a statistico-aesthetic—within advertising and marketing cultures where the aim is to imagine a coherent set of human attributes for a person with one-dimensional aspirations to consume. The statistico-aesthetic can be traced to Adolphe Quetelet's use of the bell curve to visualize what national averages of people might look like and later to Francis Galton's uses of composite photography to "see" these averages in realistic renderings for sighting genius, criminality, and racialized monstrosities of the colonial imagination (Maxwell, 2000). There are several forms of marketing research using inherited visualization techniques, including psychographic and "lifestyle" methods that aim to create "a detailed, 'humanized' portrait of the consumer . . . amenable to both quantitative analysis and to the data gathering methods of large scale survey research" (Wells, 1974, p. 320). In the early days before digital imaging, market researchers would picture the consumer using "photographs from *Life* magazine and added scrap art . . . to create individuals who emerged from . . . lifestyle data" (Piirto, 1991, p. 25). Another visualization method is found in geodemographic market research, which combines descriptive "lifestyle" analysis with geographical data to create identity maps accompanying mini-narratives of differing segments of consumers. Claritas Corporation, the most successful manufacturer of these maps, represents every American with at least one of 40 identity clusters, including such oddities as the Bohemian Mix, the Urban Renewal, Dixie Style Tenements, Norma Rae–villes, the Pools and Patio people, the Hard Scrabble, Bunker's Neighbors, Old Melting Pot, or Heavy Industry (Larson, 1994, pp. 29-57).

Each synchronic view of the marketing research complex gives us different elites to identify and different incarnations of a power structure to analyze. In the present film industry, for example, Nielsen National Research Group (NielsenNRG) controls about 80% of a US$90 million surveillance market with research that affects almost all major Hollywood releases in the United States and Europe (Milmo, 2003, p. 20). NielsenNRG has amassed a proprietary consumer database that links audience attendance to "every major motion picture released since 1982, cross-referenced by actor, director, box office, genre, studio, country and just about any other index imaginable" (Lerner, 1999, p. 18). NielsenNRG's rivals include MarketCast, OTX (Online Testing Exchange), CA Walker, and MovieFone (Dutka, 2003). Firms like OTX, a subsidiary of Ifilm.com, have expanded surveillance of Internet-using filmgoers with claims that they "can access everyone from Asian laxative users to African American women who saw a film last weekend" (quoted in Dutka, 2003). Internet consumer surveillance received a boost from a Simmons Research Consumer Study in 2002 that found "84% of all moviegoers who've seen at least one film in the last three months are now online users" (quoted in Dutka, 2003).

Another on-line research company is the Hollywood Stock Exchange (HSX), owned by a unit of Cantor Fitzgerald, a Wall Street firm. As of 2004, HSX had about a million registered users, mostly affluent young men, who trade stocks of movies and bonds of stars. "HSX was conceived as a game to take advantage of the public's obsession with box-office numbers," said one of the founders, but the real plan is to sell forecasts based on "information it has collected on the folks who frequent the site" (Bates, 2000).

Silicon Valley hardware makers also offer new spy machines concealed within Digital Video Recorders (DVR). DVRs have been advertised as a means to record television shows and bypass commercial advertisements. Initially, the major versions of these devices only worked when subscribers hooked them up to the Internet to allow service providers, TiVo and ReplayTV, to collect information on every choice, channel change, and skipped commercial. In addition to amassing a huge database of consumer information, this particular surveillance device is capable of pinpointing the identities and actions of individual television viewers (Lewis, 2001, p. 40; Rose, 2001).

The gamble of predicting the whereabouts and desires of audiences, while generating many amusing stories of blunders and missteps, creates constant pressure to innovate the techniques and enlarge the databases on which the marketing research complex depends. This structural pressure drives marketing research inexorably into ever more extensive and invasive areas of surveillance. Even billboards have been wired to relay personal information of unwitting passers-by to global positioning satellites (GPS) (Bickerton, 2003, p. 23). Other billboard experiments spy on passing cars to "deduce demographic information from the radio stations drivers are listening to and then [instantly change the billboard] advertising aimed at them based on income, sex, race, and buying habit data." Said one company official: "We can tell you the percentage of people who drove past that were married, shop at Petsmart, that make over $100,000" (Richtel, 2002, pp. C1, C5). And, of course, the latest innovation in invasive surveillance technology is M.R.I.-based neuromarketing research.

SYSTEMIC ANALYSIS

We can see that an analysis of the interests that have married corporate sales to academic psych-, bio- and neuroscience can offer interesting insights into the marketing research complex and its sociocultural influence. Yet what effective political strategy or reforms can we generate from such a study? To answer that we need to examine the underlying system that has engendered the marketing research complex. Our next "Schillerian" point of departure begins by identifying significant connections between the institutional complex and the imperial political economic system. Schiller wrote about this relationship with Joseph D. Phillips in the introduction to their book, *Super–State* (1970), and in Schiller's first book *Mass Communications and American Empire* (1969). The distinction he made between system and complex was crucial for understanding how he approached questions of strategic challenges and political reform. For example, systemic analysis would challenge the wisdom, if not legitimacy, of the allocation of resources of medical IT toward neuromarketing to serve demands of the marketing research complex. There seems to be little dispute that the M.R.I. has advanced biomedical and neurological science and helped improve medical diagnostics. But of all the alternative ways the technology might have been used for life-enhancing reasons this society has allowed transnational corporations to employ it for proving that a sports car flips the pleasure switch in a man's brain (Thompson, 2003, p. 57). This takes us to the priorities of the system that marketing research serves.

Schiller came to use the idea of "the system" to describe firmly established political economic arrangements in which university, governmental and corporate bureaucracies were integrated. The system determines the range of operations and purposes of a particular complex. Schiller gave the example of a non-systemic view of the military-industrial complex as "an outgrowth of inadvertence rather than design" (Schiller and Phillips, 1970, p. 25), the sense given by President Dwight D. Eisenhower in his famous farewell address of 1961. If the complex were instead systemically "regarded as organically inseparable from the political-economic structure that has evolved in the United States, a nodal link in *a powerful imperial system still extending its influence globally*, a very different perspective unfolds." The battle over reform of a complex "widens into a struggle for the survival of the System itself"—it "means going to the mat with the System itself" (Schiller and Phillips 1970, pp. 26–27; emphasis in original).

By extending this analogy to the marketing research complex, the links to the imperial system can be traced in a number of ways that help us think through the problems of critique and reform of marketing in the present. First, the rise of statistical analysis as a form of managing populations within European empires formed a single thread with imperial ethnological efforts to sort and subjugate the people in the colonies—the very same techniques used to define class distinctions within national populations were embraced as ways to measure difference in order to justify bloody colonialism in the world system (Maxwell, 2000). The homologies can be found in scientific formulations of race and nation, the alterations of survey research methodology to suit marketing and advertising needs of Fortune 500 companies, the polling-propaganda industry (Lewis 2001), and other system serving institutions.

Schiller's systemic analysis was also concerned with resource allocation and social tensions that arise around the distribution of resources. If we heed Schiller's concern with resource allocation we must confront how information-communication resources have historically contributed to the stratification of information haves and have-nots. In the case of the neuromarketers, to take my opening example, it is clear that as long as market criteria determine the application of the M.R.I. technology the return on investment will overshadow social demand of its life-enhancing capabilities. More generally, and probably better known, is the overt commercialism of the allocations of cultural resources. The strategic role marketing research has played in this regard is clear, in particular how it has fueled the extension of the values and assumptions of the corporate-cultural conglomerates in the content of messages produced in television and film. Schiller's United Nations Educational, Scientific, and Cultural Organization (UNESCO) report, *Communication Accompanies Capital Flows* (1979), showed the overwhelming impact of advertising on all commercial media content. Since then, other works have documented the unequal distribution of cultural resources to commercial uses (Mattelart, 1991; Wyatt 1995; Miller et al. 2001—this research tracked the trends of advertising and marketing influence in the global film and television industries).

Likewise, we might want to look at the unequal allocation of survey and marketing methods made for system-serving uses. Schiller argued that surveys and polls are predominantly used to categorize people in order to manage populations and organize public knowledge, consumption, and media use for systemic ends. "To take a poll is itself an act of social policy," Schiller wrote. "To inquire about a group's views, for *any* reason, suggests the initial mind-set of the poll-taker and implies a promise of future action or, no less significantly, inaction, somewhere in the societal decision-making apparatus" (1973, p. 105). Schiller tracked the evolution of survey techniques within the military-industrial complex and demand-side of war-related research, showing that the two main claims of the survey research industry were false—namely, that polling is a feedback loop between decision-makers and the public, thus serving democratic ends, and it produces objective facts about people and their preferences. According to Schiller, "polls have served democratic ends not poorly but disastrously. They have cultivated a deceptive guise of neutrality and objectivity. They have fostered the illusion of popular participation and freedom of choice to conceal an increasingly elaborate apparatus of consciousness manipulation and mind management" (1974, p. 123; see also Lewis, 2001).

Finally, we must tackle the global scale at which system serving consumer surveillance operates. As large marketing companies reach limits to innovation and growth, they have begun purchasing competitors and merging databases, software and licensing deals into even larger corporations to get better surveillance results. Concentration in consumer research creates global surveillance services on a sufficiently large scale and with enough variety to meet the demands of transnational corporations, whose businesses encompass interlocking interests in media, entertainment and retail industries. The globalization of consumer surveillance has resulted in unprecedented levels of capitalization in proprietary marketing research, with one multinational conglomerate rising to dominate this area in the 1990s.

We have seen that NielsenNRG dominates marketing research in testing and tracking film audience preferences. We can better understand NielsenNRG's systemic role by examining the Dutch surveillance conglomerate Verenigde Nederlandse Uitgeversbedrijven (VNU), or United Dutch Publishers. NielsenNRG is just one of 22 market research subsidiaries operated by VNU Marketing Information Group (MIG) and Media Measurement & Information Group (MMIG), which operate in over a hundred countries. VNU has become a leading business-information provider through newsletters, magazines, trade shows and directories in Europe,

Asia, South Africa and Puerto Rico. VNU also publishes *Editor & Publisher, The Hollywood Reporter, Adweek, Brandweek* and *Billboard*, among others, and owns several financial data services, a film company, ORG-MARG, the leading market research company in India. VNU was the first company allowed to track Internet use in mainland China where it is building huge databases in partnership with the data storage firm, EMC (Perez, 2002, p. 10; VNU, 2002).

By 2000, VNU had acquired Nielsen Media Research (television and Internet audience measurement), a majority share (65 per cent) in Nielsen NetRatings (Internet user measurement), and the ACNielsen Corporation, the dominant global company in consumer-behaviour surveillance and analysis (Elliot, 2000, p. C7). In addition to its Nielsen holdings, VNU consumer surveillance operations include Claritas USA (it sold Claritas Europe in 2003), Scarborough, Spectra (49 per cent), Trade Dimensions and others. Finally, as a symbol of its growing wealth, VNU signed the largest lease for New York City property in 1999 to house its headquarters in a former department store in the East Village, a deal that "came with about US$9 million in tax incentives from the city and state" (Kanter, 1999, p. 1; VNU, 2002). Through these acquisitions and partnerships VNU became one of the few firms to offer a single source for predicting "demographic, lifestyle and financial behaviour of consumers" ("Equifax", 2000). It can track box-office sales, through Entertainment Data Inc. (Nielsen EDI), video and DVD point-of-sale throughVideoScan, and sporting goods sales through Sports Trend Info (VNU, 2002).

Here the systemic analysis of VNU shows that the global marketing research complex is inseparable from the international political economic system and the entertainment conglomerates' non-stop demand for imperious measures of cultural consumption. It is important to note that, at present, globalization of audience research is still largely financed through massive surveillance of the US population. More than 50 per cent of VNU profits come from US operations. This is, in part, an effect of the non-existent or, where they do exist, shamefully pro-business privacy laws in the US, which pale when measured against the EU's protections from surveillance and for consumer rights (Maxwell, 1999). The surveillance bias towards the US cultural consumer also reflects the lack of business opportunities for marketing research firms outside the US. It is virtually non-existent in all but a few urban enclaves of the poor regions of Asia, Eastern and Central Europe, Latin America and Africa—though VNU is working to change that, especially in China and South Asia. In this way, the US population functions as a valuable asset for multinational market-research conglomerates like VNU. Understanding these systemic conditions helps explain why global consumer surveillance in general, and audience research in particular, concentrate their spying on the US population.

DEMOCRATIC PROSPECTS

The last point of departure for a "Schillerian" analysis of marketing research begins by asking whether reform of marketing research for non-dominating purposes is possible. First, it is important to note that Schiller assumed that media and communications technology ought to be used for the greater good of the world's people. Schiller argued for a balance between a universal principle in support of life-enhancing uses of technology and deep respect for the diversity of ideas and policies generated to achieve that goal, both domestically and internationally. As we have seen, Schiller offered many historical examples of commercial, governmental, and military bureaucracies putting communication technology to uses that undermined democratic communication processes in the developed West and yet-to-be-developed regions of the world. This is also the case with marketing research.

Because of this negative emphasis, there has been much confusion about Schiller's approach to mass media and information technology. Most conservative commentators accused him of being a "technophobe," a reputation that can be partly attributed to the strong bias in U.S. communication studies against political economic research on the media and related technology. This seems especially true among technophilic communication researchers who have presumed, typically without offering proof, that Herbert Schiller's name is synonymous with thoughtless machine-smashing anarchy. This, as Lai-Si Tsui has argued, is "a caricaturing of his position" that can lead to serious misreadings of Schiller's work and intent (Tsui, 1995, p. 162). It is more accurate to describe Schiller as a radical skeptic of technological determinism. That is, he questioned the principle, widespread in modern societies, that social or economic problems could be overcome with technological solutions alone. He argued instead that technology was a social construct and not a value-neutral tool serving science and industry. As such, Schiller understood technology to have, in addition to material uses, equally important organizational, symbolic, or ideological functions for American military-industrial interests (and, in later work, for transnational capitalism generally). And yet, Schiller nevertheless treated the technological infrastructure as imminently recoverable for democratic purposes, though always with the realist's assessment of the legal and political conditions that offered protection to the well-established custodians of modern communication.

On the general question of institutional reform, Schiller placed great emphasis on examining challenges to the imperial system rather than reform of bureaucratic complexes. In a pattern repeated in several of his major works, Schiller took stock of two abiding sources of transformational change, one internal and one external to the U.S. Schiller regarded the U.S.

as a key "nodal link" in the imperial system because of the dominance of the U.S. military and economy in world affairs, the imperial aspirations of 100 years of American leadership, and because U.S. domestic crises and social disruptions resonate globally. On the internal challenge, Schiller noted that the U.S. devoted ever-increasing resources to crisis management since WWII, a sign of great anxiety among the leadership over their ability to stem domestic social disruption. The U.S. is a society where there is heightened awareness of the market's false promises, spectacular waste, and frenzy-inducing consumerism. Here, the word *stress* has general currency, which Schiller added to a long list of signs of social breakdown: cost of living increases faster than per capita income; people overspend themselves into debt and work more hours to make up the difference; public education is under-funded; and risks of despair, marginalization, and ill-health are socialized, while physical and mental care are privatized. Freedom of speech, the right to dissent from this social arrangement, is doled out according to market criteria rather than public interest (Schiller, 1996, pp. 139-140).

While Schiller emphasized the military and economic aspects of crisis management, he also noted the importance of cultural regulation of dissent and how marketing, polling, and other surveillance operations of the cultural industries tracked and refashioned expressions of discontent in order to articulate the concerns of spectators and consumers to system-serving ideologies and cultural dispositions (Schiller, 1989, pp. 152-153). In this sense, marketing research's existence is predicated on the fact that people cannot be easily controlled and the mind management is essential to crisis management. The question as always is how long can the commanders of the informational-cultural complex hold off the forces of social transformation.

The external challenges to a system-serving complex like marketing research originate with socially progressive policies, socialist movements, and revolutions. Such challenges were intolerable to the U.S. leadership. The continued existence of the U.S. dominance required the continued existence of economies based on private property in the countries where [U.S. corporations] are located. Socialist revolutions must be prevented and, if possible, socialist countries must be converted to capitalism. To this end leading U.S. business circles have had a decisive part in the formulation of those policies on which the military-industrial complex is based. (Schiller and Phillips 1970, p. 25)

To meet this challenge, the U.S. leadership relied on an increasingly institutionalized war budget as the primary means of defending the system against collapse globally and domestically. These allocations to the military-industrial complex are also paradoxically a primary cause of internal instability within the American empire where they displace social allocations for education, health, the environment, and other life-enhancing areas (Schiller and Phillips 1970, p. 27).

In view of Schiller's understanding of the historical sweep of these systemic forces, the call for reform of a complex alone would have seemed to
him naive at best, deceptive at worst, unless such reforms were aimed at fundamental systemic change. To find such challenges to the marketing complex, we can survey ways people from around the world have tried to alter
the advertising and marketing apparatuses for positive social change rather
than as cultural and infrastructural supports for capitalism and U.S. imperialism.

Schiller provided an example of one such struggle, and its vulnerability.
In the Afterword to *Communication and Cultural Domination* (1976, pp.
98-109) he turned to the example of communication policy in Chile under
the Popular Unity government (1971-73), which had attempted to implement a pluralistic model of national culture-communication, one open to a
diversity of political and class interests, including commercial, non-commer-
cial, communist, socialist, and educational media organizations, among others. Popular Unity's reform included a systemic challenge—industrial elites'
holdings had been nationalized affecting U.S. military-corporate interests—
leading to reform of the communication complex: advertising became
severely restricted. This experience showed the systemic nature of marketing research—there was no structural kinship of advertising and marketing
to the socialist media, which instead derived content from interests of dominated classes of workers and peasants. The remaining commercial media,
which still functioned to extract profit from advertising directed at the dominated classes, were weakened by the new system in which the nationalized
private sector no longer supplied rich flows of advertising money. Marketing
research was in turn rendered useless by the withering demand for advertising, and many businesses were forced to close. As these tensions worsened,
Chilean industrial elites, U.S. interests, and commercial media became
increasingly intolerant of the socialistic reforms, and with the help of the
American military and CIA, mounted the coup d'etat on September 11,
1973, which ended the socialist experiment.

With this critical stance we can ask how might marketing research be
modified to serve democratic ends. We have seen that systemic reform is
very difficult, though essential to dissolving the hold of market criteria over
the marketing research apparatus. Another challenge might come from
within the cultural industries, where there is growing discontent over the
power that marketing has in determining the content of film, television, and
newer digital media. Marketing has become one of the most expensive of
Hollywood's protectionist barriers to outsiders, while the cost of marketing
has become "drain on profits" (Litman, 1998, p. 59). Hollywood invests
twice as much money in marketing activities as do other comparable industries. Directors, producers and actors have come to view marketing research
as "part of the dumbing down of the business." For a few dissenters, like

Oliver Stone or Francis Ford Coppola, who do not mind the basic principle of giving a film a final test in front of audiences, the problem is, as Stone puts it, when testing reduces filmmaking to "a product-oriented business" that ruins a film's integrity and makes the director a mere "cog in the machine" (quoted in Willens, 2000, p. 20). Actor Alec Baldwin called film marketing a "suppository into the society" on the *Charlie Rose* show (9 January 2004).

Protests from consumer groups in 2001 caused TiVo to change its relationship to subscribers, offering the mild reform of letting people opt out of surveillance, even as it partnered with VNU to improve tracking of customers who didn't opt out. Meanwhile, ReplayTV claimed it simply stopped collecting data, that is, until its owner, Sonicblue went bankrupt and sold Replay TV to a Japanese holding company (Evangelista, 2002; "ReplayTV", 2004). While corporate surveillance adjusted to these protests with an exercise of power via the legal system, the challenge mounted against them by people concerned for their freedom of cultural expression was one sign of democratic opening. There are small pools of resistance like these forming throughout the world, from everyday pirating of intellectual properties to hackers confounding cyber-surveillance.

The key to these internal challenges was expanding awareness of innocent subjects of consumer surveillance. Such challenges are pushing for greater disclosure of audience and consumer research. The burden of the added cost of disclosure is, in most cases, carried by the retailer and marketer. Were such disclosure policies broadly socialized some form of taxation would be required to pay for policing and punishment of commercial offenders, which together would probably be great enough to reduce the commercial incentive for and limit the growth of the exposed surveillance system. In this context, current EU policy on personal data protection in global data trade is instructive, in particular how it succeeds, and where it fails, in creating a mode of comprehending supra-national commitments to citizenship while accommodating the commercial logic of EU audiovisual policy, especially in defence of a right to know the surveyors, correct one's own data, and be informed when personal information is being extracted for surveillance purposes (Maxwell, 1999). Because such a policy encourages the socialisation of the economy of surveillance and display, it demands sharper inspection (see Maxwell, 1999) that would at a minimum challenge the liberal principles underlying the rights conferred upon owners of proprietary information gathered through surveillance, as well as the extremely limited freedoms of privacy protections based in the same property standards. And finally, how does such reform of marketing research avoid recapitulation of governmentality and discipline in another, apparently more humane form (Maxwell, 1996, 1996b)? In practice, marketers feel drawn to the moral authority embedded in their research technique (the protocols) or in the fees and instructions they receive from clients (the pay off).

CONCLUSION

Forms of cooperation and solidarity, however utopian they are at this time, ought to encourage individual marketing researchers to cultivate a greater ethical regard for personal information, minimising the draw of methodological purity or money. Such a principle promotes collaboration of constituencies across a number of social and cultural fields and endeavors to remove the conditions that lead marketers to deepen, and hide, their complicity with the commercial imperial system. Imagine cultural workers allying with marketing, for example, to amplify the presence of cultural labor in public discourse, to bring attention to working conditions and the process of alienation of below the line cultural workers, and to revitalise the relation between filmmaking and filmgoing. Such a modification of marketing research would convert the currently one-way surveillance of cultural consumers into a mode of sociality that raises awareness of the differences between values invested by cultural workers in making meaning and values that people derive from their own meaning-making labors. A greater ethical regard for each constituency's needs, values and desires could flow from this refunctioning of marketing research and its surveillance operations. It has the potential to end differences between the institutional identities of producer and consumer, offering instead a vision of culture work as interdependent efforts of production, distribution and consumption that bring value and meaning into the world. Such a policy would have to ensure some level of subsidy and legal freedom to organise new institutions, both domestically and through international networks. It would also need to be alert to problems confronted by new identities seeking to gain recognition and settled constituencies within the international division of cultural labor that might react to a perceived threat by silencing the newcomers.

Herbert Schiller's work inspired this essay on the imperious measures that marketing research takes in service of the contemporary political economy. The direction and use of information technology for marketing research can be analyzed using a few "Schillerian" moves that include identifying the relevant power structure, its organic ties to the imperial system, and the prospects—realistic and utopian—for democratic renewal of the marketing research complex. There are disturbances within the cultural industries themselves that raise possibilities of reform, and these ought to be embraced as potential points of alliance between critics of empire and those who labor in all areas of meaning-making affected by marketing research. Though fundamental systemic change remains beyond the horizon of current challenges, we should nevertheless be alert to opportunities for social transformations that could initiate systemic change in productive, life-enhancing directions.

REFERENCES

Bates, James (2000) "Site hopes to put profitable spin on Hollywood Fame Game." *Los Angeles Times,* 19 May: C1.

Bickerton, Ian (2003) "VNU to boost billboard technology." *Financial Times,* 18 August: 23.

Dutka, Elaine (2003) "As technology evolves and competition heats up, this is a time of great change in Hollywood market research." *Los Angeles Times,* 31 August: E8.

Elliot Stuart (2000) "Intelligex, a new web site, moves into the new world of online market-research exchange." *New York Times,* 19 December: C7.

Evangelista, Benny (2002) "Sonicblue ruling reversed; Judge says order for data invalid." *San Francisco Chronicle,* 4 June: B7.

Ewen, Stuart (1976). *Captains of Consciousness: Advertising and the Social Roots of Consumer Culture.* New York: McGraw Hill

Hurwitz, Donald L. (1983) *Broadcast "Rating": The Rise and Development of Commercial Audience Research and Measurement in American Broadcasting.* Unpublished PhD dissertation, University of Illinois at Urbana-Champaign.

Kanter L. (1999) "Dutch publishing firm colonizes US: Nielsen deal caps VNU's buying spree." *Crain's New York Business,* 23 August: 1.

Kenwood A. G. and A. L. Lougheed. (1992) *The Growth of the International Economy 1820-1990* (3rd ed.). New York: Routledge.

Larson Eric (1994) *The Naked Consumer: How Our Private Lives Become Public Commodities.* London: Penguin.

Lerner, Preston (1999) "Shadow force: Hundreds of movies have been reshaped as a result of work by Joseph Farrell's National Research Group." *Los Angeles Times Magazine,* 7 November: 18.

Lewis, Justin (2001) *Constructing Public Opinion: How Political Elites Do What They Like and Why We Seem to Go Along with It.* New York: Columbia University Press.

Litman, Barry (1998) *The Motion Picture Mega-Industry.* Boston: Allyn and Bacon.

Mattelart, Armand (1991) *Advertising International: The Privatization of Public Space* (translated by Michael Chanan). London: Comedia/Routledge.

Maxwell, Richard (1996a) "Ethics and identity in global market research." *Cultural Studies* 10(2): 218-236.

Maxwell, Richard (1996b) "Out of kindness and into difference: The value of global market research." *Media, Culture & Society* 18(1).

Maxwell, Richard (1999) "The marketplace citizen and the political economy of data trade in the European Union." *Journal of International Communication* 6(1).

Maxwell, Richard (2000) "Picturing the audience." *Television and New Media,* 1(2): 135-57.

Miller, Toby, Nitin Govil, John McMurria, and Richard Maxwell (2001) *Global Hollywood.* London: British Film Institute.

Mills, C. Wright (1956) *The Power Elite.* London: Oxford University Press.

Milmo, Dan (2003) "Biblical battle in Tinseltown." *Guardian,* 15 October: 20.

Perez, Bien (2002) "EMC to aid ACNielsen's China hopes." *South China Morning Post,* 11 September: 10.

Piirto, Rebecca (1991) *Beyond Mind Games:The Marketing Power of Psychographics.* Ithaca, NY: American Demographics Books.

"Replay TV users' lawsuit is dismissed." (2004) *Los Angeles Times,* 13 January: C2.

Richtel, Matt (2002) "New billboards sample radios as cars go by, then adjust." *New York Times,* 27 December: C1, C5.

Rose, Marla Matzer (2001) "Television industry profile," Business.Com.

Schiller, Herbert I. (1969) *Mass Communications and American Empire.* New York: Augustus M. Kelley, Paperback ed., Beacon Press, 1971; new ed., Westview, 1992.

Schiller, Herbert I., with Joseph Dexter Phillips (1970) *Super-State; Readings in the Military Industrial Complex.* Urbana: University of Illinois Press.

Schiller, Herbert I. (1973) *The Mind Managers.* Boston: Beacon Press.

Schiller, Herbert I. (1976) *Communication and Cultural Domination.* New York: International Arts and Sciences Press.

Schiller, Herbert I. (1979) "Communication accompanies capital flows." In *International Commission for the Study of Communication Problems.* The MacBride Commission. Paris: UNESCO, May.

Schiller, Herbert I. (1989) *Culture Inc: The Corporate Takeover of Public Expression.* New York: Oxford University Press.

Schiller, Herbert I. (1996) *Information Inequality: The Deepening Social Crisis in America.* New York: Routledge.

Schiller, Herbert I. (2000) *Living in the Number One Country: Reflections From a Critic of American Empire.* New York: Seven Stories Press.

Simpson, Christopher (1994) *Science of Coercion: Communication Research and Psychological Warfare, 1945-1960.* New York: Oxford University Press.

Strasser, Susan (1989) *Satisfaction Guaranteed: The Making of the American Mass Market.* New York: Pantheon.

Thompson, Clive (2003) "There's a sucker born in every medial prefrontal cortex." *New York Times Magazine,* 26 October: 54-58, 85.

Tsui, Lai-si (1995) Herbert Schiller: Clarion voice against cultural hegemony. In John Lent (Ed.), *A Different Road Taken: Profiles in Critical Communication* (pp. 155-172). Boulder, CO: Westview Press.

VNU (2002) *Annual Report.* Haarlem, The Netherlands.

Wells, William, ed. (1974) *Lifestyle and Psychographics.* Chicago: American Marketing Association

Willens, M. (2000) "Putting films to the test, every time." *New York Times,* 25 June: 11, 20.

Wyatt, Justin (1995) *High Concept: Movies and Marketing in Hollywood.* Austin: University of Texas.

CHAPTER THREE

FROM ASSOCIATIVE TO DEEP
SPONSORSHIP AT THE
MILLENNIUM DOME

Jim McGuigan

Consider, for a moment, the photograph of Ron Mueck's sculpture, *Boy*, in the Mind Zone at London's New Millennium Experience during the year 2000. *Boy* was a strangely humanistic phantom in a zone, designed by deconstructionist architect Zaha Hadid, which at the very least represented posthumanism and perhaps even the inhuman, in Lyotard's (1988) term. The Mind Zone was the most intellectual of the fourteen zones at the Dome exposition. Framing Mind's absent center was the network principle of hi-tech civilization, so thoroughly analyzed by Manuel Castells (1996), including, for instance, an ant colony, the Internet, and a sequence of criss-crossing passes leading to a Manchester United goal. At its spatial center was the enigmatic *Boy* with McDonald's logo on his back. McDonald's did not actually sponsor the Mind Zone, though the fast-food chain was a ubiquitous presence at the Dome. McDonald's sponsored Our Town Story and welcomed groups of schoolchildren from around the country on stage for their day performing at the Dome. Among McDonald's eateries on the site was the largest one in Europe situated across from the main entrance. Mind was, in fact, co-sponsored by the electronics firm Marconi and its partner company BAe Systems, the arms manufacturer.

I studied the Millennium Dome for two main reasons. First, as an exercise in multidimensional analysis (Kellner, 1997): the Dome exposition was a comparatively bounded object that lent itself to a combination of political economy, textual interpretation, and research on mediation and visitor experience, in effect, analyzing the interrelated dimensions of production, representation, and consumption. Second, from its inception, the exposition in a big tent on a southern peninsula of the Thames at Greenwich in East London, where the Meridian line cuts across the tip of the peninsula like a circumcision, was a controversial object of cultural policy. It was destined to become a big issue of public debate—in the event, bigger than I anticipated. The core thesis derived from the research, which stresses the decisive role of corporate sponsorship in how the Dome turned out, has already been published (McGuigan, 2003; McGuigan and Gilmore, 2002; see also McGuigan and Gilmore, 2001).

Here, I want to draw out some generalizations from this particular and, indeed, very peculiar case. My argument further substantiates Herbert Schiller's thesis concerning "the corporate takeover of public expressio". He noted how corporations not only commanded the communications and cultural industries, but were also invading the public sector, which was becoming engulfed by "a marketing ideological atmosphere" (1989, p. 33). Set against the marketization of everything is a tired, old, yet residually modern tradition of state intervention in the cultural field to make available to the public that which otherwise might not be provided commercially. This was the logic of expanding public arts patronage and cultural subsidy after the Second World War, though the rationales for which—and, consequentially, funding—have been undermined in recent years (Bennet, 1995). In my view, the crisis of public cultural provision—which is perhaps a seemingly trivial matter—should be seen in relation to enclosure of the global commons and the shrinking space of unbranded culture across the Earth today.

CORPORATE TAKEOVER
OF PUBLIC CULTURE

Although public culture is not, of course, reducible to the public sector and state funding, this is the area that I wish to concentrate upon. Swathes of the public sector in Britain and elsewhere have been privatized on grounds of efficiency and so forth but nobody advocates or supposes, not even in the United States, that the basic education of a whole population could be turned over to business entirely. There is plenty of partial privatization, outsourcing, and autonomous flotation in public education. Beyond these trends, however, underfunded public education is an increasingly eager host for corporate intervention, as Naomi Klein (2000) documents in *No Logo*. It is not just about Coke schools or Pepsi schools. It is also about the curriculum. Schools are eager to receive corporate donations of computing and teaching materials. Educational television, as a vehicle for advertising and marketing, most notably K-111's Channel One, is accepted with few pockets of resistance. The free gift of the ZapMe! Browser in schools is a further means of educating and surveying young consumers.

In a similar vein, Chin-tao Wu's (2002) *Privatising Culture* charts the variants of corporate intervention and takeover in the public art worlds of Britain and the United States. Modern philanthropy is one thing; postmodern corporate sponsorship, something else. The visual arts are especially suitable for corporate promotion and laundering a company's image, most notably in the case of the tobacco manufacturer Philip Morris in the United States. In London, the once radical Institute for Contemporary Arts acknowledges the generosity of Toshiba, and Tate Britain has a Nomura Room named after the Japanese investment bank that put up £1.5 million to refurbish it. Figures like the Tate's Nicholas Serota are not just curators of the public's art but cultural entrepreneurs fusing together art and business in order to make ends meet when state funding is deemed insufficient to maintain standards and expand operations. On the opening of Tate Modern in May 2000, Serota expressed "our deepest gratitude for supporting our vision" to "public and private donors" (quoted by Blazwick and Wilson, 2000).

Lines have been crossed, distinctions blurred. If the corporations will do it for no cost to the public why should the public pay at all? Well, because, in Britain, differently from the United States, these institutions of public culture would not exist were it not for public subsidy. Who exactly is supporting whom?

THE NEW MILLENNIUM EXPERIENCE

A few facts and figures: the New Millennium Experience cost in excess of £800 million of public money. This consisted of £628 million from the National Lottery granted to the New Millennium Experience Company by the Millennium Commission, at arm's length from the New Labour government, although the Dome minister said it could never be bankrupt because the government would not let that happen. A figure in the region of £200 million of tax revenue was spent on the New Millennium Experience through the urban regeneration agency English Partnerships to buy and partly reclaim the deeply toxic site of a former gasworks. The contents were sold off at knockdown prices in February 2001 shortly after closure. However, the site continued to be a public cost for maintenance for years— even after it was, in effect, given away in 2002—estimated at £250,000 a month as recently as July 2003 (Maguire and Teather, 2003, p. 1).

A number of failed attempts had been made to sell off the Dome and its site. Had the Dome been demolished, the land would have been more valuable for development. Such an admission of failure was unacceptable to the New Labour government. In the end, the government gave the place to the Meridian Delta consortium for nothing up front in the vague hope that it might eventually receive a share of profits. These are to be derived from use of the Dome as an entertainment and sports venue by the American Anschutz Entertainment Group and lucrative property development around it by Quintain Estates and the Australian Lend Lease real estate group. It is now unlikely to reopen before 2007. In addition to delays in planning permission, part of the reason for the Dome's continuing disuse is related to investigations into and lawsuits against Philip Anschutz's Quest business empire in the United States, which is suspected of artificially inflating its stock value à la Enron.

Throughout 2000, the Dome was criticized in the news media as a "fiasco," a "disaster" and a scandalous waste of public money, especially on the four occasions that the government sanctioned extra lottery grants from the Millennium Commission to keep it open. The Dome attracted just over half its projected visitor number of 12 million during the year. Only one-third of the expected visitors for January showed up in that dismal, cash-strapped month. This was given as the official reason for bailing the Dome out for the first time shortly after opening. However, the immediate financial crisis may have been as much to do with the reluctance of sponsors to pay up and, in some cases, to finalize contracts.

The actual value of sponsorship remains unclear due to commercial confidentiality agreements. It was probably around £150 million, including a nebulous "value in kind." It is evident that a number of sponsors did not pay the full tariff of association. Two sponsors—BT and Ford—actually spent much more on their zones—Talk and Journey—than was formally required by the New Millennium Experience Company (NMEC). They negotiated "turnkey" contracts that enabled them to build and run their own zones with minimal editorial interference from NMEC. In effect, both BT and Ford treated their zones, designed by the trade-show designer Imagination, as corporate promotion. For instance, there were no motorcars in Journey other than Ford.

Corporate sponsorship was a small fraction of the public money spent on the New Millennium Experience. Moreover, the estimated figure of £150 million was less than the sum of the additional tranches of Lottery funding granted during 2000. Yet, to a very large extent, corporate sponsors called the shots at the Dome. The project was launched under the last Conservative government in the mid-1990s. The general aim was to promote "British" business to the world (see Heseltine, 2000; Nicolson, 1999). The rhetoric then referred back to the Great Exhibition of 1851. When New Labour adopted the Dome, on coming into office in 1997, the historical reference point shifted to Old Labour's 1951 Festival of Britain. Yet, the fundamental constitution of the project remained the same. Sponsors were wooed desperately in the late-1990s and heeded when they revolted in January 2000 over bad publicity, resulting in the sacking of former civil servant Jenny Page as CEO and her replacement by P-Y Gerbeau, formerly of Disneyland Paris.

There were significant differences in management style and customer orientation between the two managerial regimes, but they should not be exaggerated. Gerbeau knew whom he had to please first and foremost: the sponsors. He called them "partners" (interview with the author). With the advent of the new regime, visitors were routed through the sponsors' village of small shop units—the so-called "Interactive Zone"—before being permitted to enter the Dome. Large sponsorship placards were put up in front of sponsored thematic zones so visitors should have no doubt of who the donor was. The Dome became the "Logoland" that Page said she would never allow it to become. That was somewhat disingenuous, as corporate sponsorship was at the heart of the project from beginning to end.

The Dome was supposed to explore key issues about contemporary life at the turn of the Millennium. Its zones were classified into three theme clusters at the front of the official guidebook.

The zones may be reclassified according to interpretation of how obtrusive or comparatively unobtrusive was sponsorship in particular cases and where it was absent.

Parts of the Dome attracted no sponsorship, such as the ecology zone Living Island and Play, which had its sponsorship withdrawn for not fulfilling the demands of the sponsor, BSkyB. According to MORI polling, the consistently highest visitor approval rating throughout the year was registered for the Millennium Show in the Central Arena (see McGuigan and Gilmore, 2001). The Millennium Show featured an aerial ballet choreographed by Mark Fisher with music by Peter Gabriel. It told an allegorical love story linked to the emergence, destructiveness, and collapse of industrialism. The pivotal motif of a rising and falling gasholder recalled the previous use of the Dome site. There was also a spectacular light show. It is interesting to note that the Millennium Show had no sponsor. Moreover, "a lasting legacy" from it was intended and perhaps realized. Young people had been selected and trained in the performance skills associated with the Canadian troupe, Cirque de Soleil, leaving a greater pool of modern circus talent than had previously existed in Britain.

TABLE 3.1   Official Classification of Zones

WHO WE ARE	WHAT WE DO	WHERE WE LIVE
Body	Work	Shared Ground
Mind	Learning	Living Island
Faith	Rest	Home Planet
Self Portrait	Play	
	Talk	
	Money	
	Journey	

(Millennium Experience—The Guide, p. 3)

TABLE 3.2   Alternative Classification of Zones

OBTRUSIVE SPONSORSHIP	COMPARATIVELY UNOBTRUSIVE SPONSORSHIP	LITTLE OR NO SPONSORSHIP
Journey (*Ford)	Self Portrait (*Marks & Spencer)	Living Island
Talk (*BT)	Shared Ground (**Camelot)	Play
Money (*City of London)	Mind (**Marconi **BAE Systems)	Rest
Work (*Manpower)		Faith ('The Laing Family Trust
Learning (*Tesco) Home Planet (**British Airways **BAA) Body (**Boots)		The Hinduja Foundation The Jerusalem Trust The Garfield Weston Foundation and from three other trusts and organizations associated with the
Mind (**Marconi) (**BAE Systems)		Christian Faith'— quoted from a notice at the zone)

*Official sponsor
**Official partner

ASSOCIATIVE AND DEEP SPONSORSHIP

My distinction between comparatively obtrusive and comparatively unobtrusive sponsorship is roughly a distinction between blatant propaganda—such as the employment agency Manpower's Work Zone—and subtler forms of ideological representation—such as Marks and Spencer's Self Portrait Zone. There is a further distinction to be made, however, between associative and deep sponsorship, which is not so much about the differences between the two managerial regimes as tensions within the project and a general trend exemplified by the Dome. The editorial relation between business and design in the case of the Millennium Dome illustrates an important distinction and a significant transition in a cultural project that was largely funded by the public. Although not rigidly congruent, associative sponsorship tended to be relatively unobtrusive, whereas deep sponsorship tended to be obtrusive.

Associative sponsorship is the standard form in the arts and public sector of cultural provision. Sponsors acquire kudos through association with artistic culture but are not supposed to influence content. As critics have argued, this is not what actually happens in practice (Shaw, 1993). Sponsorship exerts all sorts of subtle pressure on editorial decision making, program selection, and so on. Nevertheless, the norms of associative sponsorship are still claimed and defended in order to protect cultural integrity: for instance, sponsors of Tate Modern are not supposed to select artworks and dictate exhibition policy, though donations of money and work, to be sure, are gratefully received.

On the other hand, the purpose of *deep sponsorship* is, unashamedly, to actually construct cultural meaning in the interests of corporate business. This is evidently so in, for instance, product placement in Hollywood films and sponsorship of sporting events, where corporations have even sought to change the rules of the game. The most extreme case of deep sponsorship is autonomously created culture, usually of a popular kind so that the form itself is a vehicle for advertising, merchandizing, and public relations. Disney was a pioneer in this respect. Corporations' construction of children's culture both in entertainment and education is perhaps the most profound and widespread instance of deep sponsorship.

Several zones at the Dome were instances of deep rather than associative sponsorship: for instance, Tesco's Learning Zone, which connected its display to the supermarket chain's long-standing sponsorship of computer-aided education. Other examples of manifestly evident editorial command by sponsors included zones that were ostensibly under NMEC's control—such as Manpower's Work Zone and the City of London's Money Zone—and the two that were not—BT's Talk Zone and Ford's Journey Zone. As "Ford's Dome person" told me, "We let them [NMEC's editorial staff and advisors] believe they were influencing things but in actual fact we took no notice of them."

Although the Journey Zone's history of transport included no motor-cars other than Ford, ironically, unlike most of the Dome's contents, it afforded a sense of history. The original Dome minister, Peter Mandelson, before he was forced to resign over a loan scandal, had insisted that the Dome was to be about the future, not the past. The past was to be consigned to the dustbin of history along with Old Labour. Yet, the Dome generally failed to articulate an exciting new world. When history is abolished it is difficult to imagine the future. Curiously, though, Ford's autonomous and very expensive Journey Zone was an outstanding exception to the general obliteration rather than representation of time—past, present and future—at the Dome. The Journey Zone was designed by Imagination, the firm that had for years designed Ford's displays at the annual Motor Show in Birmingham and that had originally been hired to manage the design of the exposition as a whole. It traced the history of transport technologies, including trains, trainers and planes as well as cars, such as Ford's futuristic gas-powered vehicle, Project FC5. It polled visitors on their attitudes to transport and environmental issues. Near the end of the zone four different future scenarios for travel, devised by the University of Sussex, were presented to consider on wide, head-height monitors. On the opposite wall a notice said: "There is not one future, there are many." According to the Journey Zone, the future is a matter of choice, not predetermined. Its sponsor, Ford, one of the world's greatest manufacturers of mobile pollution, insisted on environmental friendliness. Journey felt like an exhibit in a trade show. It was also, however, the zone that did most to address the question of time, supposedly the core question of the exposition, with a chronological sense of history and comparatively intelligent speculation about the future. Ford's Journey was, then, a transparent yet somewhat sophisticated example of deep sponsorship in the construction of meaning at the Millennium Dome.

P.-Y. Gerbeau, the CEO from February 2002, did not initiate deep sponsorship at the Dome; he merely justified it in his fashionable rhetoric of "public-private partnership" and, specifically, in his argument that you cannot just take money off sponsors without allowing them to influence what is on display. Yet, the vast majority of funding did not come from corporate sponsorship but instead, from "the public purse." Lottery money, in this sense, is a kind of public subscription that was disbursed by the Millennium Commission but which failed to police editorial integrity at the exposition.

The National Lottery has, to be sure, been criticized as an informal tax on the poor to the benefit of the comparatively well off through the disbursement of funds to "good causes," especially cultural causes. A visit to the Dome was an expensive day out that attracted visitors mainly from the south east of England, the richest part of the country, though the social demography of visitors was actually quite mixed. Still, the Lottery must be regarded as a means of generating "public money" even if it is a substitute for tax revenue in the formal sense as a source of subsidy to culture and other public goods.

Clearly, the Dome was a site of tension over public and corporate control—in effect, regulation. That there were notable instances of associative sponsorship and absence of sponsorship in parts of the Dome also demonstrate the tensions in play. An example of associative sponsorship is Marks and Spencer's Self Portrait Zone, which dealt with British national identity. In this zone contradictions were set up by the juxtaposition of placard's extolling the virtues of Britishness—"creativity," 'fairplay' and so on—with Gerald Scarfe's sculptures representing the darker side of Britishness, such as a football hooligan with a boot for a head and a respectable racist. It would have been unlikely for this zone to point out that Marks and Spencer's was a "quality" and hitherto "patriotic" retail chain that was currently losing custom and turning toward outsourcing product from cheap labor around the world as part of the solution to its business problems. Nonetheless, the sponsor did allow a questioning of Britishness and an opening up of debate over national identity to be articulated in its zone and did not manifestly promote its own products there, as was so in several other sponsored zones (see McGuigan, 2004, for detailed analysis of Self Portrait).

NOT JUST PROMOTIONAL CULTURE

The Dome was undoubtedly a vehicle of promotional culture (Wernick, 1991). As Jonathan Glancey (2001, p. 26) observed: "The Millennium Experience, its entrance flanked by a branch of McDonald's proved to be an exhibition of corporate sponsorship." This was an accurate criticism, but not very deep in accounting for the political economy and ideology of corporate involvement in Britain's millennium celebrations. With very few exceptions, such as Greg Palast (2001) in *The Observer*, journalists hardly penetrated the deeper motives of corporations for sponsoring parts of the Dome. It is easy enough to see why Boots, the High-Street chemist, took the opportunity to promote pharmaceutical products at the Body Zone, but harder to see why BAe Systems put money into the Mind Zone. One of the largest armaments manufacturers in the world, BAe does not sell Hawk jets directly to the public.

Unlike the brazenness of several other sponsor/zone relations, Mind did not manifestly promote BAe's core business. Instead, the official purpose of the zone was to represent modern engineering generally and to encourage the education of engineers. However, like a number of other sponsors, BAe may have had ulterior motives for supporting the Dome. In 1997 the New Labour government promised to pursue an "ethical foreign policy", which might have meant not sanctioning the sale of armaments to the genocidal Suharto regime in Indonesia. Soon, this "unrealistic" policy was quietly dropped since the production of armaments is one of the few remaining buoyant sectors of British manufacturing and exports in what is said to be a "weightless" informational economy. The government's U-turn on foreign policy—the unrestrained issuing of export guarantees to armament manu-facturers and the conduct of diplomacy on their behalf—was of more than incidental benefit to BAe Systems. This was of much greater significance than the much commented allegation that the Hinduja brothers' modest donation to the Faith Zone bought them British passports, a story that won the journalists who broke it the journalism of the year award.

The Hinduja brothers' passports-for-sponsorship scandal was only the tip of an iceberg, the greater part of which the news media virtually ignored. As the former marketing director of one of the corporate sponsors remarked in interview, everyone had a political deal. This was apparently so of the Work Zone's sponsor Manpower, the American employment agency, in growing its business in Britain. Manpower handled human resources for the New Millennium Experience, hiring, training, and relocating employees on closure. Yet more significantly, in association with Ernst and Young, the government's favorite accountancy firm, Manpower obtained nine out of fif-teen contracts for managing employment zones around the country, a little remarked upon feature of the New Labour government's privatization of public agencies. This may just be coincidental.

There are several other coincidences to note. The supermarket chain Tesco—sponsor of the Learning Zone—must have been pleased when the government dropped its proposed legislation for taxing out-of-town carparking at retail estates. BA and BAA (British Airports Authority)—co-sponsors of Home Planet, the closest thing to a ride at the Dome—must have appreciated the government's sanctioning of Terminal 5 at Heathrow in face of popular protest by locals against its building. It came as something of a surprise when Camelot—sponsor of Shared Ground—had its National Lottery contract renewed by a Labour government that had vowed to replace its profit-making operation with a not-for-profit operator. Rupert Murdoch's BskyB—sponsor of Skyscape—has benefited from the govern-ment's light-touch policies for broadcasting and digitalization, not to men-tion its relaxed press policy. There are other examples. It may all just be coincidence. However, it is reasonable to infer that sponsorship of New Labour's Millennium Experience was more than a publicity exercise.

CONCLUSION—A SHELL FOR NEO-LIBERALISM

The Millennium exposition in a big tent at Greenwich was a multifaceted phenomenon. A great many people visited the Dome who, in spite of the media damnation, were prepared to give it the benefit of the doubt and to reflect upon its meanings in context (see McGuigan and Gilmore, 2002, on generous and reflexive visiting). However, the New Millennium Experience represented a very limited and constrained space for critical reflection on time and place due to the overweening presence of a corporate agenda. It was not so much the site for disputation characteristic of a genuinely cultural public sphere. Instead, it was the object of a pseudo–public sphere for a scandalized news media that heaped a mountain of column inches and broadcast time on top of the Dome but which somehow missed the real, underlying scandal. To put it summarily, New Labour's Millennium Experience was an "ideological shell of neo-liberalism", in Perry Anderson's (2000, p. 11) resonant phrase.

REFERENCES

Anderson, P. (2000) "Renewals." *New Left Review* 1 (2nd series), January-February: 5-24.

Bennett, O. (1995) "Cultural policy in the United Kingdom—collapsing rationales and the end of a tradition." *European Journal of Cultural Policy* 1(2): 199-216.

Blazwick, I. and S. Wilson (Eds.) (2000) *Tate Modern—The Handbook*. London: Tate Gallery.

Castells, M. (1996) *The Rise of the Network Society*. Malden MA & Oxford: Basil Blackwell.

Glancey, J. (2001) *London—Bread and Circuses*. London & New York: Verso.

Heseltine, M. (2000) *Life in the Jungle*. London: Hodder & Stoughton.

Kellner, D. (1997) "Critical theory and cultural studies—the missed articulation." In J. McGuigan (Ed.), *Cultural Methodologies* (pp. 12-41). London, Thousand Oaks & New Delhi: Sage.

Klein, N. (2000) *No Logo—Taking Aim at the Brand Bullies*. London: HarperCollins.

Maguire, K. and D. Teather (2003) "The dome—new delays, new doubts." *Guardian*, 29 July: 1-2.

McGuigan, J. (2003) "The social construction of a cultural disaster—New Labour's millennium experience." *Cultural Studies* 17(5): 669-690.

McGuigan, J. (2004) "A shell for neo-liberalism—New Labour Britain and the Millennium Dome." In S. Burnett, E. Caunes, E. Mazierska and J. Walton (Eds.), *Relocating Britishness* (pp. 38-52). Manchester: Manchester University Press.

McGuigan, J. and A. Gilmore (2001) "Figuring out the Dome." *Cultural Trends* 39: 39-83.

McGuigan, J. and A. Gilmore (2002) "The Millennium Dome—Sponsoring, meaning and visiting." *International Journal of Cultural Policy* 8(1): 1-20.

Nicolson, A. (1999) *Regeneration—The Story of the Millennium Dome*. London: HarperCollins.

Palast, G. (2001) "Ask no questions......," *The Observer—Business*, 25 March: 6.

Schiller, H. (1989) *Culture Inc.—The Corporate Takeover of Public Expression*. New York: Oxford University Press.

Shaw, R. (Ed.) (1993) *The Spread of Sponsorship—in the Arts, Sport, Education, the Health Service and Broadcasting.* Newcastle: Bloodaxe Books.

Wernick, A. (1991) *Promotional Culture—Advertising, Ideology and Symbolic Expression.* London, Newbury Park & New Delhi: Sage.

Wu, C.-T. (2002) *Privatising Culture—Corporate Art Intervention Since the 1980s.* London & New York: Verso.

SECTION TWO

INCORPORATIONS

Capturing Public Culture

CHAPTER FOUR

WHOSE GROUND ZERO? CONTESTING PUBLIC SPACE IN LOWER MANHATTAN

Vincent Mosco

In post-9/11 New York, it's not those tired 20th-century battles about pornography and blasphemy that draw blood. The new culture wars often spring from 9/11 itself, starting with the future, aesthetic and otherwise, of ground zero. (Rich, 2003, Section 2, pp. 1 and 4)

PERVERSIONS OF PUBLIC SPACE

In his 1989 book, *Culture Inc.,* Herbert Schiller demonstrated the value of a political economy approach to culture and his notable scholarly versatility by examining struggles over public space in New York City. This chapter builds on this work by taking up the political economy of one of the most significant spaces in the United States today, the site of the attacks on the World Trade Center or ground zero.

The keynote of Schiller's book is the contradiction embodied in a cover graphic, a logo announcing PUBLIC SPACE: Owned and maintained by AT&T, 550 Madison Avenue, New York City. As Schiller describes, the figure is taken from banners flying outside what was then the AT&T Building and is the result of a deal between the company and the city which provided AT&T with a zoning variance enabling it to build higher, adding 20% to the maximum volume of the building. In return, the city received an open "plaza" at the base of the building for people to sit. In characteristic fashion, Schiller comments on the assessment of *The New York Times* architecture critic Paul Goldberger and offers his own unvarnished position:

> Goldberger comes to an astonishing conclusion: "So these plazas [IBM got one too] are not really a gift to the people from the building's owners—they are much more a gift from the city itself." More accurately, the only "gift" readily evident in the transaction was the permission given to the builders to violate the zoning codes by 20 percent. The public got a couple of dubious resting places surrounded by masonry. A genuine choice might have meant an undeveloped street corner with a real park instead of . . . AT&T's massive presence. (Schiller, 1989, p. 102)

As part of my research on the transformation of New York City, I have returned several times to the site Schiller describes to carry out an ethnographic analysis. The building is no longer owned by AT&T. Another media giant, Sony, bought it and renamed the space at its base Sony Plaza. Schiller would not be surprised to learn that the marketization of public space continues unabated. As part of its deal with the city, Sony was allowed to enclose the plaza so that it is no longer an open space continuous with the street, but only accessible through a set of doors. The plaza itself has been transformed into a Sony mini-mall with shops for Sony products, the Sony Wonder Technology Lab, a museum celebrating communication technology, and an open space containing tables. Uniformed private security guards patrol the court, there to enforce what a plasticized card placed on each of tables calls

SONY PLAZA RULES OF CONDUCT:

No Loitering (Please be considerate of others waiting for a seat)
No Alcoholic Beverages
No Disruptive Behavior
No Excessive Packages
No Smoking

The only item on the list that may confuse is the stipulation against excessive packages. This has come to be boilerplate language for keeping out the homeless, who carry their worldly goods in large bags. The Plaza, which was never closed to the public when it was an open space, now operates from 7AM to 11PM.

The banners still fly outside the plaza, with two large ones announcing at the top "Sony Wonder" and at the bottom "Public Space." Smaller banners proclaim "Public Space" followed by "Sony Plaza, Public Arcade, and Sony Wonder." When Sony took over the building, perhaps to deflect criticism from its decision to glass in the plaza, it installed a coffee shop called Café Society. What was especially interesting about the shop was a huge mural over the bar with a relatively long description that could have been written by Jürgen Habermas. It described how democracy was born in the public coffee houses of Europe where people would freely gather to discuss the issues of the day. It went on to explain that Café Society was more than a place to sit and sip, but an essential force for equality and civic participation. In that spirit it took the name Café Society to honor and extend that tradition. Café Society is no longer a part of Sony Plaza. Coffee is now sold at a Starbucks inside a shop selling only Sony products in one corner of the Plaza. The Berkeley Bar and Grill, an upscale restaurant, replaced Café Society. This "Yup-Scale" bistro (the actress Gwyneth Paltrow gave it her blessing at its opening) cut further into the main plaza, diminishing the number of tables.

Culture Inc. also discussed the IBM building, which is located across the street from Sony Plaza at 590 Madison Avenue, attached to the new Nike Town emporium. In another media twist, the building became headquarters of the Freedom Forum Media Foundation, which hung a banner outside the building proclaiming Free Press, Free Speech, Free Spirit. IBM built a glass-enclosed atrium in return for its zoning variance, but soon fled the city that had subsidized its New York location and sold out to a real estate developer and art collector. Right under the nose of the Freedom Forum banner we find another proclamation on each of the Atrium's tables announcing "Rules of the Atrium":

> Sleeping and Smoking are Prohibited
>
> Drinking of Alcoholic Beverages is Prohibited
>
> Shopping Carts and Large or Obstructive Packages are Prohibited
>
> Sitting on Atrium Floors or Heating Vents is Prohibited
>
> Leave Chairs and Benches Clear of Personal Items
>
> No Radio Playing
>
> Gambling, Card Playing, Solicitation, Handbilling, and Disorderly Conduct are not Permitted
>
> No Loitering
>
> Disregard of These Rules will Subject You to Your Removal
>
> Thank you for your cooperation.

Schiller's analysis of the struggles over public culture and the increasing threat posed by marketization was part of a wider interest in reaching out to cultural practitioners including artists, librarians, policymakers, teachers, students, trade unionists, journalists, and film makers. This is one reason why critics who pegged Schiller as a one-dimensional thinker, an economic determinist who saw capitalism as an omnipotent singularity, miss the mark. Admittedly, he concentrated on the power of global capitalism, particularly the growth of transnational media, information, and cultural businesses. Without a doubt, events have more than justified this focus. However, he also recognized that capitalism was a complex beast and that there was no necessity nor inevitability to its triumph. In the last decade of his life, Schiller expanded his research to examine the cultural significance of media in city streets and parks, billboard advertising, museums, libraries, and a host of other places that demonstrated for him that "a community's economic life cannot be separated from its symbolic content" and that "speech, dance, drama, music and the visual and plastic arts have been vital, indeed necessary, features of human experience from the earliest times." (Schiller, 1989, p. 31)

THE POWER OF THE PAST

Building on the view that a community's economic life cannot be separated from its symbolic content, this chapter turns to the case of New York's ground zero and what we can learn from the political economic and cultural struggles over who will control it. The World Trade Center was arguably the first material manifestation of the postindustrial society idea. It was driven by an intense commitment to create a hub for what Manuel Castells (1989) has called "the Informational City", a space of flows or portal that simultaneously produces, manages, and distributes data, messages, and ideas. People began to call New York a Global City to describe its ability to command and control the international production and distribution of resources, particularly information (Sassen, 1992). As Eric Darton eloquently describes it, the World Trade Center project was wrapped up in the "dawning awareness of political and business leaders of the beginning of a service economy . . ." Its construction would not just add office space to lower Manhattan, "its emergence on the skyline would broadcast the news that New York had ...wrenched itself free of its murky industrial past . . . [T]he towers would serve as symbols of the financial center's manifest destiny and would secure the city's position as the vital hub of the coming postindustrial world." (Darton, 1999, pp. 74-75) It would indeed provide the first utopian or sublime space of the information age.

As captured in two types of accounts, the World Trade Center itself embodied the technological sublime. The first is the mythic history represented in Angus Gillespie's *Twin Towers* (a book written before 9/11 but reprinted and distributed widely after the attacks), which contains several themes that lend transcendence to the process of building them and to the structures themselves. The story of their construction is one of overcoming all obstacles, from the political wrangling between governments to the use of new design and engineering concepts, each of which challenged the view that, as Chapter 2 of Gillespie's book announces, "It Can't be Done." If the process of constructing the towers is embodied in the "against all odds" myth, then the structures themselves are rendered in the glow of a populist myth: although elite critics universally disliked them, they were beloved among ordinary folk. "Pick up almost any serious book on American architecture," Gillespie tells us, "and you will look in vain for mention of the World Trade Center. The few books that do mention the building do so with disparaging language." (2001, p. 162) And yet, it "is recognized by ordinary people as an icon for the City of New York." (p. 179) Put simply, in the subtitle of his chapter on architecture, it was "beloved by all except the experts." In spite of all the difficulties, including the savage criticism of an architectural elite, the Towers succeeded. These were no mere office buildings; they embodied the populist myth of the American Dream.

Michel de Certeau provides a different sense of the sublime, less the mythic history and more the mythic spectacle, in his essay "Practices of Space." From the perspective of the 107th floor of one tower, he finds that "On this concrete, steel, and glass stage, bounded by the cold water of two oceans (the Atlantic and the American) the tallest letters in the world create this gigantesque rhetoric of excess in expenditure and production. To what erotics of knowledge can the ecstasy of reading such a cosmos be connected?" He goes on to admire "the pleasure of looking down upon, of totalizing this vastest of human texts" (de Certeau, 1985, p. 122). The spectacle summons the language of vastness in geography and discourse, a language of eros and cosmos, to capture the totalizing force of the vision from the near heavenly perch of the observation deck.

Notwithstanding the mythic discourse, ground zero was born in the tumult of social conflict and the banality of political economy, all of which help to explain contemporary struggles over the site. The Trade Center project actually grew out of a fierce debate in the 1950s and 1960s, when a dispute about urban redevelopment, that is what to do with lower Manhattan, effectively became the surrogate for an argument about the meaning and significance of a postindustrial society. In brief, on the one side were proponents of strengthening the existing mixed economy of blue-and white-collar labor and affordable housing. On the other were supporters of a postindustrial monoculture of office towers and luxury housing. The latter, led by David and Nelson Rockefeller, won out over a movement that included the noted urban specialist Jane Jacobs (1961) and other critics of the view that

New York City would inevitably lead the way to a postindustrial service economy (New York City Planning Commission, 1969; Regional Planning Association, 1968).

New York City once provided one of the best examples of a diverse, what would come to be called "post-fordist," socioeconomic order, led by small and medium-sized enterprises and a strong public infrastructure, long before Piore and Sable (1984) made the so-called second industrial divide popular and before scholars and planners flocked to Bologna to document the success of "The Third Italy" (Best, 1990). All of this ended between 1960 and 1990 with the elimination of 750,000 industrial jobs. In 1967 alone, as Danny Lyon powerfully documents in his now deeply haunting photographic essay, over 60 acres of buildings in lower Manhattan were destroyed, an area four times larger than the site of the Trade Center attack (Lyon, 1969, p. 3). As a result, lower Manhattan, including the World Trade Center and the luxury housing complex Battery Park City, which literally rose out of the Hudson River from material dug out of the ground to create the towers, became the icon for a postindustrial society (Darton, 1999; Doig, 2002; Fitch, 1993).

Before construction of the World Trade Center, the area it came to occupy was mainly occupied by light manufacturing firms, primarily electronics shops and the businesses serving them, giving the area the informal designation of "Radio Row" or the Electrical District, bounded by the Wall Street financial area on the east and a thriving port on the south and west. Today, one reference work looks back on the area in the pre–Trade Center days and calls it "seedy" (http://www.infoplease.com/spot/wtc1.html). Indeed, Trade Center lore suggests that the towers were built to redevelop and revitalize lower Manhattan. But there is another view, based on a different approach to urban development, which questioned the need to build the towers and argued that they did more harm than good.

Radio Row, that "seedy" electrical district, was a major Manhattan employer. In fact, the "clearance" required to build the towers eliminated 33,000 jobs and small businesses from the region. Seedy it may have been, at least from the perspective of the pure, clean spaces of glass encased in the Towers and their surrounding structures, but Radio Row was also "one of Manhattan's most vibrant shopping areas." In fact, as commentators describe, the protest against the World Trade Center development project from merchants, trade unionists, and social activists based in Radio Row was unprecedented in both its strength and in the nature of the coalition that mounted the resistance (Glanz and Lipton, 2002, p. 36). Protesters formed a coalition that was also backed by a handful of powerful New Yorkers such as Lawrence A. Wien, one of the owners of the Empire State Building, who established the Committee for a Reasonable World Trade Center, which attacked the proposed towers as excessive and radical. In 1964 he raised the now chilling warning that an airplane might someday strike the Center with disastrous consequences. Sometimes operating independently, sometimes joined by Jane Jacobs and the Radio Row protesters, Wien's group was a formidable opponent to the Rockefeller interests which pushed for the full Trade Center.

It is impossible to calculate precisely the consequences of losing Radio Row. One of the leading historians of New York City, Mike Wallace, suggests that the loss of this center of the city's electronics industry may very well be one reason why Silicon Valley sprouted in California and not in New York, the city that gave birth to the telecommunications and broadcasting industries (Wallace, 2002). Moreover, the firms based in Radio Row were part of a wider district that included the docks, rail freight yards, and associated markets that made up what Fitch calls "the infrastructure of blue-collar New York" (Fitch, 1993). In turn, this district was characteristic of the New York City economy as a whole, which was made up of a diverse mix of manufacturing and service industries, many small and medium-sized enterprises, and a varied strata of blue-and white-collar jobs, which grew organically in agglomerative districts. Affordable housing dotted these areas, which led to retail shops that added further diversity to the mix. But instead of advancing New York City's version of diverse, flexible specialization, of mixed land use and support for blue-and-white collar families, the city's power brokers and planners decided to dismantle it (Doig, 2002). The neighborhood known as SoHo was one of the few areas spared the redevelopment wrecking ball, thanks in part to Jane Jacobs' successful movement to stop Robert Moses' plan to build a lower-Manhattan expressway. Facing a power elite of New Yorkers who were driven to realize the postindustrial society myth, she was not as successful when it came to the World Trade Center.

The WTC was built to open a second major office district comparable, if not larger and more important, than the one in midtown Manhattan, and thereby literally cement the City's claim as the capital of a postindustrial world. It was a centerpiece of David Rockefeller's redevelopment plan initiated in 1958 and was executed by his creation of the Downtown Lower Manhattan Association. The project would eliminate manufacturing firms, working class housing, the civic associations and retail outlets that served them, and replace them with financial services and related firms, along with upper class housing. The World Trade Center construction vastly expanded the district's office space, and landfill from the site was dumped into New York harbor to extend Manhattan island for a World Financial Center and upper income housing in what came to be called Battery Park City (Gordon, 1997). To attract residents, a state-of-the-art park was built on the Battery Park waterfront, at a time when most of New York's parks were suffering from neglect, and one of the city's premier public high schools, reserved for the best of the city's students, was moved into the district and placed in a brand new building costing $300 million, at a time when New York's public schools were also suffering from years of dereliction.

In spite of the Rockefeller family's leadership and the support of the banking and services sectors, there was public skepticism about the strategy of building office space. Not everyone bought into the postindustrial myth, choosing instead an alternative myth, a vision of industrial society renewed through new forms of customized manufacturing and worker cooperatives. For example, in 1955, John Griffin, a City University professor, rattled the city's elites, in part because his research received Rockefeller Foundation financial support, by publishing a study criticizing city planners for failing to provide support for manufacturing companies beginning to leave the city. Griffin called for the revitalization of blue collar industry, particularly in lower Manhattan where new and second generation immigrants lived and depended on manufacturing jobs. Challenging the reigning elite wisdom that industrial clearance and office construction were the solutions, a strategy that meant moving the working class out of Manhattan to find jobs in the outer boroughs and the suburbs rather than bringing the jobs to them, Griffin set out a plan for industrial renewal in lower Manhattan, including the development of industrial cooperatives.

Furthermore, a series of studies produced by a group of Harvard University researchers, particularly Hoover and Vernon's *Anatomy of a Metropolis* (1962), demonstrated the strength of the city's flexible manufacturing base and further argued that the city would not benefit from what amounted to the office monoculture that elites had in store for much of Manhattan. But the ten volumes of research produced by Vernon's Harvard team, commissioned to provide the basis for the city's master plan, were instead shelved and replaced with studies and recommendations provided by the city's Regional Planning Association and the noted urban planner William H. Whyte, which contended that blue collar jobs and the city's working class would naturally decline and that the city should prepare for a postindustrial shift to white collar work (Regional Planning Association, 1968). All of this was cemented by a close political alliance between New York Mayor John Lindsay, Governor Nelson Rockefeller, and his brother, banker David Rockefeller.

The city's 1969 planning document put all of the plans together, including the clearance of businesses, particularly manufacturing firms remaining on the lower west side of the city, and elimination of the docks, one of the key elements of New York's global trade infrastructure, as commercial enterprises. It also called for development of Battery Park City and construction of the World Trade Center (New York City Planning Commission, 1969). With manufacturing firms eliminated and no port to transfer goods out of the city, New York ended its long run of economic diversity in favor of office and upper-income residential construction.

The redevelopment of the WTC district was widely touted as a victory for free markets and private enterprise. However, this attempt to directly connect postindustrialism on the ground with the myth of the market does not exactly fit, because most of the project was driven by government agencies that provided considerable financial help, mainly in the form of government bonds and real estate tax abatements. Moreover, these were not just any government agencies but new forms of public-private partnerships, led by the New York and New Jersey Port Authority, which combined public finance power with limited accountability and the power to expropriate land and property. The Authority used its public status to raise funds to finance major projects, but was not subject to the same public responsibilities as were traditional government agencies (Doig, 2002). In effect, the Port Authority, which today remains owner of the WTC site, has represented the major real estate development interests in the project, which since he leased the site from the PA in 1999 have been led by developer Larry Silverstein. Furthermore, businesses benefited from significant real estate tax abatements at the WTC and enjoining properties such as Battery Park City. From 1993 to 2001, city budget documents reveal, real estate tax abatements to the WTC totaled $595.5 million or $66.2 million per year, and Battery Park City enjoyed $788.3 million in abatements or $87.6 million a year (City of New York, 2001, p. 39). Over this period, these two adjacent sites enjoyed the most substantial tax abatements of any areas in New York City.

Power politics certainly had a great deal to do with why the Trade Center was constructed. The story of how Nelson Rockefeller stacked the Port Authority with family and party loyalists after his election as governor in 1958 is a classic case study in brute political power (Darton, 1999, p. 82). But it was always encased in a supportive mythology as well. Much of this had to do with purifying and cleansing the perceived blight of lower Manhattan and, specifically, Radio Row. For the Trade Center's primary architect, Minoru Yamasaki, it was simple and downright Manichean. On the one hand was his design of the Towers, evoking in his mind "the transcendental aspirations of a medieval cathedral." On the other was Radio Row, in his words, "quite a blighted section, with radio and electronics shops in old structures, clothing stores, bars and many other businesses that could be relocated without much anguish." With thoughts of translucent towers filled with people running the digital world, he concluded: "There was not a single building worth saving." (Glanz and Lipton, 2002, p. 38) But not everyone bought into this purification project. For example, architecture critics did not quite get the cathedral metaphor in the Trade Center design. Perhaps because Yamasaki had to bow to the pressures of his financial backers and increase the towers' height from his proposed 90 stories to over 100, critics lambasted the designs as "graceless," a "fearful instrument of urbicide," and, as for the bit of ornamentation at the base, it was viewed as

"General Motors Gothic" (p. 39). Even today, after the attacks that repuri-
fied the WTC, architecture critics continue to assail the structures, with one
referring to their design as "one of the more conspicuous architectural mistakes of the twentieth century." (Goldberger, 2003, p. 78)

The most significant problem facing Trade Center supporters, one that
was readily apparent soon after construction was completed in 1973, was
how to fill over ten million square feet of office space. From the start, city,
state, and federal agencies made up for the huge shortfall by moving in entire
departments to fill the Towers' empty spaces, particularly in the late 1970s
when economic problems, which would eventually bankrupt the city, significantly depressed the commercial real estate market. Fifty floors of one
tower were occupied by New York state offices, and the Port Authority
filled some of the other tower. As one analyst concluded, "The Trade Center
never had enough tenants in international trade to be worthy of its name."
(Goldberger, 2002, p. 91) The general office glut would continue even as the
construction, sparked by subsidies and tax abatements, also continued
throughout the 1980s. Between 1988 and 1995 New York City lost 57,000
jobs in banking alone, and by the mid-1990s, 60 million square feet of office
space lay empty in the downtown area (Wallace, 200, pp 15-16).

Things got better as Lower Manhattan benefited from the dot-com
boom, and a high tech district known as Silicon Alley emerged in the late
1990s to occupy some of the office space vacated by financial service and
related firms after the major economic restructuring of the early 1990s
(Longcore and Rees, 1996). New Internet companies filled office buildings
left vacant by financial services firms that relocated and replaced workers
with new technologies. Once again, New York City, out of bankruptcy but
also out of manufacturing alternatives, enjoyed a postindustrial economic
allure. Indeed, Silicon Alley embodied a cyber version of the phoenix myth;
in this case the city reborn from the ashes of its industrial past. Even so, it
also propelled a transformation of urban politics and power as corporate-
controlled bodies like Business Improvement Districts remade public spaces
into private enclaves and rewrote the rules of policing, civic activity and
public spectacle. Moreover, much of the new entrepreneurial spirit was
made possible by government financial subsidies that opened prime rental
space at well below market prices and helped to retrofit older buildings with
the technologies necessary to run an aspiring dot-com firm. For a time, the
growth of Silicon Alley revived Lower Manhattan, bringing as many as
100,000 new jobs into the area and its appendages, through 5,000 new media
firms. By 1997, journalists were calling it a "juggernaut" (Chen, 1997, p.
B12; Mosco, 1999). But by 2001, Silicon Alley practically vaporized in the
dot-com bust, leaving the new media industry in New York to familiar conglomerates like AOL-Time Warner and IBM, which could withstand the
bust better than any of the many small firms that gave the city its hip atti-

tude in the 1990s (Kait and Weiss, 2001). With the dot-coms disappearing and the economy declining in the first nine months of 2001, the office glut returned, and visionaries now turned to biotechnology to provide the next boost to the city economy, repeating a story spreading in cities whose dot-com hopes were turning into vaporware (Pollack, 2002; Varmus, 2002). On the day before the towers fell, there were 8.9 million square feet of vacant office space available in lower Manhattan alone. The goal of turning lower Manhattan into an office monoculture was failing even before two jetliners struck the twin towers. In the months that followed, in spite of losing 13.45 million square feet in the attack, the amount of available downtown space actually grew, the result of a declining economy and fears of new attacks.

STRUGGLE FOR CONTROL OF THE SITE

Before determining what is to be done with ground zero, it would be useful to determine how the disaster happened. But there does not appear to be much hope for a thorough investigation. Most analysts agree that for one to succeed it will take a commitment along the same lines that followed the attack on Pearl Harbor and the Kennedy Assassination. In those cases, legislation approved the formation of independent investigative commissions that conducted wide-ranging studies which, if not satisfactory to their numerous critics, were certainly more open and thorough than the best of what has appeared to date with respect to the World Trade Center attacks. Until 2003, the highest level investigation was a joint House-Senate Intelligence Committee review carried out in secret. Even at that, the findings released have proven embarrassing because they revealed numerous previously undisclosed warnings of an impending attack. Intense lobbying, particularly from the families of victims, led to an agreement for an independent investigation that would go forward, but the Bush Administration, most likely fearing that it would reveal more major intelligence failures, was reluctant to give its approval. And when it did, the choice of Henry Kissinger to chair the investigation met with widespread criticism, particularly about whether a committee under his direction would likely pursue politically charged issues like the failures of U.S. intelligence agencies and the role of the Saudi Arabian government in the 9/11 attacks. The controversy over Kissinger ended almost as quickly as it began when the former Secretary of State withdrew from consideration because of his reluctance to meet the government's ethical guidelines. The full committee membership was named in December of 2002 and it began to hear testimony in March 2003. But with a relatively small budget, $3 million, a fraction of the $40 million spent by special prosecutor Kenneth W. Starr to investigate former

President Clinton and Monica Lewinsky, it is not surprising that the committee's final support left many questions unanswered. Those parts of the report that were particularly revealing, such as a section on the role of Saudi Arabia in the attacks, were kept from public view by White House edict (Johnston, 2003).

There is more optimism about the actual site, owing largely to the generally favorable response to the selection of a design by Studio Daniel Libeskind whose plan focuses on the pit excavated at the base of what was the trade center and it is to be ringed by glass towers that swirl upward to a spire 1,776 feet tall. Specifically, the pit describes a four-and-a-half acre memorial space 30 feet below street level into which people will descend and walk around the area that bore the weight of the collapsed buildings and observe the walls that held back the subterranean waters of the Hudson River and saved Lower Manhattan from massive flooding. Although it will not be as deep as originally planned in order to accommodate new infrastructure, the pit and its walls will retain their power to remind visitors of what turned the purified space of the Twin Towers into ground zero. But it is more than just a reminder. The walls, specifically the western so-called slurry wall that held back the Hudson will continue to restrain the river's force even as visitors walk by. As one design critic put it, "There will be . . . no firm demarcation of what was and what became. Where the wall was, it still is, and in such a place memory is a live event. History plays out in real time" (Johnson, 2003). But it is not only the Hudson's waters that need to be kept back. There is also the danger of re-mythologizing or even fetishizing this space with visions of the sacred and a new purity that echoes the purification that Towers' architect Minoru Yamasaki tried to impose on Radio Row. This process of creating a new myth has already begun as these almost prayerful words about the Libeskind pit attest: "New Yorkers need to stand watch to ensure that the final plans sanctify this space deep in the earth. Although unasked for, it is our Parthenon, our Stonehenge. Purified by loss, it is ours to shape and renew" (Meyerowitz, 2003, p. A31).

Perhaps. But the overall planning process for what to do with the site leaves little room to expect anything resembling a fundamentally new direction. There is certainly no reason to expect an open debate about diversifying the site and the local economy. The commitment to a post-industrial office monoculture, in spite of massive overproduction of office space, appears safe. Like all of the other design teams, Studio Libeskind was required to incorporate enormous amounts of office space, settling on 7.63 million square feet along with another 900,000 square feet of commercial retail space. The stipulation was put in place by the Lower Manhattan Development Corporation, the body that the state and city put together to make decisions about the future of the site. The LMDC, with the power to condemn land and override city land use regulations, is comprised of people appointed by the Governor of New York State and the the city's Mayor. Almost every member of the committee is from the banking and real estate sector, including the one labor representative from the Building and Construction Trades Council. There is no one in authority likely to even whisper what one scholar concluded in his analysis of the planning for the site. According to Angotti (2002), "Before rushing to create new office space, it would be best to consider the millions of square feet of vacant office space that followed construction of the World Trade Center in the 1970s. Would it make sense to once again build for a market that never was there in the first place?" In the view of one architecture critic, persistent answers to the effect that it would indeed make sense represent the interests "of New York's largest corporate architecture firms and the politically connected real estate-development industry they serve" (Muschamp, 2002a). One 2003 report questioned whether they represent the interests of the city which, it concludes, has suffered the "doomed strategy" of utter dependence on a few industries like finance and real estate (Center for an Urban Future, 2003). Although the resolution of the design competition did make some things clear, as another account put it, "battle lines are already being drawn over other issues." These include how the memorial will be paid for, when the commercial buildings will go up, or even "whether the towers will look much like the buildings in the design" (Wyatt, 2003a).

One factor that might shape final decisions is a declining economy that, even with massive government help in the form of subsidies, tax abatements, and the waiving of environmental rules, makes it difficult, if not impossible, to make money from a new set of towers. Between February 2001 and February 2003, New York City lost 176,000 jobs (Eaton, 2003). In November 2002, there was 15.4 million square feet of vacant office space in downtown Manhattan, more than the entire commercial market of Atlanta and businesses continued to relocate from the area and out of high rise office buildings generally (Bagli, 2002). Another is a public uproar. When the Development Corporation put its weight behind initial designs resulting from a competition that was even more strictly controlled to guarantee not only massive office construction but dull buildings, concerned social groups and the general public reacted against what was clearly an effort to repro-duce the office monoculture (Wyatt, 2002). The result was a new competi-tion which chose new design teams with more flexible guidelines (along with warnings that public protests will slow down the entire process of rebuild-ing lower Manhattan). The result was a major improvement in design but no change in the office monoculture. So it is understandable that, in spite of some optimism, one noted design critic remains cautious because "we have learned in the past year that the development corporation needs to be watched closely, every step of the way. Blink, and the new design study could turn out to be no more than another set of sideshow distractions from an overly politicized process" (Muschamp, 2002b, p. B7). And, according to a report released in September 2003, not blinking is no guarantee of seeing everything going on. The report finds that "scores of changes to Daniel Libeskind's design, both major alterations and minor refinements," have been made including shrinking parks "that in reality are little more than streets with flower beds" (Wyatt, 2003c). The wishes of the elite Lower Manhattan Development Corporation and Governor Pataki, who want to rebuild the office monoculture, have darkened the glow from the town hall meeting of 2002 when more than 4,000 New Yorkers spent a long summer day debating urban planning and the fate of ground zero. Fearing that the Libeskind design would limit full commercial development of the site, developer Larry Silverstein openly clashed with the architect and then explicitly reigned in Libeskind's authority. The public face-saving meeting did little to quiet public concerns. Indeed, the haste to paper over differences and start rebuilding has resulted in numerous clashes, the most embarrassing of which pitted 15 members of victim family members blocking trucks carrying construction materials onto the ground zero site to protest rebuilding on the nine and a half acres that encompass the "footprint" of the towers and they want a memorial on the site to begin 70 feet below street level, on the bedrock on which the towers sat (Slackman, 2003; Wyatt, 2003b).

New Yorkers are also very wary because much of the federal money promised in financial relief has simply failed to come forward. The Federal Emergency Management Agency has been criticized severely in an internal review for mishandling its front line mission, providing emergency economic assistance (Chen, 2003). In fact, as one report put it, "many victims, elected officials, business executives and others are both confused and angry about why, more than a year after the most serious terrorist attack on American soil, less than a quarter of the federal government's promise of financial assistance has been realized. . . ." (Wyatt et al., 2002, p. A1) Moreover, more than one-third of federal emergency grant money earmarked for small business has gone instead to big investment banks, brokerage firms, and big law firms. Small retail outlets in the immediate vicinity of the attacks have received a small fraction of their claims (Wyatt and Fried, 2003).

In his farewell address to the city former Mayor Giuliani promised to push for a "soaring, monumental" memorial on the WTC site (Cardwell, 2001). Such a memorial to the victims is essential. But memorials are supposed to be about learning from the past and, as local authorities race to repeat past mistakes, or replicate cyberspace myths about an "informational city," not much learning is taking place. A complete memorial would including rethinking the site and adjoining neighborhoods. It would start with an investigation that would determine exactly how and why so many lost their lives and many others their livelihoods in the attack. Furthermore, it would include revisiting Jane Jacobs' call for diversifying the local econo-my and its social class composition. Or even, as one historian has suggested, a combination of Jacobs' philosophy with a dose of her nemesis Robert Moses. For all of his near obsession with megaprojects that undermined local neighborhoods, Moses had a keen sense of how public investment in the transportation infrastructure and in recreation facilities spread the bene-fits widely. That he and others were able to accomplish so much of this dur-ing the Great Depression is also a model for how government can rebuild on a massive scale even when the national economy is severely eroded (Wallace, 2002). But, barring some significant change in the political climate, it is unlikely that we will see this kind memorial.

REFERENCES

Angotti, T. (2002) "The Makeup of the Lower Manhattan Redevelopment Corporation." http://www.gothamgazette.com/landuse/

Bagli, C. (2002) "Tall tower near Ground Zero is proposed." *New York Times,* 12 November.

Best, M. (1990) *The New Competition: Institutions of Industrial Restructuring.* Cambridge, MA: Harvard University Press.

Cardwell, D. (2001) "In final address, Giuliani envisions soaring memorial." *The New York Times,* 28 December.

Castells, M. (1989) *The Informational City.* Oxford: Blackwell.

Center for an Urban Future (2003) *Engine Failure.* New York: Center for an Urban Future, September.

Chen, D.W. (1997) "New media industry becoming juggernaut," *The New York Times,* 23 October.

Chen, D. W. (2003) "FEMA criticized for its handling of 9/11 claims." *New York Times,* 8 January.

City of New York, Office of Management and Budget (2001) Statement of the Mayor, New York, 25 April.

Darton, E. (1999) *Divided We Stand: A Biography of New York's World Trade Center.* New York: Basic Books.

de Certeau, M. (1985) "Practices of space." In M. Blonksy (Ed.), *On Signs.* (pp. 122-145). Baltimore, MD: Johns Hopkins University Press,

Doig, J. W. (2002) *Empire on the Hudson: Entrepreneurial Vision and Political Power at the Port of New York Authority.* New York: Columbia University Press.

Eaton, L. (2003) "With 176,000 jobs lost in 2 years, New York City is in grip of a recession." *New York Times,* 19 February.

Fitch, R. (1993) *The Assassination of New York.* New York: Verso.

Gillespie, A. G. (2001) *Twin Towers.* New Brunswick, NJ: Rutgers University Press.

Glanz, J. and E. Lipton (2003) *City in the Sky: The Rise and Fall of the World Trade Center.* New York: Henry Holt.

Goldberger, P. (2003) "Eyes on the prize." *New Yorker,* 10 March: 67-82.

Goldberger, P. (2002) "Groundwork." *New Yorker,* 20 May: 86-96.

Gordon, D. (1997) *Battery Park City: Politics and Planning on the New York Waterfront.* Amsterdam: Gordon and Breach.

Hoover, E. and R. Vernon (1962) *Anatomy of a Metropolis.* New York: Doubleday.

Jacobs, J. (1961) *The Death and Life of the Great American Cities.* New York: Random House.

Johnson, K. (2003) "The very image of loss." *The New York Times,* 2 March.

Johnston, D. (2003) "Classified section of Sept. 11 report faults Saudi rulers." *New York Times,* 26 July.

Kait, C. and S. Weiss (2001) *Digital Hustlers: Living Large and Falling Hard in Silicon Alley.* New York: HarperCollins.

Longcore, T.R. and P.W. Rees (1996) "Information technology and downtown restructuring: The case of New York City's financial district." *Urban Geography* 17(4): 354-372.

Lyon, D. (1969) *The Destruction of Lower Manhattan.* New York: Macmillan.

Meyerowitz, J. (2003) "Saving the wall that saved New York." *New York Times,* 27 February.

Mosco, V. (1999) "New York.com: A political economy of the 'informational' city." *The Journal of Media Economics* 12(2): 103-116.

Muschamp, H. (2002a) "Rich firms, poor ideas for Towers site." *New York Times,* 18 April.

Muschamp, H. (2002b) "Ground Zero: Six new drawing boards." *New York Times,* 1 October.

New York City Planning Commission (1969) *Plan for New York City.* New York: Author.

Piore, M. J. and C. F. Sabel (1984) *The Second Industrial Divide.* New York: Basic Books.

Pollack, A. (2002), "Cities and states clamor to be bio town, U.S.A.." *The New York Times,* 11 June.

Regional Planning Association (1968) *The Second Regional Plan.* New York: Author.

Rich, F. (2003) "Ground zero or bust." *The New York Times,* 13 July.

Sassen, S. (1992) *The Global City: New York, London, Tokyo.* Princeton, NJ: Princeton University Press.

Schiller, H. I. (1989) *Culture Inc.* New York: Oxford.

Slackman, M. (2003) "15 to block Ground Zero in protest of development." *New York Times,* 3 September.

Varmus, H. (2002), "The DNA of a new industry." *The New York Times,* 24 September.

Wallace, M. (2002) *A New Deal for New York.* New York: Bell and Weiland.

Wyatt, E. (2002) "Slowing down at a cost." *New York Times,* 22 July.

Wyatt, E. (2003a) "Design chosen for rebuilding Ground Zero." *New York Times,* 27 February.

Wyatt, E. (2003b) "Architect and developer clash over plans for Trade Center site." *New York Times,* 15 July.

Wyatt, E. (2003c) "Ground Zero plan seems to circle back." *New York Times*, 13 September.
Wyatt, E. et al. (2002) "After 9/11, Parcels of money, and dismay." *New York Times*, 30 December.
Wyatt, E. and J. P. Fried (2003) "Downtown grants found to favor investment field." *New York Times*, 8 September.

CHAPTER FIVE

BUSINESS USERS AND THE INTERNET IN HISTORICAL CONTEXT

Dan Schiller

Visionary executives, brilliant engineers, and even federal telecommunications regulators have each been credited with pioneering U.S. telecommunications system development. In contrast, to this day, business users of network systems and services scarcely have been noticed as a shaping force. Nevertheless, for nearly a century, industrial, financial, and commercial telecommunications users have played a formative, and at key points a determining, role in this infrastructure's evolution. Opportunities for their exercise of influence were occasioned by both repeated cycles of network innovation around business applications, and sustained and successful lobbying efforts to alter existing public policy, above all, to expedite the growth of computer communications. To explicate these points, albeit only in a preliminary way, requires engagement with a little-known history.

BUSINESS USERS AND THE NEW DEAL SETTLEMENT IN U.S. TELECOMMUNICATIONS

The history of telecommunications has been written largely from the supply side, so as to stress the role of the carriers that provision society with access to different network systems and services. From the beginning of the American republic, however, the demand side of the telecommunications equation also has been pivotal; business users have repeatedly made critical contributions to the structure and policy of telecommunications. Prospective business user demand thus helped justify rapid expansion of an increasingly encompassing post office system throughout the early national period (John, 1995), and generated momentum for continuing technical and organizational innovation in the supply of network services throughout the later nineteenth century. The fledgling telegraph was disproportionately used by large-scale enterprises oriented toward a truly national political economy: banks, commodity traders, news agencies, railroads (Chandler and Cortada, 2000; Duboff, 1980; Yates, 1989). Telephony too originated largely as a business — or, better, a business class — service (Fischer, 1992; Schiller, 1998).

Network applications were unevenly generalized across the field of big business, which in turn came to rely increasingly on a wide swath of telecommunications services. Like a privileged minority of early residential telephone users, businesses made use of the public switched telecommunications network. Unlike residential users, businesses also came to depend vitally on a category of service aimed solely at organizational users: leased lines, or private wires, as the specialized facilities proffered by carriers beginning with Western Union are called. By 1878, private wire contracts for Morse service had proliferated to the point that one vendor specializing in service to banks and brokerages rented 300 private lines with 1,200 miles of wire in and around New York City (Duboff, 1983, p. 268). The Bell telephone system likewise quickly moved into leased line service.[1]

Provision of this specialized class of service — "the greatest source of revenue of the telegraph companies," reported the *Wall Street Journal* in 1909 ("Telegraph Business," 1909) — was apparently lucrative. By one account, 31% of Western Union's net income derived from "sources other than toll messages" in 1896; but the proportion ranged upwards of 60% by 1906-08 ("Railroads West," 1909).[2] A Western Union official stated to a Congressional panel (reporting in 1909) "that this business was so much more profitable than handling messages that the company had considered a suggestion that it cease to handle messages entirely and turn its entire attention to leased-wire business" (US Congress, 1909, p. 22; see Duboff, 1983, p. 268).

Business users of leased lines were led by brokers, who possessed systems "covering the entire country." Apart from the railroads, however, Standard Oil was accounted to be the largest individual business user, followed by "the packers," and then U.S. Steel, all of whose plants and subsidiaries, a newspaper reported, "are connected by private telegraph wire." The Associated Press also was a very heavy user of leased lines ("Railroads," 1909, p. 6).

As their reliance on telecommunications deepened, business users began to organize themselves, at first on an *ad hoc* basis, into a pressure group to demand changes in the structure and policy of telecommunications provision. During 1904-1905, to take what is probably the leading instance of this trend, private consultations were undertaken between New York Telephone, the Bell affiliate, and a "Telephone Committee" established by the Merchants' Association of New York to conduct "an exhaustive examination" of telephone service and charges there. The Committee stated in its report that New York Telephone had obligingly "consent[ed] to open its books and to supply the Committee with all necessary details of investment, gross earnings, operating expenses, and net earnings." The immediate result was a series of rate adjustments and service changes (Merchants' Assoc., 1905, pp. 7, 8-9). But the more important consequence was to drive toward a new policy regime.

Facilities-based competition in telephone service provision had erupted unevenly throughout most of the United States in the years following the lapse of the Bell patents in 1894, so that by 1907 around half of all subscribers accessed networks operated by non-Bell carriers. The Committee, however, faulted this emergent competitive system for furnishing an inadequate and overpriced service (Merchants' Assoc., 1905, pp. 37-38, 39). It was willing to lend support to the Bell, if in return the telephone trust promised to acquiesce to legally structured rate regulation and, in the Committee's own eyes as important, "consistent and reasonable publicity" for supplier charges and services (Merchants' Assoc., 1905, pp. 37-38, 39).

The importance of New York City–based businesses to the entire country's finance, commerce, and manufacturing gave this shift more than merely local resonance. Business users elsewhere also intervened, with similar intent, throughout this formative period of telephone system development (Lipartito, 1989; Weiman and Levin, 1994). In opposition to concerns that continued to be expressed by trade unionists, political reformers, and other groups, the Committee's rejection of competition therefore went far, as Alan Stone suggests, to shift "elite opinion . . . definitively in the direction of local monopoly's provision of telephone service," and toward what he calls the "regulated network manager system" that AT&T soon succeeded in dominating once more (Stone, 1993, p. 160; also Schiller, 1998).

More than a decade later, the role of business telecommunications users was enlarged to encompass international objectives. U.S. diplomats hoped to use a post–World War One conference on international electrical communications as a basis for projecting U.S. power more effectively in this increasingly critical sphere. The National Foreign Trade Council, representing U.S. exporters, overseas traders, and executives, wrote to the U.S. Department of State in November 1919 to demand that business interests be expressly represented in these deliberations. Other leading trade associations, such as the

American Manufacturing Export Association, once more the Merchants' Association of New York, the National Association of Manufacturers, and the U.S. Chamber of Commerce met, in the run-up to the conference, "to develop a unified position in international communications." They succeeded not only in agreeing on an agenda, but also in impressing the latter forcefully on U.S. diplomats, who altered their negotiating positions to accommodate users' concerns (Schwoch, 1987, pp. 293, 294).

It is therefore correct to claim—in contrast to those would lay this achievement largely at the door of AT&T executives—a critical role for business users in establishing the system of U.S. national and international telecommunications that began to cohere in the years around World War I, and that was consolidated during the New Deal period.

This was not a simple process of consensus-building, even just *within* the business community. Business users of telecommunications converged on radio technology during the 1920s and advanced unprecedented claims on the still-forming nationwide system, especially in regard to the high-frequency, short-wave spectrum band that was just beginning to be exploited commercially. The Federal Radio Commission, established in 1927, made available for assignment portions of this new band (extending between 6,000 and 23,000 kilocycles), reporting that "a constantly increasing number of applications for the use of these frequencies has flooded the commission, covering a wide variety of services and experiments." As a result of this discrepancy between available supply and demand, the agency determined to undertake an extensive investigation of the properties of the high frequency band, "the needs and merits of the types of service seeking accommodation in the band, and the application of the standard of 'public interest, convenience, or necessity' to these questions." Absent such "a scientific and orderly plan" for the exploitation of these higher frequencies, the Commission explained, "congestion equal to that which has been the root of all evils in the broadcast band would obtain" here as well (FRC, 1928, p. 26).

A public hearing on these issues was held early in 1928. In attendance were all of the major executive agencies with a direct and indirect interest in communications, from the Departments of State, War, Navy and Commerce to the Bureau of Lighthouses. Also represented, not surprisingly, were the leading radio manufacturers and the domestic and transoceanic communication companies. But the range of organizations touched by high frequency allocation policy went far beyond this. The FRC observed: "The following groups, represented in many cases by eminent radio engineers and lawyers, were called upon in turn and each made an earnest plea for accommodation in the high-frequency band":

Newspaper services.

. . . .

Airplane operating companies.
Navigation companies.
Railroads.
Department-store chains.
Electric railways.
Interurban bus systems.
Electric power transmission systems.
Lumber companies.

. . . .

Motion picture producers.
Police and fire-alarm systems.
Forest and watershed patrols.
Ranch owners.
Remote resorts and hotels.
Operators of facsimile transmission services.

. . . .

Mining and oil companies.
Packers and shippers.
Geologists.

Disparate organizations and associations presented themselves before regulators: the American Petroleum Institute; Firestone Tire and Rubber and its rival, Goodyear; retailers R.H. Macy and Bamberger Co.; media companies including Universal Pictures, Hearst Publications, McGraw Hill, *The Los Angeles Times, The San Francisco Examiner, The New York Times, The Chicago Tribune* and other newspapers; the American Railway Association. Marked disagreement ensued, as rivals vied for spectrum with which to satisfy "such strikingly different services as transoceanic and transcontinental communication, railroad needs for communication between locomotive and caboose on a freight train and between office and switch engine, the claims of oil companies not only for communication purposes but also for prospecting for oil, and of power companies for emergency purposes." The welter of competing interests and demands indeed was such that the Commission determined to allocate frequencies at first only in what it termed the transoceanic high frequency band, "in order that these frequencies should not be appropriated by other nations to the disadvantage of the United States" (FRC, 1928, pp. 27, 28).

While unhappy would-be users pursued their cases in the Court of Appeals, the Commission got started on allocation of the so-called "continental high-frequency band" (1,500 to 6,000 kilocycles) the following year. Applications were made by "several large concerns desiring to establish public systems of point-to-point radio communication in the United States, duplicating the wire systems between the larger cities." Under consideration, once again, were likewise "a large number of applications from more or less private interests desiring to set up a more limited system of communication, such as between chain stores, brokers' offices, mail-order houses and their branches, oil companies, mines, and the like" (FRC, 1928, p. 33). And industrial demand for radio frequencies seemed only to increase. The Commission reported (FRC, 1929, p. 19) in 1929 that applications had been entered "for the assignment of literally thousands of frequencies more than are available . . . " It promised weakly to bring "[t]he best engineering talent in the country" to bear on the policy issues it confronted (FRC, 1928), p. 34).

A varied group of business users was beginning to formulate a qualitatively new demand: access to specialized communication facilities and services, to be integrated into large business operations as a private matter outside the sphere of common carrier provision. Protesting to legislators that the established carriers remained inert, unwilling or unable to meet their emerging telecommunications needs at a suitable price, business users also were beginning to organize themselves into a permanent pressure group and policymaking force.

By the late 1920s, in turn, the Federal Radio Commission began to grant business users a sporadic right to develop specialized network services. This deference was accorded, however, only on a selective—even an exceptional—basis: it did not yet involve the reorganization of the overall public switched telecommunications network. We have little historical research into these initiatives, each of which expressed and built toward segmented industrial telecommunications needs. The geophysical exploration and pipeline services innovated by oil companies comprise one case in point; another is the shared radio services developed by Aeronautical Radio, Inc., a consortium of airline companies. In the context of such forays, however, AT&T's well-known deal with fledgling network radio broadcasters— which gave to the telephone company a monopoly over radio program transmission services, in exchange for its own promise to back out of radio broadcasting markets—may be seen as averting efforts to develop still another such special-purpose industrial system. Radio networks, and the television networks that succeeded them, thus agreed (in the latter case only under duress) to contract for private line service from AT&T rather than build their own proprietary networks.

Other industries presumably followed a similar course. During the mid-1930s, AT&T furnished about 1,000 private line systems to business users, including 250 used by banks and financial houses; in 1936, private line toll services supplied $32,590,337 in revenue to AT&T—some 10.5% of its overall intra- and interstate toll revenues, and around one-quarter of its interstate

Long Lines revenues (Herring and Gross, 1936, p. 56; U.S., FCC, 1938, pp. 419, 613). In New York City, private branch exchange attendants—women workers operating switchboards in hotels, large offices, hospitals, stores, and other businesses—by this time outnumbered telephone company operators three to one (Dilts, 1941, pp. 69, 132).

Business users thus were attaining an expanding political and economic status in telecommunications. As regards system development policy, however, business users' needs continued to be relegated to the edges of the evolving regulated, public switched network over which AT&T and, increasingly residually, Western Union, presided.

Even before the New Deal, a palpable shortage of the critical enabling resource—spectrum—helped justify the Federal Radio Commission's decision to place business users' demands for access to radio frequencies after those of the common carriers. "Those applicants proposing to engage in the communication business serving the entire public or a particular class of the entire public, and assuming the duties, obligations and responsibilities of common carriers are deemed to be in a better position to meet the standard of public interest than any of the other applicants," was the Commission's considered opinion in one precedent-setting early case.[3] In another, it explicitly endorsed its originating position, "that applications would not be granted for service which would duplicate that already furnished by land-line companies." The reasoning behind this second decision is of considerable interest:

> It may be that the commission owes the wire telegraph companies no duty to protect them from competition by radio services. But there is a much broader consideration than this. The commission, while encouraging the development of radio, should nevertheless, in applying the statutory standard, take into consideration the possibility of a radio company competing unfairly with a wire service to such an extent that the general public may suffer . . . .
>
> Obviously there is no constant relationship between the capital, personnel, and maintenance expenses of a wire circuit on the one hand and its volume of traffic on the other. The company's cost of a wire circuit between small communities is not always justified by the income from traffic. The offices in small communities must be maintained to preserve the utility of the entire service to all the people of the Nation. The charges for message traffic over the more profitable circuits between large centers of population must include some charge for the maintenance of the less profitable circuits. The wire companies' charges for their readiness to serve are thus equitably distributed.
>
> With the wire communication companies thus situated, the commission can not, from the standpoint of national welfare, encourage the establishment of radio communication systems based solely upon the selection of the most profitable points of communication. Radio compa-

nies taking the "cream" of the business at reduced rates might impair the utility and the economic structure of the wire companies, for the latter, in order to meet competition, might be compelled to abandon unprofitable circuits . . . .

Upon the same considerations, the commission must not lend itself to the establishment of radio circuits which will rely upon the handling at reduced rates of the bulk traffic of individual large corporations between their various offices, to the practical exclusion of the less profitable occasional traffic of the general public, especially under circumstances where the wire communication companies are prevented by law or regulation from making such preferential and discriminatory arrangements.[4]

Such language offered a premonition of the concern to develop a more comprehensive telecommunications system that would shape the New Deal settlement in this field. It also portended that the limited mandate of the Federal Radio Commission would have to give way to a broader regulatory warrant, one that explicitly encompassed common carriage as well as broadcasting.

Business users engaged in this attempt to create a more powerful and far-reaching federal regulatory agency. Lacking effective rate regulation for international radiotelegraphy, a group of business users allied themselves in a "cable and radio users' protective committee" to insist in hearings over the Communications Act of 1934, that a new Federal Communications Commission, with ratesetting oversight, in fact was needed. Through a revealing set of exchanges, these large users charged that the carriers were colluding with the British Post Office to extort higher charges. Rate reductions had resulted from technical change (shortwave radio and loaded permalloy cables) and the accompanying overcapacity that had developed on North Atlantic routes; only by preserving these lower rates could the very large telecommunications expenses borne by the complainants—some 50-odd banks, stock and commodity exchanges, and import/export houses—be kept within restraint. But the carriers instead had ostensibly combined in hopes of enforcing a mutually beneficial rate *increase*. In these depressed times, such a predatory imposition was especially onerous. "Unfortunately there exists in this country," wrote the chairman of the Cable & Radio Users Protective Committee to Senate Interstate Commerce Committee chair Clarence C. Dill, "no tribunal with adequate powers to consider and determine this conflict of opinion between the companies and their customers." "That such a body be promptly established," the user group concluded, "is our only request."[5] Urged on by the State Department, Congress passed the enabling legislation; and, to the chagrin of AT&T executives (who opposed it), the FCC was established.

In the context of the Great Depression, which everywhere brought the question of how to overcome economic stagnation to the forefront of policymaking, emboldened New Deal regulators commenced upon a top-to-bottom review of the process of telecommunications system development.[6] They began by taking a hard look at the internal economic workings of the AT&T monopoly (in the process, providing a foretaste of the broader investigations of U.S. industry that would soon be undertaken by the Temporary National Economic Committee) through the so-called "Telephone Investigation" of 1935-39. Altered policies followed hard on the heels of this unprecedented scrutiny, which was to produce some 75 boxes of material (now housed at the National Archives). Though hardly revolutionary, substantial policy changes were set into motion.

The FCC sought to erect an effective procedural framework through cooperation with existing state public utility commissions; and thereby to develop a capacity for end-to-end regulatory oversight of the nation's telecommunications network. Forever frustrated in its attempts to actualize this vision, the agency nevertheless could and did employ the new framework to achieve substantive policy change. Above all, perhaps, it was able to boost demand by systematically lowering prices, especially during the long boom that followed World War II, when the chronic under-supply of local residential telephone service at last was relieved. (Congress also contributed, through passage of legislation that aided rural telephone system development and thereby further extended the existing national network.) Inclusive, or "universal" household access to the telephone thus became the signal achievement of the New Deal settlement. But there were also others. New Deal labor reforms, for example, impinged importantly on telecommunications. Between passage of the Wagner Act in 1935, the momentary ascent of the Left-led CIO union, the American Communications Association during the decade that followed, and the formation of the rival CIO affiliate, the Communications Workers of America in 1947, the principle of collective bargaining rights by independent trade union organizations, which AT&T executives had held at bay for a generation, took firm root (Schacht, 1985). As well, a federal antitrust case brought against AT&T in 1949 added to pressure on the company to acquiesce to a vision of public service responsibility.

Attempting to contribute to this emerging settlement, the war-time FCC nevertheless continued to defer to "industrial" radio[7] applications, as well as to employ a policy of limited competition in administering the provision of telegraph services aimed at business users. Now, however, the agency also embarked on a more encompassing planning process. The perceived need was to formulate requirements and make recommendations pertaining to "the increased demands for frequency use for all purposes which would follow the conclusion of the war" (Joint Technical Advisory Comm.,

1952, p. 13). Dampened demand by businesses for special-purpose networks during the Depression, followed by the overarching need to focus on wartime communications needs, had permitted the agency to avoid general policymaking in this critical area. Spiraling demand and hothouse innovation during the postwar decades, in contrast, would compel the FCC repeatedly to revisit the question of specialized communications systems for business users—above all, to effectuate integration on preferential terms of a new and increasingly fundamental piece of office equipment: the electronic digital computer.

In that process, the New Deal settlement in telecommunications came under increasingly fierce pressure.

BUSINESS USERS AND THE EMERGENCE
OF COMPUTER COMMUNICATIONS

World War II and the Cold War that followed it gave a powerful spur to innovation in electronics, telecommunications, computers, and aerospace. System development in these high-technology fields received another boost from the settlement, within two days of each other in 1956, of antitrust cases brought against AT&T and IBM by the U.S. Department of Justice.[8] The Justice Department thus succeeded in what Stanley N. Barnes, the Department's then antitrust chief, called a "program to open up the electronics field," among other things by compelling AT&T and IBM to license their patents on easy terms ("I.B.M. Trust," 1956).

Building not only on "cost-plus" contracts for cutting-edge computing technologies from military agencies but—increasingly—on demand for cost-efficient applications by a diversifying base of industrial, commercial, and financial users of punched-card data processing equipment, during the 1950s the U.S. computer industry took off. Revenues garnered by IBM— the industry leader by a long shot—for its newer electronic computer systems exceeded those from conventional punched-card systems only in 1962, prompting executives to bet the company on a new generation of electronic computers (the 360 line, introduced in April 1964) (Pugh and Aspray, 1996, p. 14). But it was not only conducive policies on the supply side that produced this boom. "The return to a 'peace-time' economy" after World War II, write Pugh and Aspray (1996, pp. 9, 10), "opened a flood gate of demand by industries that had been deprived of equipment during the war, and new uses and methods devised during the war further increased demand as customers applied them to peace-time activities." Prosaic but vital processes began to be networked, in whole or in part, reaching functions such as payroll, personnel files, insurance records, accounting, banking, inventory control, and manufacturing production scheduling (Cortada, 1996, pp. 20-21).

Jump-started by the military's Project Sage, an air-defense system developed by MIT in partnership with several major corporations, but targeting a wide range of existing and prospective business applications, digital data transmission using telephone lines in turn became an increasingly pressing focus (Pugh and Aspray, 1996, p. 11). Business users, in particular, sought to develop computer communications networks to spread the benefits of their centralized data processing resources more widely throughout their organizations; and to innovate remote-processing applications, such as the cutting-edge Sabre system developed by American Airlines in partnership with IBM (Copeland et al., 1995).

The telephone network had been engineered for voice applications, however, and did not lend itself unproblematically to data traffic. "The voice common-carrier communications systems of today," wrote Paul Baran— one of the engineers who designed the Internet's underlying technology of packet switching—in 1967, "were designed primarily to provide a voice-to-ear or typewriter-to-typewriter link between humans. Today's communications regulation doctrine still regards the computer merely as another user of these existing telephone, typewriter, and telegraph networks. It isn't merely the matter of jamming a size ten foot into a size five shoe. The fundamental desired communications characteristics are so different that we are living on a procrustean operation basis" (Baran, 1967, pp. 12-13).

Adapting and adjusting the nation's telecommunications system therefore posed basic problems of public policy. Should computer networks be incorporated into a regulated, heavily unionized, public utility telecommunications system, which functioned to provide end-to-end service and stressed voice service for residential users? Should new network technology be categorized for system development purposes as a "computer utility," as many engineers, system designers, and policymakers were calling it? Under whose auspices might the vibrant and expansive field of data communications be most adequately developed?—The telecommunications industry that was dominated by AT&T? Or a punched card data processing business that was feverishly transforming itself into an electronic digital computer industry—but that was almost equally fully monopolized by IBM?

As we know, the answer turned out to be neither. What accounts for this outcome, which created the political-economic space in which what we know as the Internet was to grow?

A report written by a staff member of the Federal Communications Commission somewhat self-servingly avers that, "in providing fertile ground for the growth and development of data networks over the nation's communications infrastructure," over a period of 35 years beginning in the mid-1960s the FCC determined through a series of proceedings "that computer-based services offered over telecommunications facilities should not be subject to common carrier regulation"; in so doing, it asserts, "the Commission set forth the necessary unregulated landscape for the growth and development of the Internet" (Oxman, 1999, p. 6). Was the FCC, then, a far-sighted and consistent (de)regulator?

The claim possesses nominal validity. The FCC *did*, in fact, contribute through an episodic series of vital decisions, to the emergence of computer communications in general and the Internet in particular. But to leave the matter here is to neglect the vitally relevant fact that these selfsame FCC decisions were predicated on and, in case after case, prompted by specific, concrete demands put to the agency by business users of telecommunications, generally in alliance with a small but rapidly growing group of independent equipment and service companies. Large business users, working together as a super-lobby comprised both of existing peak trade associations and newly established specialized organizations, therefore must be accorded pride of place in explaining the modernization of U.S. telecommunications around data networks. The root cause of Internet development is thus not simply that the FCC chose to expedite development of data communications, but that business users effectively destabilized, and ultimately supplanted, the regulated network manager system that they themselves had earlier helped to erect.

Why? By three vital standards—an essential role in coordinating increasingly dispersed corporate units at a moment of sweeping economic expansion, concurrently escalating operating expense, and a cascade of new applications' strategic importance to further growth—network systems were transforming into an ever more vital business infrastructure during the 1950s and 1960s. It is this essential fact that, I think, explains decisions to intervene in policymaking by corporate telecommunications users, who were no longer content with access to an expensive, general-purpose, regulated network. As business user dependence on merged computer-communications deepened, while AT&T continued to operate within the terms of the New Deal settlement, consensus over system development policy for the nation's telecommunications system eroded. Disagreements developed over the specific uses to which the public network might be put, the need for special-purpose equipment and services, and the prices at which different services would be provided. Relatively early on, however, attention fastened on the more basic issue: the further evolution of telecommunications as a public utility industry. Elsewhere I have traced the spiral of policy change, beginning in the late 1950s, through a series of related telecommunications regulatory disputes that pitted AT&T against its biggest customers at the Federal Communications Commission.[9] Such users increasingly demanded, and the authorities in turn duly provided them with, "the same latitude in the use and implementation of [their] communications facilities that [they] enjoy in the use and implementation of the many thousands of other tools, facilities and services necessary to the conduct of [their] business" (U.S., FCC, 1957, pp. 849-850, 850, 851).

Deliberation over the future of U.S. telecommunications system development reached a watershed during the period 1966-1971.

EXECUTIVE BRANCH INTERVENTION, 1967–69

Business ratepayers generated 58% of domestic long-distance revenues in 1976, and the largest 3.9% of their number accounted for over three-fifths of this total (U.S. Congress, House, 1981, pp. 87-89). Mobilized and channeled by business users as a pressure group, this massed demand lent added weight to already formidable political power—power that was not available to small residential ratepayers. For this reason, the result seems utterly predictable: If the line of business demand for proprietary control of network technology traces an unbroken ascent from the late 1950s, then the curve of political response was almost as smooth; indeed, it is difficult to identify a single major FCC decision from this point forward in which a defense of the older regulated network manager system carried the day.

Was this, however, because regulators and courts simply rubberstamped the unremitting liberalization for which business users pressed? No; political (and cultural) mobilization also came into the process. I shall try here only to estimate the latter's political coordinates.[10]

Sporadic effort in fact was made to enlarge the mandate of the New Deal settlement, so as to make room for computer communications. Throughout his tenure as an FCC Commissioner, Nicholas Johnson, a maverick Democrat, entreated his colleagues to consider seriously the view that "Public utility telephone regulation should be approached in terms of the social-economic-political consequences of decisions, in addition to (or perhaps rather than) conventional 'rate of return' and other seemingly isolated financial issues." Johnson's plea was the closest the postwar FCC ever came to laying down updated and explicit principles of public responsibility for regulators to rely upon in shaping, rather than only responding to, the computer age.[11] The quest proved fruitless. No FCC docket was ever opened "In the Matter of Extending the Public Service Conception from Telecommunications to Data Processing."

At the same time, however, the momentum gathering behind proposals for telecommunications liberalization was generated mainly by Democrats, working within Democratic Administrations. Gerald Faulhaber explains that,

> in the early to mid-1960s, the FCC retained a number of young econo-
> mists, whose procompetitive, anti-big business view was shared by
> other regulatory economists who came to professional maturity in New
> Deal and post-New Deal America. . . . According to them, bigness tends
> to breed abuses, and, since the Bell System was the biggest of all, it was
> guilty of the greatest abuses. The cure was to encourage new firms to
> enter telecommunications, protecting them if necessary against preda-
> tion by Bell. . . . While many of these economists had left the FCC by
> the early 1970s, and a new generation of economists took over, the pos-
> itive view of competition and the negative view of Bell had become
> ingrained in the FCC staff. (Faulhaber, 1987, p. 50)

In 1968, Democratic FCC Commissioner Johnson was authorized to
write the pivotal Carterfone decision, which extended broad rights of foreign terminal attachment to the public telephone network. The ideological
climate of antipathy to the regulated network manager system thus emerged
as a liberal anti-monopoly construction directed against AT&T. The cohe-
siveness and extent of partisan insurgency should not be overstated (the
FCC's Carterfone vote was unanimous, for example), but it seems certain
that, during its early phases, Democrats spearheaded and shepherded
telecommunications liberalization.

An Executive Branch initiative undertaken by a Democratic administration—that of Lyndon Baynes Johnson—played a decisive part in making the
perceived need for telecommunications liberalization into an emerging elite
consensus. A Task Force on Communications Policy convened by President
Johnson in 1967 endorsed limited competition in private line service in the
waning months of his administration, and prescribed that telecommunications policy "should seek to develop an environment always sensitive to
consumer needs" (President's Task Force, 1968, p. 6). The Task Force, which
drew together members of over a dozen federal departments and agencies,
and employed research contractors at universities and think tanks for advice,
was initially established to address a discrete policy problem; internal
memos corroborate that its substantive purpose was to assess U.S. satellite
policy. This was in itself a complex and delicate matter. There were two outstanding issues (each giving on to ancillary questions that need not concern
us): First, to determine who, if anyone, should own and operate a domestic
communications satellite system, such as had been proposed by several
applicants, notably including the Ford Foundation (which hoped to set up a
nonprofit domestic satellite system whose profits would help fund public
television); second, to determine whether the United States should have a
single "chosen instrument" in international communications, which would
require a merger between established international satellite and terrestrial
carriers. Both questions bore directly on the nature of U.S. participation in
the International Telecommunications Satellite Consortium, whose signato-

ries were about to renegotiate their still-provisional arrangements; whereas the latter question, if answered affirmatively, would also entail legislative amendment of the Communications Satellite Act of 1962.[12]

Simply to raise such issues served notice on AT&T that its successful effort, in the early 1960s, to extend into satellite technology innovation so as to protect its own prior investment in domestic landlines had become newly vulnerable. Task Force scrutiny likewise signaled, as observers quickly noted, that "the responsibility for resolving the question of establishing a domestic satellite communications system will not rest wholly with the Federal Communications Commission" ("Task Force . . . ," 1967, p. 1). In a draft memo to President Johnson, in the context of satellite issues, W. DeVier Pierson linked the need for a Task Force to the fact that the "FCC has asserted substantial regulatory authority—of a nature posing real problems for the executive branch."[13]

Indeed there is evidence that a wider Executive Branch concern about prospective FCC policymaking motivated the launch of the Task Force. DeVier Pierson, the President's Special Counsel and a close advisor, directed early on in the Task Force's existence that "priority attention" be given to "the Task Force relationship to the FCC and applications pending before it."[14] Days before it reached the conclusion of its deliberations, the Task Force Chairman himself reiterated, in a memo to President Johnson:

> It takes a long time to get a Task Force of this kind established and into motion. The opportunity should not be wasted. In my view, the line of policy laid out . . . is moderate, balanced, and right, and its articulation in a Task Force Report could help to influence the pattern of decisions by the F.C.C., by industry, and by Congress in a constructive way for a long time to come. Our efforts and the discussion of the draft chapters have already had a marked effect both on the F.C.C. and on A.T.&T. policy.[15]

It may be conjectured that these allusions were to the FCC's Carterfone decision, which had been handed down scarcely six months earlier (in June, 1968) and to its ongoing deliberations in the Computer Inquiry, each of which made decisive contributions to the process of liberalizing corporate access to the U.S. telecom infrastructure.

Notwithstanding its initial brief, the Task Force's chairman, Undersecretary of State Eugene V. Rostow, certainly interpreted his mandate broadly and commenced to undertake what he boasted was "the most fundamental and broad gauged study of communications policy in forty years."[16] His move to "rear back and look at communications as a whole" spurred intense disagreement among Task Force members during the fall of 1967, but Rostow ultimately gained the authorization he wanted to broaden the study to encompass domestic common carrier (and broadcasting) issues.[17]

As a result of this enlargement of its warrant, the Task Force became subject to ferocious counterpressure from AT&T. Agitated by (accurate) rumors that an attempt to force AT&T to divest its manufacturing subsidiary, Western Electric, was under consideration by Task Force staff, for example, AT&T lobbyists attempted to intercede at the highest levels of the Executive Branch; this option got no further.[18] And serious thought was being given into the final days of the Task Force's existence to suppressing completely two chapters of its report, which dealt with domestic common carrier and television issues.[19] A few months before its work reached completion, a memo to President Johnson from DeVier Pierson and other top communications advisors had recommended this course, the major "disadvantage" of which—they conceded—would be that "the opportunity would be lost to move the FCC toward better regulatory practices in the omitted fields."[20] Ultimately, however, the chapters *were* included in the Task Force's Report, and they underlined a need for dramatic changes in the structure of domestic telecommunications provision. Indeed the reforms called for included virtually all the contemporaneous liberalizing initiatives under review by the Federal Communications Commission.

Explicitly underscoring that it wished to preserve "integrated provision" of domestic public message telephone service, the Task Force nevertheless specifically recommended that the FCC endorse "the removal of unnecessary restraints to promote innovation and to encourage greater responsiveness to consumer needs" in the case of "services which supplement those of the basic public message telephone network."[21] The Task Force likewise purported to consider "teleprocessing" merely a "supplemental" service, for which "the removal of tariff restrictions on the sharing of communications lines, on splitting or resale of channels, and on message switching, seems compatible with maintaining the integrity of the basic communications network"; and it also supported more generous foreign attachment provisions.[22] A report produced a year or two later, which relied on studies undertaken in the context of the President's Task Force on Communications Policy and the FCC's Computer Inquiry, explicitly linked the Task Force's liberalization agenda to a fledgling technology known as the ARPA network—a key antecedent of today's Internet:

> It is not clear that operation and systems management of the ARPA network by a common carrier would optimize other factors. . . .
> Competition in contractor selection would be effectively eliminated, with probable adverse effects upon both cost and system performance. Although the carriers certainly have or could acquire the expertise to operate and continue the evolutionary development of this network, the problems which must be solved are fundamentally those of computer

systems design and operation rather than problems of the traditional communications engineering nature. Accordingly, it is plausible to assume that certain firms in the computing industry may be better qualified and/or motivated than the common carriers to perform this task well. Furthermore, such organizations, being more familiar with and responsive to the needs of the computing industry, might be more likely to carry this interactive computer network concept into other areas of business and scientific application, thus fulfilling a major objective of ARPA research project support: to develop and encourage the application of advanced technological concepts, in industry as well as in the military. Therefore, ARPA favors the removal of the prohibitions against communications line resale, to reduce communications cost and increase flexibility in the supply of end-product communications services such as the ARPA network. (Mathison and Walker, 1970, p. 134)

It therefore seems clear that, despite assurances that computer networking would develop as a *supplementary* service domain, the goal of "carry[ing] this interactive computer network concept into other areas of business"—that is, of generalizing networks and network applications—already functioned as an explicit policy objective.

The language of assumption and argument employed by the Task Force report, finally, itself possesses considerable significance, for it helped launch "competition" as an ascending orthodoxy in U.S. telecommunications: "The main concern of policy in this field should be to improve the effectiveness of regulation where regulation is necessary, to remove unnecessary restraints on private initiative, and to provide as free a field as possible for the imagination and enterprise of innovators."[23] Thus the Task Force urged that the FCC approve licenses for telecommunications companies such as MCI, which wished to compete with AT&T in providing voice and data systems to large commercial and institutional customers, and that the Commission base its judgment in such cases on a need to reject rate-averaging in favor of marginal cost pricing for customers with high-volume needs.[24] While it acknowledged that the proliferation of such private communications systems "could raise serious problems for the integrated network," moreover, the Task Force specifically asserted that "these problems can be met by allowing the established carriers sufficient flexibility in rates to meet competition, and by strengthening regulatory capabilities to prevent destructive competition." The overriding threat was, a majority of its members felt, AT&T's increasingly thoroughgoing departures from cost-based pricing, which purportedly "encourage[d] inefficient investment in communications."[25] The Task Force thus bridged toward a language of formal economic doctrine and, by the same token, away from the New Deal settlement's more substantive public service conception.

Business users' prime demands for system development in fact struck at the heart of this existing settlement. First, they proposed that the cost economies achieved by introducing new technology into the telephone network should be passed largely on to them, instead of being directed toward other ends (such as protecting low local residential telephone rates): acceptance of this tenet would (and did) dramatically destabilize the comprehensive rate structure that had been developed to build out inclusive network access. Even more radically, they proposed that business users themselves, in partnership with emerging specialized providers, should be accorded proprietary control over a large and increasing segment of the networking process: agreement would (and did) subvert the New Deal norm of comprehensive, or end-to-end, public utility regulation of "the" public switched network. Contrariwise, a renewal of the public service conception to accommodate computer-communications networks would have inescapably reinvigorated that doctrine. What—and whose—needs should such an emboldened public interest principle address? How should it be updated; what policies should it seek to embody? Should the requirement of universal telephone service, just coming into its own in practice, be enlarged to include comprehensive public access to networked information services? Should nondiscrimination mandate comparable service for all users of computer communications? Should public utility status be conferred on the computer industry? Such were the vital questions that the FCC bypassed in consequence of business user intervention; yet, fundamental decisions about ownership and control of such networks nevertheless were taken. Phrasing the new norm bluntly, Internet pioneer Paul Baran declared in 1967 that "In essence . . . computer 'utilities' are not utilities" at all (Baran, 1967, p. 9).

"All bulk users of communications services may benefit if the task force's recommendations are followed," commented an article in *Business Week* shortly before this blue-ribbon body released its final report. And, significantly, the article continued:

> Taken in its entirety, the proposed reshuffling of the communications industry is so sweeping the report might have been treated as a hot potato by the Administration that set it in motion. And a new Republican Administration might be expected to be even more reticent about asking Congress to translate its recommendations into law.
>
> But the problems that led to formation of the task force in the first place are so acute that any Administration will have to try to solve them. Thus, the chances are good that the report—as the product of the most concentrated investigation of the subject—will carry weight with Nixon decision makers. ("Making New Waves," 1968)

For the first time, indeed, a presumption of bipartisan approval for liberalized policies now could be made. With Nixon's appointment of Dean Burch to chair the FCC, Republicans, who hitherto had tended to defer to AT&T, joined the disestablishmentarians.

A fateful trajectory was therefore set. Through one proceeding after another, in the wake of the First Computer Inquiry, regulatory controls over the use of telecommunications for computer-communications offerings were consistently pared down or relaxed. The process of liberal deconstruction therefore moved from the periphery of the public switched network to its center. As ownership and control of network technologies were lifted out of the web of obligations that had encased the regulated network manager system, AT&T's own strategic thinking ultimately transformed into that of just another private competitor. The federal antitrust suit that instigated the 1982-1984 breakup of what used to be called "the telephone company" only climaxed this ongoing series of regulatory and judicial actions. Curtailing the system of end-to-end general-purpose service offered by a regulated monopoly provider, as Alan Stone underlines, the divestiture concurrently signaled "the atrophy of the public service principles" that had infused the New Deal settlement (Stone, 1989, p. 338).

INTERNET TAKE-OFF

Thus was crafted the space in which a decentralized network of networks could be sculpted. But the uses that were made of this space were by no means already uniformly evident; the Idea of the Internet was not simply waiting to be born. Nor is the sudden eruption of the Internet during the 1990s to be associated simply with the surge in popularity of World Wide Web access, and the fast-paced widening of the e-mail habit. Behind both of these, rather, lies the complex rise of the personal computer industry during the 1980s, and the succeeding ascent of the local and wide-area networks which in turn transformed these stand-alone instruments into a new communications medium. These developments bring us back to business users. The proliferation of PCs, and the widespread competency training that went with them, occurred first and foremost as a desktop business-office aid.[26] Throughout the 1980s and 1990s, local area networks connecting PCs, peripherals, and other computing resources then mushroomed in huge numbers throughout major corporations. Urs von Burg (2001) has shown how these electronic warrens were stimulated by a canny vendor strategy of relying upon a nonproprietary, or "open," technical standard for their local area network products (Ethernet).

Under the terms of the FCC's Computer Inquiries, these LANs constituted "data-processing" networks, free to be developed as a strictly private
matter—free, that is, of common carrier regulation—by host companies and
computer industry vendors. By 1986, as intra-organizational networks and
private value-added networks of different kinds burgeoned within this
growing deregulated domain, only two-thirds of U.S. network investment
was made by public network carriers—down from nearly 100% as recently
as 1980 (Noam and NiShuilleabhain, 1996, p. xvii). By the late 1980s, in turn,
the annual expenditures of the top 100 telecommunications users ranged
from a low of perhaps $20 million, to a high of around $1 billion, with the
average outlay falling between $50 and $100 million (U.S. Congress, OTA,
1990, p. 37). But this was merely a preface to the network investment boom
that crested at the millennium, and that transformed information technology in general, and the Internet in particular, into the core of the political
economy overall.

The proliferation of corporate local area networks helped spur an accelerating further demand for cheap, wider-area interconnectivity. As von Burg
suggests, the Internet—employing another nonproprietary standard,
TCP/IP—offered a prospective solution and, during the 1990s, corporate
LANs "quickly became important on-ramps to it" (von Burg, 2001, p. xiii).
Perhaps two-thirds of the spectacularly increased Internet investment that
occurred through the 1990s was undertaken by businesses, principally to
erect walled-off private systems known as intranets,[27] while only one-third
of such investment went to the enlargement of the public internet (Cerf,
1999). Indeed, intranets and their further extensions, extranets linking
organizations, purportedly constitute the most rapid take-up ever for a network technology. Not coincidentally, far and away the larger share of
Internet e-commerce flowed between businesses, rather than between businesses and consumers (Cross, 1999, p. 109; see also Schiller, 1982a). Signs
abounded that this emergent system would directly cannibalize the public
switched telecommunications network, as major corporate users joined with
ISPs and backbone providers to route voice calls over a combination of
intranet and public Internet facilities. Such an outcome would signal the
final eclipse of the New Deal settlement, as public utility rate regulation of
common carrier services gives way to unregulated carriage, offered on privately negotiated price- and service terms (Committee on the Internet, 2001,
pp. 151-176). Around the Internet, in turn, what we might call the corporate
reconstruction of the telecommunications infrastructure proceeded apace.

NOTES

1. Whereas, around 1904, AT&T was garnering 28% of the industry's private-wire revenue, by 1914 AT&T had doubled its share of this market (to 56%). Railroads were especially significant users of these private wire systems, and often enjoyed access via special, shared arrangements with Western Union. In 1914, exclusive of railroads, four-fifths of telegraph-service private wire leases were held by bankers and brokers; and an additional 9% of leases were held by meat packing, iron, and steel companies. These private wire systems were located disproportionately in the northern states stretching from the Atlantic coast to the Missouri River. Some of the larger systems linked locations in both the U.S. and Canada (Interstate Commerce Commission, 1918, pp. 734-35, 738-39).

2. Thanks to Richard John for these two *Wall Street Journal* references.

3. By-Products Coal Co. v. Federal Radio Commission, No. 4984, in Third Annual Report, p. 37.

4. Intercity Radio Telegraph Co., appellant, v. Federal Radio Commission, No. 4987 etc., in Third annual Report, p. 40.

5. Grayson. M.-P. Murphy, to Honorable Clarence C. Dill, March 17, 1934, in U.S. Congress, Senate, 1934, pp. 217-218. Also see pp. 142-153, 173-176.

6. The New Deal settlement in telecommunications is a major focus of my current book project, tentatively titled *A Hidden History of U.S. Telecommunications.*

7. As a pioneer in communication scholarship noticed, perhaps because he had served during this period as Chief Economist at the FCC itself. See Smythe, 1957.

8. A third antitrust case had been brought against RCA.

9. The following paragraphs draw on material published in Schiller, 1982a, 1982b.

10. In the longer work-in-progress on which this chapter draws, I devote attention to a succession of popular cultural projects that concurrently heaped scorn on AT&T—the core of the regulated network manager system.

11. 18 FCC 2d 953, 977 (1969).

12. Lyndon Baines Johnson Presidential Library, Austin, Texas, "Memorandum for the President" May 12, 1967, from DeVier Pierson [draft], in Office Files of DeVier Pierson, Container No. 30, Comsat—1967-1968. The Ford Foundation, under its president McGeorge Bundy, had filed a highly publicized comment with the FCC in April, concerning the utility of a domestic satellite system for efficient networking of public television signals. See U.S., FCC, 1967.

13. LBJ Presidential Library, "Under cover of 'Memorandum for Harry McPherson, Douglass Cater, Leonard Marks From W. DeVier Pierson,'" May 9, 1967, p. 1. See also "Memorandum for Harry C. McPherson, Douglass Cater from: W. DeVier Pierson," May 3, 1967, both in WHCF Oversize Attachment 3619, DeVier Pierson Communications Satellite.

14. LBJ Presidential Library, "Memorandum for Honorable Eugene Rostow," from DeVier Pierson, October 2, 1967, in Office Files of DeVier Pierson, Container No. 18, Communications—Misc. Material.

15. "Memorandum For the President From the Chairman of the President's Task Force on Communications Policy," 2 December 1968, p. 7, in National Security

File, Subject File, Communications Policy—Task Force on, LBJ Presidential Library.
16. "Memorandum For the President From the Chairman of the President's Task Force on Communications Policy," December 1968, p. 3, in National Security File, Subject File, Communications Policy—Task Force on, LBJ Presidential Library.
17. Nicholas Johnson, "The Public Interest and Public Broadcasting: Looking At Communications As a Whole," Remarks Prepared for Delivery to the Resources for the Future and the Brookings Institution Conference on the Use and Regulation of the Radio Spectrum, Airlie House, Warrenton, Virginia, September 11, 1967, pp. 1, 3; "Memorandum for the President from the Chairman of the President's Task Force on Communications Policy," December 1968, p. 3, in National Security File, Subject File, Communications Policy—Task Force on, LBJ Presidential Library.
18. See, for example, "Memorandum for: the President," 21 June 1968, From James Rowe, in White House Central Files, Confidential File, Container 35, FG 600/Task Force on Communications Policy: 3; "Memorandum for the Secretary of Commerce Subject: International Communications," August 26, 1968, from Fred Simpich, in White House Central Files, Container No. 363, Ex FG 600/Task Force/Communications Policy; and "Memorandum for the Record, from Douglass Cater, Subject: Meeting with Ed Crossland, Vice President of AT&T," July 5, 1968 in WHCF Oversize Attachment 3619, DeVier Pierson Communications Satellite, LBJ Presidential Library.
19. "Memorandum for the President from the Chairman of the President's Task Force on Communications Policy," 2 December 1968, in National Security File, Subject File, Communications Policy—Task Force on, LBJ Presidential Library Memorandum, pp. 4-9. Considerable evidence of horsetrading among the panelists exists. Perhaps the most controversial issue the group addressed concerned the establishment of a monopoly provider of international telecommunications service, free of influence from the entrenched carriers—which some members of the Task Force, for whom the proposed monopoly was "necessary but repugnant," insisted should be balanced by competitive strictures, in order to prevent the creation of "an industry-oriented Report, rather than one which dealt directly with some of the deeper public interests in the field" (p. 8). W. DeVier Pierson, who transmitted the Final Report to the President, confided in his memo that the Task Force "has completed its work in a curious fashion. There was intense disagreement within the task force membership as to whether some issues—specifically, those dealing with the domestic common carrier industry and opportunities for television—were appropriate subjects for study within the mandate of the Task Force. . . . The task force did not resolve these issues and, in fact, did not meet during the final months of its deliberation.

"Consequently, the attached report is largely the report of the Chairman and the staff—not of the entire task force." Pierson recommended that the President, rather than release the Report as a public document, transmit it to the Budget Bureau "as an informational tool for a possible legislative program in this area" by the incoming Republican Administration. "Memorandum For The President," December 9, 1968, from W. DeVier Pierson, in White House Central

Files, Container No. 363, FG 600/Task Force/Communications Policy, LBJ Presidential Library.
20. "Memorandum for the President September 26, 1968, from Leonard Marks, Douglass Cater and DeVier Pierson," in White House Central Files, Container No. 363, Ex FG 600/Task Force/Communications Policy, LBJ Presidential Library.
21. Final Report, Chapter One, pp. 17, 20.
22. Final Report, Chapter One, p. 21; Chapter Six, pp. 26-28, 29-36.
23. Task Force On Communications Policy, Final Report, Chapter One, p. 9.
24. Final Report, Chapter Six, pp. 9-25.
25. Final Report, Chapter Six, pp. 16-17.
26. During Fall, 2001, around 24 million U.S. inhabitants possessed T1 or higher-speed Internet access lines in their offices, and fewer than 9 million enjoyed broadband, or highspeed, connections at home; thus the cultural habit of Net access, now including broadband access, continues to be nurtured at work, and only secondarily at home (Grenier, 2001, p. B8).
27. By which is denoted an intraorganizational network that makes use of Internet technologies: routers and TCP/IP, as well as, typically, the HTTP application, often with additional applications such as e-mail and file transfer protocols.

REFERENCES

Baran, Paul (1967) "The coming computer utility — laissez-faire, licensing or regulation?" Santa Monica, CA: Rand Corporation P-3466, April.
Cerf, Vinton (1999) "Transforming impact of internet." Internet and the Global Political Economy Conference, University of Washington Center for Internet Studies, 23 September.
Chandler, Alfred D. and James W. Cortada (Eds.) (2000) *A Nation Transformed by Information.* New York: Oxford University Press.
Committee on the Internet and the Evolving Information Infrastructure, Computer Science and Telecommunications Board, National Research Council (2001) *The internet's coming of age.* Washington, DC: National Academy Press.
Copeland, Duncan G., Richard O. Mason and James L. McKenney (1995) "Sabre: The development of information-based competence and execution of information-based competition " *IEEE Annals of the History of Computing* 17(3): 30-56.
Cortada, James W. (1996) "Commercial applications of the digital computer in American corporations, 1945-1995." *IEEE Annals of the History of Computing* 18(2).
Cross, Kim (1999) "B-to-B, by the numbers." *Business 2.0,* September 1999.
Dilts, Marion May (1941) *The Telephone in a Changing World.* New York: Longmans, Green.
DuBoff, Richard B. (1980) "Business demand and the development of the telegraph in the United States, 1844-1860." *Business History Review* Winter: 459-79.
DuBoff, Richard B. (1983) "The telegraph and the structure of markets in the United States, 1845-1890." *Research in Economic History* 8.

Faulhaber, Gerald R. (1987) *Telecommunications in Turmoil: Technology and Public Policy.* Cambridge: Ballinger.

Fischer, Claude (1992) *America Calling.* Berkeley: University of California Press.

Grenier, Melinda Patterson (2001) "Record number of office workers used web broadcasts last month" *Wall Street Journal,* 15 October: B8.

Herring, James M. and Gerald C. Gross (1936) *Telecommunications Economics and Regulation.* New York: McGraw-Hill.

"I.B.M. trust suit ended by decree; Machines freed" (1956) *The New York Times,* 26 January: 1, 18.

Interstate Commerce Commission Reports (1918) "Decisions of the Interstate Commerce Commission of the United States May 1918 to August 1918," Volume 50. Washington, DC: GPO.

John, Richard (1995) *Spreading the News.* Cambridge: Harvard University Press.

Joint Technical Advisory Committee, Institute of Radio Engineers and Radio-Television Manufacturers Association (1952) *Radio Spectrum Conservation: A Program of Conservation Based on Present Uses and Future Needs.* New York: McGraw-Hill.

Lipartito, Kenneth (1989) *The Bell System and Regional Business: The Telephone in the South, 1877-1920.* Baltimore: Johns Hopkins.

Mathison, Stuart L. and Philip M. Walker (1970) *Computers and Telecommunications: Issues in Public Policy.* Englewood Cliffs: Prentice-Hall.

"Making new waves in communications" (1968) *Business Week,* 16 November.

The Merchants' Association of New York (1905) "Inquiry into telephone service and rates in New York City by The Merchants' Association of New York." New York, June.

Noam, Eli M. and Aine Nishuilleabhain (1996) "Introduction." In E. Noam and A. Nishuilleabhain (Eds.), *Private Networks Public Objectives.* Amsterdam: Elsevier.

Oxman, Jason (1999) "The FCC and the unregulation of the internet." Office of Plans and Policy, FCC, OPP Working Paper No. 31, July.

President's Task Force on Communications Policy (1968) *Final Report.* Washington, DC: USGPO, 7 December.

Pugh, Emerson W., and William Aspray (1996) "Creating the computer industry." *IEEE Annals of the History of Computing* 18(2): 9-14.

"Railroads west said to be unable to get all the telegraphers needed" (1909) *Wall Street Journal,* 31 August: 6.

Schacht, John M. (1985) *The Making of Telephone Unionism 1920-1947.* New Brunswick, NJ: Rutgers University Press.

Schiller, Dan (1982a) "Business users and the telecommunications network." *Journal of Communication* 32(4): 84-96.

Schiller, Dan (1982b) *Telematics and Government.* Norwood, NJ: Ablex.

Schiller, Dan (1998) "Social movement in telecommunications: Rethinking the public service history of U.S. telecommunications 1894-1919." *Telecommunications Policy* 22(4/5): 397-408.

Schwoch, James (1987) "The American radio industry and international communications conferences, 1919-1927." *Historical Journal of Film, Radio and Television* 7(3).

Smythe, Dallas (1957) *The Structure and Policy of Electronic Communications.* Urbana: University of Illinois Press.

Stone, Alan (1989) *Wrong Number: The Breakup of AT&T.* New York: Basic Books.

Stone, Alan (1993) *Public Service Liberalism: Telecommunications and Transitions in Public Policy.* Princeton, NJ: Princeton University Press.

"Task force to study development of new national communications policy established by President Johnson" (1967) *Telecommunications Reports 33*(36), 21 August.

"Telegraph business west" (1909) *Wall Street Journal,* 30 December: 6.

U.S. Congress, House of Representatives (1981) *Telecommunications in Transition: The Status of Competition in the Telecommunications Industry.*

U.S. Congress, Office of Technology Assessment (1990) *Critical Connections: Communications for the Future,* OTA-CIT-407. Washington, DC: USGPO, January.

U.S. Congress, Senate (1909) "Investigation of Western Union and Postal Telegraph-Cable Companies." 60th Congress, 2d Session, February 16. Document No. 725, Committee on Interstate Commerce, Washington, DC: GPO.

U.S. Congress, Senate (1934) "Hearings Before the Committee on Interstate Commerce on S. 2910, Federal Communications Commission." 73d Cong., 2d Sess., 9, 10, 13, 15, March, Washington, DC: GPO.

U.S., FCC (1928) *Second Annual Report of the Federal Radio Commission to the Congress of the United States.* Washington, DC: USGPO.

U.S., FCC (1929) *Third Annual Report of the Federal Radio Commission to the Congress of the United States.* Washington, DC: USGPO.

U.S., FRC (1938) Proposed Report: Telephone Investigation (Pursuant to Public Resolution No. 8 74th Congress). Washington, DC: GPO.

U.S., FRC (1957) "In the matter of allocation of frequencies in the bands above 890 Mc.," Docket 11866, Comment of the Automobile Manufacturers Association, 15 March.

U.S., FCC (1967) "In the matter of the establishment of domestic communications satellite facilities by non-governmental entities," Docket No. 16495, Supplemental Comments of the Ford Foundation, 3 April.

von Burg, Urs (2001) *The Triumph of Ethernet: Technological Communities and the Battle for the LAN Standard.* Stanford: Stanford University Press.

Weiman, David and Richard Levin (1994) "Preying for monopoly: The case of Southern Bell, 1884-1912," *Journal of Political Economy* 102, February: 103-126.

Yates, JoAnne (1989) *Control through Communication.* Baltimore: Johns Hopkins.

CHAPTER SIX

PRIVATIZATION
AND IDENTITY

The Formation of a Racial Class

Oscar H. Gandy, Jr.

Among the many targets of Herb Schiller's critical reflections on the character and quality of communication theory and research, he reserved a special place for what he considered to be a lost opportunity for meaningful engagement with the study of audiences. In his view, the bulk of mainstream audience research seemed to have been designed either to ignore or to explicitly deny the corrosive influence of corporate-controlled media on global culture and human social development (Schiller, 2000). Of course, the celebration and exemplification of active audiences, playfully and creatively resisting the influence of media conglomerates, might be seen as a defensive flanking maneuver performed by the vanguard of an army of neoliberal intellectuals and academics. Mobilized perhaps in response to charges of cultural imperialism, and threatened by signs of a spreading oppositional movement (Nordenstreng, 1993) calling for the establishment of a New World Information and Communication Order (NWICO), this cadre was joined by a well-meaning, but woefully misguided band of cultural theorists (Kubey, 1996). Knowledgeable observers agree that the "takeoff of cultural studies to growth is almost exactly coterminous with neoliberalism's dominating economic and social policy" (Murdock, 1995, p. 91). Political economists of communication largely resisted this siren's song, and as a result, came to be isolated on the fringes of an evolving research tradition (Mosco, 1996).

Although efforts at the repair and rehabilitation of the rift that emerged between political economists and cultural theorists by means of polite conversations in public and in print may have enjoyed some limited success (Garnham, 1995), no clear path toward a collaborative future seems to have been established (Hagen and Wasko, 2000). Much of the terrain that remains to be crossed is likely to be filled with highly charged debates over the nature of identity and its relationship to the consumption of media products (Slater, 1997). Those debates are likely to be the most troublesome when the basis of identity is race and ethnicity.

Grossberg (1996, p. 90) suggests that most "work in cultural studies is concerned with investigating and challenging the construction of subaltern, marginalized or dominated identities." On the other hand, when political economists of communication have paid any attention at all to matters of identity formation, most have tended to focus their lens on the development of class consciousness, while giving short shrift to racial identity. In part, this may be understood as a rejection of the idea that racial oppression could be the basis of a politicized identity from which a progressive social movement could be expected to emerge (Gandy, 1998; Mosco, 1996; Murdock, 2000). This neglect is unfortunate for a number of reasons, not the least of which is the fact that racial and ethnic identity continues to serve as a primary framework through which a broad range of social policies are assessed and used as the basis for political mobilization (Dawson, 2001; Hochschild, 1999; Kinder and Sanders, 1996).

As I will try to argue, a political economy of communication that is sensitive to the role that identity plays in both production and consumption could further our understanding of the ways in which corporate control of media and other cultural institutions (Schiller, 1989) helps to reproduce inequality through the formation of an isolated racial class (Negus and Román-Velázquez, 2000). This racial class, composed largely of African Americans (Gans, 1999), is likely to take shape within the confines of a hermetically sealed and hopelessly "corrupted" public sphere of the sort that reliance upon advertising all but guarantees (Baker, 2002). The task before us is to develop a challenge to the dominant paradigm of media policy research that sees no alternative to a marketplace logic in the sphere of information (Schiller, 1996; Sunstein, 2001). This chapter is designed to be a first step in response to that challenge.

CONSUMPTION AND IDENTITY FORMATION

In the context of a cultural studies–based emphasis on consumers as agents that proceeds almost without regard to the structural factors that help to determine which goods and services are made available within markets, there tends to be an assumption that commodity consumption may be a more important determinant of collective identity than any other aspect of capitalist relations. That "you are what you eat" has acquired the status of an ontological truth.

Although he has little to say about the sorts of complications we face when consideration of race and ethnicity enters into the relations between consumption and identity formation, Warde (1994) underscored the importance of the appearance of choice in the leading accounts. In assessing the contributions that Anthony Giddens, Zygmunt Bauman, and Ulrich Beck make to our understanding the role that choice plays in identity formation, Warde calls our attention to a number of problems that emerge along the way. These problems are related to the ways in which choices made under conditions of uncertainty and risk come into conflict with the more traditional ways in which an individual's attachment to a social group may be formed. These conflicts are especially salient when these "routine choices" take place within markets that develop under the influence of advertising.

Because of their commitment to the idealized competent agent, the choices that matter most are those that are made under the assumption of autonomous affirmative acts, rather than passive consent or tolerance. At the same time Warde (1994) emphasizes the critical distinction that exists between choice and selection. He suggests that only choices are marked by substantial anxiety about the consequences of being wrong.

Neither Giddens, Bauman, or Beck invite much consideration of the sorts of social pressures toward conformity that are linked to group membership. For many, feelings of accountability and responsibility to a primary group are part of the ties that bind and thereby limit a whole host of choices about what to consume (Allen, 2003; Cornell and Hartmann, 1998). Indeed, each of these theorists of social risk tends to see the absence of stable attachments as evidence of postmodern autonomy and as a mark of accomplished individuality. For them, this postmodern consumer is likely to be identified with a lifestyle, rather than a community. As a result, "social membership is reduced to identities one puts on and takes off at a whim" (Slater, 1997, p. 87).

Yet, evidence abounds that the salience of racial and ethnic group membership is in fact quite high, even if it varies among people as a function of social location and context (Cornell and Hartmann, 1998; Jaret and Reitzes, 1999). Allen (2003) provides numerous examples of the myriad ways in which attachments to groups, whether professional or primordial, tend to be marked by a high degree of "accountability" to the group for choices that have been made. This sense of accountability treats as legitimate an expectation among group members that any individual member will provide justifications for any choices they have made that appear to be outside the boundaries of "good form." Thus, the burden of accountability helps to explain why choices about consumption, at least those which can be observed or inferred, are so marked by a sense of personal risk. At issue, then, is the extent to which media-guided consumption may help to reinforce group ties marked by accountability.

It seems likely that identification with a racial group, understood as a relationship involving feelings of accountability to the group, is reflected in the strategies used by marketers to influence consumer decisions in ways that reinforce the power of these socioeconomic ties. Thus, in order to understand the critical role that is played by commercial media, we need to determine the extent to which commercial messages, framed in the context of racially targeted advertising campaigns, are able to incorporate the chains of accountability and the associated threat of group sanction as a way to reinforce a consumer's identification with a commodity (Hecht, Jackson, and Ribeau, 2003).

Although this sort of marketing strategy is not explicitly political, there are a great many examples of political mobilization in which members of social groups have used their identity as consumers as a basis for issuing economic and political demands. Cohen (2003) describes a number of successful corporate campaigns that have been organized by African Americans. Many of these campaigns have involved the use of the consumer boycott as tools in an effort to pry loose a bit of respect from American business leaders. Often, these boycotts were directed against retail establishments that refused to employ African Americans. Campaigns against Sears, Woolworth, and A&P instructed Black consumers to shop wisely. Admonitions along the lines of "Don't buy where you can't work" made both economic and political sense, and as a result were quite successful in bringing about reforms in racist business practice (Cohen, 2003, pp. 44-46).

Black consumer concerns have also been mobilized in support of the development of an "independent African American economy." This largely unrealized social goal featured a unique admixture of black capitalist entrepreneurs and black-owned cooperatives of the sort favored by W. E. B. Du Bois (Cohen, 2003). According to Cohen (2003, p. 325), the "shift from incorporating blacks into mass markets to setting them apart through racially based market segmentation, then, paralleled the larger evolution of civil rights from integration to black power. . . ." Ironically, economic separatism under the control of African Americans has devolved into a form of market segmentation that now operates under the control of multinational media conglomerates (Gandy, 2003).

As I will argue a bit further on, the consequences of market segmentation for the development of progressive social movements in the United States are not promising. As Cohen observed "as market segmentation gave capitalists and rebels alike a shared interest in using consumer markets to strengthen—not break down—the boundaries between social groups, it contributed to a more fragmented America" (Cohen, 2003, p. 331). In addition, the same techniques that have been used to segment and target consumers are increasingly being used to segment the public sphere and target or ignore individuals who have been identified as members of socially constructed groups (Gandy, 2001a).

TASTES AND PREFERENCES

Any attempt to understand the role that commercial media play in the formation of racial and ethnic identities must come to terms with the complex ways in which tastes and preferences for media content come to be shaped over time. Only the most dogmatic adherents to mainstream economic doctrines still suggest that consumer preferences emerge fully formed at birth, and only a scant few more still express the view that preference formation is external to the market (Reder, 1999). Instead, economists have reluctantly come to agree that preferences are learned within markets as well as in nonmarket environments that are also shaped by the strategic efforts of marketers who seek to influence individuals' expectations and experiences with consumer goods (Baker, 2002).

Within cultural studies, on the other hand, the underlying rationale for studying media consumers defined by ethnicity and race has been a desire to provide examples of critical resistance to domination (Cottle, 2000; Ferguson, 1998; Ross and Playdon, 2001). Although this work may serve to balance that small part of mainstream media effects research that has been concerned with assessing the impact of representation on audiences of color (Gandy, 1998; Gunter, 2000), very little scholarship from any camp attempts to examine the ways in which the economics of supply and demand help to determine the quantity and character of these representations over time (Gray, 1995, 2000).

Only a very small body of work has been concerned with assessing the tastes and preferences of media consumers without at the same time characterizing them as either "cultural dupes" or the loyal opposition. Jones (1990) offered an early assessment of the characteristics of the audience for Black Entertainment Television (BET)—the only national television network that was, at least in its early days, being programmed specifically with an African American audience in mind. Jones' examination of the tastes and preferences of BET viewers confirmed earlier research that had suggested that African Americans preferred to watch programs that featured black actors and themes (Frank and Greenberg, 1980). She also observed that racial identity (group orientation) and age predicted the level of satisfaction viewers derived from BET programming.

More recently Edwards (2001) observed a strong preference for programs with African American characters in urban settings among most of her young black female respondents. She utilized a variation of Milton Rokeach's Terminal and Instrumental Values scales to determine the extent to which particular values might predict television program preferences. She observed that an index of "self-oriented values" predicted frequent viewing of a subset of programs, and an index of "other-directed values" predicted rejection or avoidance of these programs.

Although racial identity, at least that variant that indicates a sense of "linked fate" (Dawson, 1994), is strongly associated with reading the African American press, there is only a slight tendency for this form of identity to predict viewing of commercial television programs that have a majority of black characters (Gandy, 2001b). A preference for such programs also seems to reflect class positions, in that those viewers "with preferences for African American programs tend to have household incomes well below the national average" (Brown and Cavazos, 2002, p. 237). Understanding the relationship between the social class of a group of media consumers and the quality of the content they consume is at the heart of any political economy of racial class formation. This relationship reflects the ways in which the locus of financial control determines the nature of the commodities supplied to the market.

THE ROLE OF ADVERTISING

Although there is a well-developed literature on the influence of market structure on the performance of media systems (Doyle, 2002; Napoli, 2001, 2003), and although the performance of actors within those markets is also of central importance (Crouteau and Hoynes, 2001), it is the way in which the costs of production, marketing, and distribution are financed that ultimately determines the ways in which those organizations behave (McManus, 1994; Picard, 2002). Although political economists have tended to focus their attention on the ways in which ownership influences the behavior of media systems (Mosco, 1996), the influence of advertisers should be understood as shaping the day-to-day decisions within those media that rely on this form of "third party payment."

Baker (1994, 2002) provides a well-developed analysis of the ways in which reliance upon income from advertising has contributed to the decline in the quality of the press. Reliance upon advertising can even be shown, in the United States at least, to have hastened a reduction in the amount of direct competition that newspapers face. Reliance on advertising also leads the newspapers to avoid providing coverage and analysis of issues that advertisers would rather not be associated with. Baker is explicit (1994) in suggesting that the interests of advertisers are often in conflict with the interests of consumers. And because he interprets the purpose of the First Amendment as serving the interests of the citizen-consumer over that of the corporate person, he has proposed taxing the income from advertising at a higher rate then the income derived from circulation.

It is no longer considered a radical idea to suggest that media are in the business of producing audience attention for sale or lease to advertisers. There has been some innovative theoretical work designed to elaborate the notion of audience attention as an economic resource (Goldhaber, 1997). There is little doubt that the attention of individuals is a scarce and valuable resource. There is something useful to be gained from thinking about advertising in terms of a transaction in which something of value is exchanged for audience attention. This was a fundamental part of the contribution that Dallas Smythe made to our thinking about the audience as a commodity (Smythe, 1977). Although critics suggest that the metaphoric construction of "watching as working" was rather quickly pushed to its conceptual limits (Meehan, 1993), the renewed attention being paid to the study of this audience suggests that that conclusion was unwarranted (Napoli, 2003).

We have come to recognize that there are a great variety of techniques and strategies that are used by communicators to attract and hold the attention of audiences. There is a substantial literature that explores the ways in which aesthetic and technical "devices" achieve measurable success in capturing and holding the attention of audiences defined by age, gender, and social class (Gunter, 2000). Barnhurst (1994), for example, has explored the ways in which the strategic use of graphic resources that include photographs, color, charts, and the general layout of the newspaper, have been used to capture and control the movement of the readers' attention throughout sections of the newspaper.

For our purposes, what matters most for our understanding of the role that advertising plays in the creation of a racial class is an appreciation of the ways in which advertisers are able to influence the racial composition of the audiences that different media tend to attract. The use of content and production techniques that attract audiences that are more homogeneous by race and social class is referred to as audience segmentation, and its contribution to the reproduction of social distinctions is too important to ignore.

SEGMENTATION AND SEGREGATION

Consumer segmentation is one of the most important strategies used by commercial firms in an effort to exercise more effective and efficient control over the "choices" that consumers make (Turow, 1997). I have suggested that an unintended outcome or an external effect of media segmentation is the reinforcement and normalization of patterns of racial and ethnic segregation (Gandy, 2003). Segmentation produces this racial effect through a complex process that involves the reproduction of racial stereotypes (Entman and Rojecki, 2000), which in the case of African Americans transforms pigmentation into stigma (Loury, 2002).

Stigma generates two forms of discrimination, one, which Loury calls "contract discrimination," has arguably been brought under the control of legal and cultural norms. The other, discrimination in contact, continues to explain much of the still substantial variation in income, wealth, and influence that divides African Americans from other groups in the United States (Gans, 1999). In Loury's view, "past racial discrimination in contract, together with present discrimination in contact, disadvantages blacks by impeding their acquisition of skills" (Loury, 2002, p. 125). Loury (2002) argues, and substantial evidence suggests, that much of the disparity in knowledge and skill that we observe between whites and African Americans is the product of social exclusion—exclusion that is in large part, but not entirely, the result of contact discrimination on the part of whites.

It seems clear that patterns of routine social contacts and interaction enable the formation of social networks through a process that Giddens refers to as structuration (Gregory, 1989). These networks can be understood in terms of the social and cultural capital that is reproduced and distributed to their members (Cornell and Hartmann, 1998). Geographic and social segregation along racial lines works to reproduce stigmatizing markers of difference that reinforce an avoidance response that we might recognize as "aversive racism" (Dovidio, 2001) when it is applied to those who are "other" to African Americans.

Although a rationale for contact discrimination on the part of African Americans can be understood as having a basis in safety and security and solidarity in the past, it is not so clear that the balance of accounts continue to favor such discrimination in the present.

Although it is important to understand the role that African American leadership plays in the reproduction of racially homogeneous social networks, it is even more important for us to understand the role that segmented media play in the social amplification of the risks of segregation (Kasperson, Jhaveri, and Kasperson, 2001). As I have suggested, it is primarily advertisers, rather than African American leaders, who control the ways in which this media system does its work.

Media segmentation not only reinforces segregation by race and class, it also reproduces the same sorts of distribution bias that we observe elsewhere in society (Danna and Gandy, 2002). Media that are targeted to African Americans are likely to be characterized by lower quality editorial content and an oversupply of advertisements for potentially harmful commodities (Gandy, 2003). This tendency is explained by the fact that African American audiences are not valued as highly as other audiences, in part because African Americans have less income available for the consumption of commodities that serve largely expressive ends.

We would not expect those in the business of producing audiences for sale to invest in programs that attract large numbers of African Americans, especially if those programs were not also attractive to large numbers of upscale, non-black audiences. The television programs that are least likely to be attractive to this more highly valued audience are those with primarily African American casts. One estimate suggests that television networks could expect to receive $16,704 less for each 30-second spot they offered in programs featuring an African American cast (Brown and Cavazos, 2002, p. 238).

Because African American consumers are not valued at the same level in the market for advertising as white consumers (Napoli, 2003; Ofori, 2001a), a marketplace logic suggests that there should be fewer resources "wasted" in attracting, or "producing" them. A marketplace logic ensures that African Americans are likely to be ill-served, because a commercial media market will not supply much of the content they would prefer to consume (Wildman and Karamanis, 1998).

It is not necessary to argue that the undersupply of programs of interest to African Americans reflects some sort of racial animus (Gandy, 2000). To the extent that programs that interest African Americans are attractive to a relatively small number of consumers, minority status alone is enough to produce an undersupply of content in the context of a capitalist market. It is likely, however, that the extent of the undersupply will be greater under conditions of finance through advertising than it would be under some form of direct purchase, such as through cable television subscriptions (Wildman and Karamanis, 1998).

Unfortunately, because the literature that is concerned with the social impact of segmentation and targeting is relatively underdeveloped at this point in time (Napoli, 2003), we have little empirical evidence to support any claims about the ways in which reliance upon targeted advertising would also determine the extent to which specific content or subject matter of importance to African Americans would be supplied. However, there is a basis in logic, theory, and economic history for developing some troublesome expectations.

The assumptions that advertisers make about the nature of African American consumers help to shape the strategic behavior of advertisers of different classes of goods and services, as well as for different media formats. For example, because of assessments of the nature and extent of the "digital divide" (Hoffman, Novak, and Venkatesh, 1998; Ofori, 2001a), online businesses were less likely to see African Americans as potential customers (Zaret and Meeks, 2000), and were therefore less likely to place advertisements in black-targeted media (Appiah and Wagner, 2002).

Mainstream economic theory suggests that the size of the market determines the amount of capital that is available to producers and distributors for investment in the development of content. Without other considerations we would assume that the larger the potential market, the larger the pool of resources that might be invested in producing the content that either would be supplied to the audience, or used as bait to attract their attention for advertisers. As a result of the combined influence of limited wealth and relatively small numbers, those media organizations that are committed to an African American audience will have fewer resources to invest in the acquisition and production of content. This means that the content they do acquire will necessarily be of lower quality in terms of production values or in terms of currency.

In the case of those black-targeted media organizations that are reliant on advertiser support, it seems likely that they may have to rely on income from the supply of audience attention to the vendors of more troublesome commodities, such as cigarettes and beer.

This is likely to be the case because in addition to refusing to pay a fair price for access to minority audiences, some advertisers actively seek to avoid attracting black and Latino consumers (Ofori, 1999). Although some observers question the ethics of targeting so-called vulnerable consumers with harmful products (U.S. Court of Appeals, 2001), others suggest that it is just good business strategy (Smith and Cooper-Martin, 1997). The result, unfortunately, is that African Americans are scarred through contact with both edges of this twin-edged sword.

This is nowhere more obvious than in the case of black-oriented radio. Citing a general trend, publishers of *The Black Commentator* described the decline in the investment being made in news production in Washington, DC—a city with so many African Americans that it had been referred to affectionately as "Chocolate City." Thirty years ago, at the heart of the Civil Rights movement, when the black press responded to the demands of its community (Owens, 1996), there were 21 reporters employed by Black-oriented radio stations in the city. Now, there are only four reporters at two stations, with three of them at Howard University's popular commercial station, WHUR ("Who Killed Black Radio News," 2003). As the publishers note, the current situation is not a matter of black ownership, because Cathy Hughes, the African American owner and founder of the 66-station Radio One chain, doesn't employ a single newsperson at any of the four stations she runs in the nation's capitol. Indeed, news workers are hard to find at any of the stations in the 22 cities in which her chain has established a dominant market presence. We are invited to keep in mind that by herself, Hughes controls more black-oriented stations than the giant Clear Channel enterprise, although they differ very little in terms of their failure to invest in the production of news for their African American listeners. Critics suggest that by adopting the business plans and economic logic preferred by mainstream media, black radio executives have contributed to the "relentless decline in Black political power" ("Who Killed Black Radio News, 2003, p. 4).

Of course, not all observers agree that the absence of local news coverage targeted to the African American community necessarily leaves that community without a meaningful alternative. Squires (2000) provides a case study of a black owned-and-operated talk radio station in Chicago (WVON) that she believes meets the community's needs. It seems likely, however, that WVON is rather unique among commercial stations in that its connection with its community is such that over a three-year period (1995-1998) financial contributions from listener "subscription" drives generated in excess of $180,000. She claims that "WVON and its listeners have created a media environment whose commercial and community goals overlap" (Squires, 2000, p. 90). Unfortunately, small community-oriented stations like WVON are frequently the targets of the drive toward consolidation that produces multi-market media conglomerates like Clear Channel and Radio One. It should also be noted that in 1996, WVON had an average quarter hour (AQH) audience of 8,800, whereas the number one black-oriented station in Chicago (WGCI-FM) had an AQH of 68,700 listeners (Duncan, 1997).

THE BLACK PUBLIC SPHERE

Squires (2002) identifies three distinct forms that "subaltern" public spheres might take as they provide meaningful alternatives to the idealized, but unrealized public sphere that Habermas associates with democratic political systems (Habermas, 1989; Jacobs, 2000). Although each of the alternative forms can be identified, they are not equally likely to be subject to the distorting influence of advertising. The least likely alternative is the "enclaved" public sphere.

Squires suggests that an "enclaved" public sphere for African Americans emerged during periods in American history when there was a strongly felt need to develop "safe" places in which black people could develop both an oppositional identity, as well as a political strategy for survival. The expectation was, as Fraser (1992) suggests, that enclaved groups would eventually emerge into the larger public sphere as claimants on the rights enjoyed by other citizens.

The "counterpublic sphere" that Squires identifies comes closest to more generally accessible formations that critics of Habermas have identified (Jacobs, 2000). Counterpublic spheres not only facilitate the development and expression of otherwise marginalized perspectives, but it is part of their political function to introduce these alternative perspectives into mainstream discourse. The third form that Squires labels "satellite" public spheres exist to support the separate, but not clandestine existence of communities that are within the nation, but not an integral part of it. The Nation of Islam is a separatist movement with its own media. Although not shrouded in secrecy, its discourse is designed for its members and its mission, and there is little interest in accommodating or attempting to substantially influence the mainstream political system. It seems likely that both counterpublic and satellite public spheres are subject to the distorting influence of commercial sponsorship.

It remains to be seen whether new media forms, such as those enabled by the competitive Web-hosting market, will support the development of truly independent forums. The fact that only a tiny fraction of Web sites are supported by advertising revenue (Ofori, 2001a) has meant that operators of African American sites in search of commercial sponsorship have begun to enter into "network agreements" so as to make themselves more attractive to the marketers. This business strategy seems likely to reduce both the diversity of perspectives, as well as the force of the critique that the upscale target audiences will encounter on the Web.

Squires' (2002) elaboration of issues at the heart of debates about the nature of alternative and oppositional public spheres also provides an entry point for examining the role being played by a small, but increasingly visible cohort of black conservatives (Dawson, 2001). Rather than using the criticism that is often directed toward these individuals from the black mainstream as evidence of the collapse of an African American political agenda on civil rights, Squires suggests that the popularity of these voices within the mainstream media can be taken as evidence of an emergence of a "Black conservative counterpublic" (Squires, 2002, p. 465).

Although these black conservatives enjoy their greatest visibility within mainstream, white-targeted media, financial support from conservative organizations has also enabled these conservative voices to be heard within newsweeklies targeted to the African American community. Black billionaire media mogul Bob Johnson has been identified as an active participant in efforts by conservatives to funnel support to black-identified organizations willing to support right wing social policies ("Trojan Horse Watch," 2002).

Support from primarily white, conservative organizations has allowed Black-identified organizations such as The Black Alliance for Educational Options to nearly dominate issue-advertising expenditures in Washington DC in 2001. In excess of $4 million was spent on television and print advertising in the majority black community of the District of Columbia (DC) in an effort to mobilize support for a conservative policy goal—the establishment of school voucher programs. Much of the funding for the Black Alliance campaign came from primarily white, conservative foundations (Falk, 2002).

POLARIZATION AND THE FORMATION OF A RACIAL CLASS

One consequence of segmentation and targeting on the basis of racial group membership is the widening of a racial divide between African Americans and other members of minority racial and ethnic groups. Gans (1999) suggests that there is a strong possibility that the multiracial hierarchy that presently exists will be transformed into a bimodal structure with two primary groups, black and non-black. Although there might be a residual category for groups such as immigrants of color and for the products of mixed marriages, Gans sees the increasingly voluntary nature of racial identification in the United States (Zuberi, 2001) as facilitating the eventual adoption of white identity. This newly established flexibility would even accommodate those "multiracials" clearly possessing that "one-drop" of "black blood" that would have previously defined them as black in the United States (Davis, 1991; Nobles, 2000). There seems to be little doubt that the adoption of white identity among Hispanics will continue, despite the appeals made by critical race theorists (Haney-López, 1996).

Edley (1996) and Dawson (2001) identify distinct political orientations among African Americans. These differences are especially meaningful when examined in relation to social policies that not only divide whites and African Americans, but generate tensions among black people. Edley makes a simple distinction between what he refers to as universalist and nationalist perspectives on racial difference, where universalists are informed by a belief that racial differences are increasingly less important determinants of the relations between people, and nationalists tend to underscore the importance of group identity and cohesion. Both nationalism and universalism exist in strong and weak forms that Edley labels in the extreme as responsible or pathological.

Dawson (1999) suggests that the values of black popular culture, including rap music, have only limited political utility. They "cannot substitute for the mobilization, organization building, and political, economic, and social struggle through which societies are transformed and social justice won" (p. 336).

What remains uncertain is the extent to which the mass media can provide a sufficiently powerful basis for the development of a common identity based on racial commitment that is reinforced through the consumption of commercial goods and services that are marketed through targeted media. Commercialized African American culture transformed by privatized media seems likely to establish even more severe limits on the political utility of this corrupted public sphere.

THE CHALLENGE THAT REMAINS

Herb Schiller's powerful and relentless criticism of the myriad ways in which an evolving capitalist information industry spreads its tentacles into the whole of our social being (Webster, 2002) has helped us understand how the commoditization of information has contributed to the widening of disparities between the haves, and the have-nots we recognize in terms of their social class position.

Yet, I have become convinced that we need to look more closely at some of the other ways in which hosts of dividing practices that have been normalized through their integration into a corrupted public sphere constrain the development of a progressive movement for social change. Schiller concluded not long ago that given "the erosion of democratic institutions and processes that have been detailed, the multiplying crises in American life are less and less likely to be overcome by democratic means" (Schiller, 1996, p. 140).

In his more recent writing (Schiller, 2000), he sought to frame an observable lack of social cohesion among Americans as a threat to the nation's ability to maintain its status as "Numero Uno." Yet, the apparent willingness of the American superpower to "go it alone, if necessary" against any who challenged its authority would suggest that the ruling elites are not at all concerned about the development of any substantial, or sustainable oppositional social movement concerned about inequality.

The signs are far too numerous and too sharply outlined for any but the fatally distracted to ignore the broad outlines of a uniquely American "final solution" to the social crisis that African American poverty represents in a nation of committed consumers. The reframing of affirmative action programs designed to narrow the gaps in competence and confidence that are the products of a racist past (McWhorter, 2001) as a policy of enlightened self-interest in the benefits of "diversity" as an input in educational production function is just one of the signs that the American polity appears ready to accept the "disappearance" of African Americans from the agenda of legitimate and pressing concerns.

Although attempts to eliminate racial categories from official statistics are being carried forward as part of a conservative political agenda (Guinier and Torres, 2002), racial and ethnic classification shows little sign of being set aside as a strategic resource in the rationalization of social, economic, and political activities. Although it is primarily critics who introduce racial statistics into public debates in order to indicate the extent to which racial disparities continue to reflect the burdens of racism (Fairclough, 2002; Gandy, 2003; National Research Council, 2004), the very same statistics are used to justify other discriminatory acts that reinforce these disparities. The most troublesome of these activities take place within the sphere of commoditized information (Danna and Gandy, 2002), and we have barely begun to appreciate how important it is for us at least to question, if not to act against the spread of corrupt segmentation along racial lines.

The political economy of communication, the academic specialty that Herb Schiller has done so much to develop, seems to me to be an ideal platform from which to mount a critical engagement with these issues.

There are plenty of empty spaces for those who care to join in the effort.

REFERENCES

Allen, Anita L. (2003) *Why Privacy Isn't Everything: Feminist Reflections on Personal Accountability.* Lanham, MD: Rowman & Littlefield.

Appiah, Osei and Matthew Wagner (2002) "Differences in media buying by online businesses in black and white targeted magazines: The potential impact of the digital divide on ad placement." *The Howard Journal of Communications* 13: 251-266.

Baker, Edwin C. (1994) *Advertising and a Democratic Press.* Princeton, NJ: Princeton University Press.

Baker, Edwin C. (2002) *Media, Markets, and Democracy.* New York: Cambridge University Press.

Barnhurst, Kevin G. (1994) *Seeing the Newspaper.* New York: St. Martin's Press.

Brown, Keith S. and Roberto J. Cavazos (2002) "Network revenues and African American broadcast television programs." *Journal of Media Economics* 15: 227-239.

Cohen, Lisbeth (2003) *A Consumers' Republic: The Politics of Mass Consumption.* New York: Alfred Knopf.

Cornell, Stephen and Douglass Hartmann (1998) *Ethnicity and Race: Making Identities in a Changing World.* Thousand Oaks, CA: Pine Forge Press.

Cottle, Simon (Ed.) (2000) *Ethnic Minorities and the Media: Changing Cultural Boundaries.* Philadelphia: Open University Press.

Croteau, David and William Haynes (2001) *The Business of Media: Corporate Media and the Public Interest.* Thousand Oaks, CA: Pine Forge Press.

Danna, Anthony and Oscar H. Gandy (2002) "All that glitters is not gold: Digging beneath the surface of data mining." *Journal of Business Ethics* 40: 373-386.

Davis, Floyd J. (1991) *Who is Black? One Nation's Definition.* University Park: Pennsylvania State University Press.

Dawson, Michael C. (1994) *Behind the Mule: Race and Class in African-American Politics.* Princeton: Princeton University Press.

Dawson, Michael C. (1999) "'dis beat disrupts': Rap, ideology, and black political attitudes." In Michele Lamont (Ed.), *The Cultural Territories of Race: Black and White Boundaries* (pp. 318-342). Chicago: University of Chicago Press, .

Dawson, Michael C. (2001) *Black Visions: The Roots of Contemporary African-American Political Ideologies.* Chicago: University of Chicago Press.

Dovidio, John F. (2001) "On the nature of contemporary prejudice: The third wave." *Journal of Social Issues* 57: 829-849.

Doyle, Gillian (2002) *Understanding Media Economics.* Thousand Oaks, CA: Sage.

Duncan, James H. (1997) *American Radio 1997 Small Market Edition.* Cincinnati, OH: Duncan's American Radio.

Edley, Christopher (1996) *Not All Black and White: Affirmative Action and American Values.* New York: Hill and Wang.

Edwards, Lynne (2001) "Black like me: Value commitment and television viewing preferences of US black teenage girls." In Karen Ross and Peter Playdon (Eds.), *Black Marks: Minority Ethnic Audiences and Media* (pp. 49-66). Burlington, VT: Ashgate.

Entman, Robert and Andrew Rojecki (2000) *The Black Image in the White Mind: Media and Race in America.* Chicago: University of Chicago Press.

Fairclough, Adam (2002) *Better Day Coming: Blacks and Equality, 1890-2000.* New York: Penguin.

Falk, Erika (2002) *Print and Television Legislative Issue Advertising in the Nation's Capital [sic] in 2001.* Washington, DC: Annenberg Public Policy Center.

Ferguson, Robert (1998) *Representing "Race": Ideology, Identity, and the Media.* New York: Oxford University Press.

Frank, Ronald E. and Marshall E. Greenberg (1980) *The Public's Use of Television: Who Watches and Why.* Beverly Hills, CA: Sage.

Fraser, Nancy (1992) "Rethinking the public sphere: A contribution to the critique of actually existing democracy." In Craig Calhoun (Ed.), *Habermas and the Public Sphere* (pp. 109-142). Cambridge, MA: MIT Press.

Gandy, Oscar H. (1998) *Communication and Race: A Structural Perspective.* New York: Oxford University Press.

Gandy, Oscar H. (2000) "Audience segmentation: Is it racism or just good business?" *Media Development* 2: 3-6.

Gandy, Oscar H. (2001a) "Dividing practices: Segmentation and targeting in the emerging public sphere." In W. Lance Bennet and Robert M. Entman (Eds.), *Mediated Politics: Communication in the Future of Democracy* (pp. 141-159). New York: Cambridge University Press.

Gandy, Oscar H. (2001b) "Racial identity, media use, and the social construction of risk among African Americans." *Journal of Black Studies* 31: 600-618.

Gandy, Oscar H. (2003) "The irrationality of rational choice: Audience segmentation and the real digital divide." In Joseph Harper and Thom Yantek (Eds.), *Media, Profit, and Politics: Competing Priorities in an Open Society* (pp. 249-264). Kent, OH: Kent State University Press, .

Gandy, Oscar H. (2003) "Journalists and academics and the delivery of race statistics: Being a statistician means never having to say you're certain," *Race and Society:* 149-160.

Gans, Herbert J. (1999) "The possibility of a new racial hierarchy in the twenty-first century United States." In Michele Lamont (Ed.), *The Cultural Territories of Race: Black and White Boundaries* (pp. 371-390). Chicago: University of Chicago Press.

Garnham, Nicholas (1995) "Political economy and cultural studies: Reconciliation or divorce?" *Critical Studies in Mass Communication* 12: 62-71.

Goldhaber, Michael H. (1997) "The attention economy: The natural economy of the net." *First Monday* 2(4) (http://www.firstmonday.dk/issues/issue2_4/goldhaber).

Gray, Herman (1995) *Watching Race*. Minneapolis: University of Minnesota Press.

Gray, Herman (2000) "Black representation in the post network, post civil rights world of global media." in Simon Cottle (Ed.), *Ethnic Minorities and the Media* (pp. 118-129).. Philadelphia, PA: Open University Press.

Gregory, Derek (1989) "Presences and absences: Time-space relations and structuration theory." In David Held and John B. Thompson (Eds.), *Social Theory of Modern Societies: Anthony Giddens and his Critics*. New York: Cambridge University Press.

Grossberg, Lawrence (1996) "Identity and cultural studies: Is that all there is?" In Stuart Hall and Paul duGay (Eds.), *Questions of Cultural Identity* (pp. 87-107). Thousand Oaks, CA: Sage.

Guinier, Lani and Gerald Torres (2002) *The Miner's Canary: Enlisting Race, Resisting Power, Transforming Democracy*. Cambridge, MA: Harvard University Press.

Gunter, Barrie (2000) *Media Research Methods: Measuring Audiences, Reactions and Impact*. Thousand Oaks, CA: Sage.

Habermas, Jurgen (1989) *The Structural Transformation of the Public Sphere*. Cambridge, MA: MIT Press.

Hagen, Ingunn and Janet Wasko (Eds.) (2000) *Consuming Audiences? Production and Reception in Media Research*. Cresskill, NJ: Hampton Press.

Haney-López, Ian F. (1996) *White by Law: The Legal Construction of Race*. New York: New York University Press.

Hecht, Michael L., Ronald L. Jackson, and Sidney A. Ribeau (2003) *African American Communication: Exploring Identity and Culture*. Mahwah, NJ: Erlbaum.

Hochschild, Jennifer L. (1999) "Affirmative action as culture war." In Michele Lamont (Ed.), *The Cultural Territories of Race: Black and White Boundaries* (pp. 343-368). Chicago: University of Chicago Press, .

Hoffman, Donna L., Thomas P. Novak, and Alladi Venkatesh (1998) "Diversity on the internet: The relationship of race to access and usage." In Amy K. Garmer (Ed.), *Investing in Diversity: Advancing Opportunities for Minorities and the Media* (pp. 125-192).. Washington, DC: The Aspen Institute.

Jacobs, Ronald N. (2000) *Race, Media and the Crisis of Civil Society*. New York: Cambridge University Press.

Jaret, Charles and Donald C. Reitzes (1999) "The importance of racial-ethnic identity and social setting for blacks, whites and multi-racials." *Sociological Perspectives* 42: 711-737.

Jones, Felicia G. (1990) "The black audience and the BET channel." *Journal of Broadcasting and Electronic Media* 34: 477-486.

Kasperson, Roger, Nayna Jhaveri, and Jeanne X. Kasperson (2001) "Stigma and the social simplification of risk: Toward a framework of analysis." In James Flynn, Paul Slovic, and Howard Kunreuther (Eds.), *Risk, Media and Stigma: Understanding Public Challenges to Modern Science and Technology.* Sterling, VA: Earthscan Publications.

Kinder, Donald R. and Lynn M. Sanders (1996) *Divided by Color: Racial Politics and Democratic Ideals.* Chicago: University of Chicago Press.

Kubey, Robert (1996) "On not finding media effects: Conceptual problems in the notion of an 'active' audience (with a reply to Elihu Katz)." In James Hay, Lawrence Grossberg, and Ellen Wartella (Eds.), *The Audience and its Landscape* (pp. 187-205). Boulder, CO: Westview Press.

Loury, Glenn C. (2002) *The Anatomy of Racial Inequality.* Cambridge, MA: Harvard University Press.

McManus, John H. (1994) *Market-driven Journalism: Let the Citizen Beware?* Thousand Oaks, CA: Sage.

McWhorter, John (2001) *Losing the Race: Self-sabotage in Black America.* New York: Harper Collins.

Meehan, Eileen (1993) "Commodity audience, actual audience: The blindspot debate." In Janet Wasko, Vincent Mosco, and Manjanuth Pendakur (Eds.), *Illuminating the Blindspots: Essays Honoring Dallas W. Smythe* (pp. 378-397). Norwood, NJ: Ablex,

Mosco, Vincent (1996) *The Political Economy of Communication.* Thousand Oaks, CA: Sage.

Murdock, Graham (1995) "Across the great divide: Cultural analysis and the condition of democracy." *Critical Studies in Mass Communication* 12: 89-95.

Murdock, Graham (2000) "Reconstructing the ruined tower: Contemporary communications and questions of class." In James Curran and Michael Gurevitch (Eds.), *Mass Media and Society* (pp. 7-26).. New York: Oxford University Press.

Napoli, Philip (2001) *Foundations of Communications Policy.* Cresskill, NJ: Hampton Press.

Napoli, Philip (2003) *Audience Economics.* New York: Columbia University Press.

National Research Council (2004) *Measuring Racial Discrimination.* Washington, DC: National Academies Press.

Negus, Keith and Patricia Róman-Vélazquez (2000) "Globalization and cultural identities." In James Curran and Michael Gurevitch (Eds.), *Mass Media and Society* (pp. 329-345). New York: Oxford University Press.

Nobles, Melissa (2000) *Shades of Citizenship: Race and the Census in Modern Politics.* Stanford, CA: Stanford University Press.

Nordenstreng, Kaarle (1993) "New information order and communication scholarship: Reflections on a delicate relationship." In Janet Wasko, Vincent Mosco, and Manjunath Pendakur (Eds.), *Illuminating the Blindspots: Essays Honoring Dallas W. Smythe* (pp. 251-273). Norwood, NJ: Ablex.

Ofori, Kofi A. (1999) *When Being No. 1 is Not Enough: The Impact of Advertising Practices on Minority-owned and Minority-formatted Broadcast Stations.* Washington, DC: Civil Rights Forum on Communications Policy. Report to the Federal Communications Commission.

Ofori, Kofi A. (2001a) In the Black: African-American web entrepreneurs and internet advertising." In America Rodriguez (Ed.), *Reinventing Minority Media for the 21st Century* (pp. 19-35). Washington, DC: The Aspen Institute.

Ofori, Kofi A. (2001b) *Minority-targeted Programming: An Examination of its Effect on Radio Station Advertising Performance.* Washington, DC: National Black Media Coalition.

Owens, Reginald (1996) "Entering the twenty-first century: Oppression and the African American press." In Vernice T. Berry and Carmen L. Manning-Miller (Eds.), *Mediated Messages and African-American Culture: Contemporary Issues* (pp. 96-116). Thousand Oaks, CA: Sage.

Picard, Robert (2002) *The Economics and Financing of Media Companies.* New York: Fordham University Press.

Reder, Melvin W. (1999) *Economics: The Culture of a Controversial Science.* Chicago: The University of Chicago Press.

Ross, Karen and Peter Playdon (Eds.) (2001) *Black Marks: Minority Ethnic Audiences and Media.* Burlington, VT: Ashgate Publishing Company.

Schiller, Herbert I. (1989) *Culture, Inc.: The Corporate Takeover of Public Expression.* New York: Oxford University Press.

Schiller, Herbert I. (1996) *Information Inequality: The Deepening Social Crisis in America.* New York: Routledge.

Schiller, Herbert I. (2000) *Living in the Number One Country: Reflections from a Critic of American Empire.* New York: Seven Stories Press.

Slater, Don (1997) *Consumer Culture and Modernity.* Cambridge, MA: Blackwell.

Smith, N. Craig and Elisabeth Cooper-Martin (1997) "Ethics and target marketing: The role of product harm and consumer vulnerability." *Journal of Marketing* 61: 1-20.

Smythe, Dallas (1977) "Communications: Blindspot of Western marxism." *Canadian Journal of Political and Social Theory* 1: 1-27.

Squires, Catherine R. (2000) "Black talk radio: Defining community needs and identity." *Press/Politics* 5: 73-95.

Squires, Catherine R. (2002) "Rethinking the black public sphere: An alternative vocabulary for multiple public spheres." *Communication Theory* 12: 446-468.

Sunstein, Cass R. (2001) *Republic.com.* Princeton, NJ: Princeton University Press.

"Trojan horse watch: Bob Johnson's message invades black radio" (2002) *The Black Commentator,* October 17. http://www.blackcommentator.com/14_thw_pr.html

Turow, Joseph (1997) *Breaking up America: Advertisers and the New Media World.* Chicago, IL: University of Chicago Press.

United States Court of Appeals for the Third Circuit (2001) Jesse Brown v. Philip Morris, et al. No. 99-1931: Lexis Nexis, 9734 (May 17)

Warde, Alan (1994) "Consumption, identity-formation and uncertainty." *Sociology* 28: 877.

Webster, Frank (2002) *Theories of the Information Society* (2nd ed.). New York: Routledge.

Wildman, Steven S. and Theomary Karamanis (1998) "The economics of minority programming." In Amy K. Garmer (Ed.), *Investing in Diversity* (pp. 47-65). Washington, DC: The Aspen Institute.

"Who killed black radio news?" (2003) *The Black Commentator.* http://blackcommentator.com/44/44_cover_pr.html

Zaret, Elliot and Brock Meeks (2000) "Kozmo's digital dividing lines." (April 4). MSNBC.com. http://www.msnbc.com/news/373212.asp.

Zuberi, Tukufu (2001) *Thicker than Blood: How Racial Statistics Lie.* Minneapolis: University of Minnesota Press.

SECTION THREE

GLOBALIZATIONS

Breaching The Walls

CHAPTER SEVEN

CULTURAL GLOBALIZATION AND AMERICAN EMPIRE

John Sinclair

The McDonald's on every corner; the Hollywood blockbusters on simultaneous release in all the multiplexes; the sound and image of pop icons like Madonna emanating from the franchised music store in the mall; at home, the TV program guide peppered with *Desperate Housewives* and *Oprah* — throughout the world, these are the kind of encounters people experience every day with the commercial popular culture of the United States. Over the last 50 years or so, these and other cultural forms have expanded their reach, first from the United States to the rest of the West, and more recently, into the postcommunist and former "Third World." American cultural domination seems a self-evident fact of life in the global era.

Ever since the 1960s and 1970s, social theorists have sought to explain and interpret the significance of such cultural influence in terms of deeper economic and political transformations at work in the world. There have been two main critical paradigms employed to do this: firstly, that of "cultural imperialism," which was prevalent in the 1970s and 1980s, and then, after the end of the Cold War, cultural flows have been understood more as an integral dimension of globalization. This chapter begins by reviewing the cultural imperialism perspective, and examining the reasons why "cultural globalization" emerged as a more valid way of conceptualizing how cultural influence works. It will also take account of how certain key assumptions and concerns of the cultural imperialism approach nevertheless have persisted into the present, including the belief that cultural globalization is really a process of "Americanization." Finally, by way of a case study, the chapter provides an assessment of the impact of marketization upon the television industry of Latin America, a major world region long subject to the hegemony of the United States.

DEPENDENCY AND IMPERIALISM: A BACKWARD GLANCE

No doubt because of this hegemony, the crucible of cultural imperialism theory was in fact Latin America. When the "Development Decade" of the 1960s did not produce the social and economic changes predicted by the post–World War II U.S. and European advocates of "modernization," Latin American theorists looked for their own explanation. They found this in "dependency" theory, essentially the idea that the continued economic and social problems of the region were due to the inability of Latin American national economies to develop independently of foreign investment and technology. This general theory was given a cultural emphasis by a number of Latin Americans who cast it in terms of the "dominant ideology thesis," the most influential theoretical paradigm in communication, media, and cultural studies throughout the 1970s and well into the 1980s. The basis of this view was Marx's perception that the class that owned the means of the production and distribution of ideas in a society, which includes the media, could thereby control the flow of beliefs in that society in accordance with its own interests (Collins, 1990, pp. 1-24). In the Latin American "cultural dependency" version, social inequalities were seen to be legitimized and perpetuated by the ideas and images that circulated in the media of the dependent societies, and much media content was imported, particularly from the United States. In one view, the United States was "the generating hub of the capitalist ideology and culture that is being diffused" (Dagnino, 1973, p. 137).

In various national settings in the region, this neo-Marxist theoretical critique of ideology was applied to research on imported media content, especially television. The most significant case was Chile, where the supporters of Latin America's first elected Marxist president, Salvador Allende (president 1970-73), sought to defend his regime against destabilizing ideological influences, both from inside and outside the country. Prominent in this defense was Armand Mattelart, a Belgian, who in his own right and in conjunction with various collaborators was involved in prolific theoretical, research, and media production activities. These included the classic ideo-logical analysis of Disney comics, *How to Read Donald Duck* (Dorfman and Mattelart, 1975). Mattelart went on to become the most articulate and active theorist of cultural imperialism in Europe, preferring that term for his analysis, but explicitly acknowledging his debt to dependency theory (Mattelart, 1980). Other Europeans sought to focus the critique more specifically, notably Oliver Boyd-Barrett with his variant of "media imperialism" (1977), whereas Cees Hamelink concerned himself with "cultural synchronization" (1983).

In the United States, Herbert Schiller had already taken up the metaphor of imperialism in his seminal *Mass Communications and American Empire* (1969). This spelled out the connections Schiller saw between the overseas activities of U.S. corporations, and the role of U.S. foreign policy in facilitating their interests. That role included making the world safe for the commercialization of foreign markets with consumer goods. Schiller saw the media as having some key functions in this process, both directly through advertising, and indirectly through the diffusion of images of a "consumerist" way of life displayed as a social ideal.

The concept of cultural imperialism went on to acquire an influence in actual world events far beyond the ambit of international media critics. The term was adopted by the bloc of nonaligned countries in the United Nations in the 1970s as a way of formulating their concerns about how media flows between nations were dominated by the West. As they saw it, the European and American news agencies monopolized news flows; U.S. advertising agencies were engaged in the "homogenization" of national cultures as they sought to transform them into new markets for transnational consumer goods manufacturers; and Hollywood and the U.S. networks dominated world film and television screens. Their critique developed into a set of demands for a "New World Information and Communication Order" (NWICO) through UNESCO. These demands shared the theorists' assumption that populations in the dependent countries were vulnerable to ideological manipulation because the media were structured in favor of the West, and especially the United States.

CULTURAL IMPERIALISM AS CLASSIC CRITIQUE

The era when the cultural imperialism perspective really did make sense of the world ended with the demise of the Cold War, which had given it its rationale. Since then, there have been some definitive critiques of the concept. British theorist John Tomlinson argues that the cultural imperialism perspective was not so much a paradigm, a theory, nor a thesis, but rather a "discourse": that is, a certain set of ways of talking about cultural influence between nations (1991, pp. 34-56). This reminds us that "cultural imperialism" was invented as a rhetorical term to rally and to challenge: it was never intended just to analyze and theoretically comprehend the workings of the process as such. Consequently, the cultural imperialism discourse largely consists of a series of more or less explicit assumptions that underlie a certain worldview, so critiques of it tend to proceed by constructing a "straw man" composite; or by specifically addressing the works of a representative exponent, such as Schiller; or both. That is what will be done here, but it may be asked: why rehash a debate around a discredited critical orthodoxy of decades past?

For one reason, traces of some key assumptions of the old discourse often can be seen in the new. For another, to revisit the world in which cultural imperialism was a plausible paradigm is to establish something of a baseline against which can be measured both the real-world changes of the last few decades and the theoretical responses that have been made to them. So, this section will briefly review the major tenets of "classic" cultural imperialism discourse. We can then proceed to canvas the criticisms that have been made of these positions and consider the subsequent reformulations, before going on to review the case for cultural globalization as a more fitting way of understanding current realities.

First, there is the foundational belief in the universal, inevitable, and deliberate domination of the United States, the center of world wealth and power, over the rest of the West and the peripheral Third World. Hence the term "imperialism," but not in the sense of the Holy Roman Empire, nor the European colonial empires, nor even the way in which Lenin saw it as "the highest stage of capitalism." Rather, imperialism is intended more as a rhetorical trope for how the United States has used communication technologies to transform such past modes of domination, and is defined simply as "a system of exploitative control of people and resources" (Schiller, 1991, p. 17). Thus, cultural imperialism is systemic in that it involves the transfer of structures, notably the commercial model of broadcasting as developed in the United States, but it is not just the blind, unintended consequence of the implantation of such structures. On the contrary, the control that emanates from the center is "deliberate management of the sphere of consciousness" (Schiller, 1976, p. 19), made necessary by the functional relationship that is seen to exist between the economic "world system" and the "cultural-communications sphere." These functions are both instrumental, in promoting consumption, and ideological, in securing popular support for capitalist values (Schiller, 1976, p. 6).

Secondly, as is already implicit in its functionalist perspective, such classic formulations of the cultural imperialism paradigm assume a model of how media influence works, in the form of the "dominant ideology thesis" alluded to earlier. In addition to the basic premise that the media propagate capitalist ideas, there is the conviction that the media have such a powerful effect that these ideas can be made to prevail over whole populations, regardless of other social and cultural influences, through media "manipulation." Furthermore, whereas the dominant ideology thesis was initially developed as a critique of national societies, in the cultural imperialism perspective it becomes writ large as an international phenomenon:

> America's media managers create, process, refine, and preside over the circulation of images and information which determine our beliefs and attitudes and, ultimately, our behavior. (Schiller, 1973, p. 1)

The third main precept in the discourse of cultural imperialism follows from this rather mediacentric model, and that is the belief that the impact of "the worldwide advance of North American consumerist ideology" (Schiller, 1973, p. 6) is the same for everyone everywhere: hence the notion of "homogenization." Although rarely argued explicitly, this is the implicit assumption that the influx of news, entertainment, and advertisements from the center that is carried over the peripheral airwaves has an irresistible and uniform effect upon its recipients. Furthermore, there is a tendency in cultural imperialism discourse to regard the ideological meaning of such media contents as self-evident and transparent. Audience effects tend to be read off as a function of ideological content, yet there is scant regard given as to exactly how ideological effects are produced by specific contents, and even the actual process of cultural production is viewed in formulaic terms. That is, media products are themselves seen as homogenized, "made to identifiable specifications and with ascertainable ingredients," with predictable, inevitable ideological effects (Schiller,1973, p. 6).

A corollary of the homogenization thesis is that national cultures are under threat from foreign cultural incursion, and that this poses a threat to national sovereignty. In an age in which satellite television was first appearing and "transborder data flow" was an emergent issue, this was one point on which both the theoretical critics and the leaders of peripheral nations could readily agree. Even before satellites, the spread of Western, mainly United States, information and entertainment via television in particular threatened "the cultural integrity of weak societies" and their "national, regional, local or tribal heritages" with extinction (Schiller, 1969, p.109). The argument went that because the fostering and defense of its national culture was the responsibility of each nation-state, the inflow of foreign cultural products, especially where the government had no control over it, was therefore a fundamental challenge to the integrity of its national culture and hence its very national sovereignty.

FROM CULTURAL IMPERIALISM
TO GLOBALIZATION

Although there was cogent but constructive critique of the cultural imperialism discourse even in its heyday (Tunstall, 1977), the case against it has
largely been built with the wisdom of hindsight and rests mainly on the former paradigm's inability to incorporate real-world changes since the end of
the Cold War, nor to deal with new developments in media theory and
research. This section will review the core premises of cultural imperialism
discourse in the light of such changes, leading up to the advent of cultural
globalization as a new paradigm for understanding the flows of cultural
influence in the contemporary world.

To take firstly the issue of U.S. dominance, there can be no argument
against the fact that the collapse of the former Soviet Union has left the
United States as the single most powerful nation in the world, with no coun-
tervailing force. Nor can it be contested that the United States remains the
pre-eminent nation economically, not least in the world flows of cultural
products and services, especially the audiovisual media sector, which figures
so significantly in its export activities. However, the notion that the United
States is at the center of a single world system of cultural and media influence is not sustainable, as the cultural industries at the center of world
regions once considered peripheral have colonized these regions for themselves. These several new centers have developed very much on world-
regional linguistic and cultural differences, yielding geolinguistic markets
based on Mandarin, Hindi, Arabic, Spanish, and Portuguese, to name the
major ones (Sinclair, Jacka, and Cunningham, 1996). Although not threaten-
ing the ultimate dominance of the United States, the new flows not only
make for more complex, multilevelled choices for audiences in the markets
affected, but also introduce a relativism to the particular realities of foreign
cultural influence. For example, small countries may see their national and
cultural sovereignty as being threatened more by a large neighbor than by
the United States, or even large countries by their rivals: consider Indian television spilling into Sri Lanka, or Pakistani television into India. Elsewhere
in Asia, Japan has emerged as a major source of cultural influence (Iwabuchi,
2002).

A related issue is that both capital and labor have become "deterritorialized" from the nation-states in which they have their origin, and particularly in the era of marketization, media corporations foment and implement
their global strategies without the benefit of the support of their national
governments. A striking example is News Corporation, which, along with
its ruling family, the Murdochs, is Australian in origin. Yet it makes no sense
to call it "Australian," as 90% of its shareholders live outside Australia

(Frew, 2003); most of its operations are outside Australia, including the Fox network in the United States; no part in its expansion has been played by the Australian Government; and its Chairman, Rupert Murdoch, has become an American citizen. Even more instructive has been the case of Sony's acquisition of the former U.S. majors CBS Records and Columbia Pictures at the end of the 1980s, which showed Americans that foreign cultural incursion was something that could happen to them too. Yet, today, it is simply not helpful to think of Sony as "Japanese": rather, it is a prime example of a truly "global" corporation, made so through what Lash and Urry call "international horizontal integration" (1994, p. 130).

This is much the point that Herb Schiller himself conceded around this time: or at least, he argued that no longer was cultural domination driven by the power of the United States as a nation-state, but rather, by "transnational" (though not yet for him, "global") corporations acting in their own interests. Similarly, although insisting there was a collective logic to such large-scale corporate behavior, Schiller also recognized that the size, dispersal, and complexity of these entities meant that there could be "no general coordination of the system at large" (1991, p. 21). Finally on this aspect, Schiller retained the concept of imperialism, and the view that "media-cultural imperialism" was an integral part of economic imperialism, but he no longer put this in functionalist terms. Above all, he reintegrated the media back into an "all-encompassing cultural package" of commercial culture, which also embraced the shopping mall, the theme park, and the fast-food restaurant (Schiller, 1991, p. 15). There had been a stage in the debate when it had been helpful to distinguish between the media and other forms of cultural imperialism, because so much of that debate was focused on international news and the world expansion of television in particular, but Schiller was here restoring the most valuable insight in cultural imperialism discourse: the connection between the economic and the cultural spheres. The ongoing debate now, both in the political economy tradition that Schiller did so much to found and more widely in discourse about cultural globalization, is more about how that connection should be theorized and how it can be observed in practice.

The next assumption of the old cultural imperialism discourse that has come up for re-examination concerns the meaning that imported media content has for audiences, and its effects. At worst, there is the notion that the masses are manipulated as mere ideological dupes of omnipotent media that hold them in thrall. Against this "dominant ideology thesis," theory and research since the 1980s has led to something of a paradigm shift away from a conception of powerful media effects acting upon a passive audience to a view of an "active audience." The latter is based on naturalistic empirical investigation of how actual audiences seek out media experiences for themselves and how social differences within audiences such as gender, race, and class can bear upon the different interpretations they make of media messages. This view also entails the insight from semiology that messages themselves carry more than one meaning and that the gaps and contradictions within a message allow audiences to construct their meaning from it, rather than it having a single unambiguous interpretation that imposes itself on them.

Indeed, John Fiske, the main figure identified with such a "revisionist" view, talks of a "semiotic democracy" in which audience members can resist or subvert ideological meanings; others argue that this can only occur within strict limits, what David Morley calls a "structured polysemy" (cited in Curran, 1990). Yet even the more moderate version of this line of critique exposed the total disregard that cultural imperialism discourse had shown towards the meanings carried in media content, and how audiences made sense of them. In this respect, Schiller remained unrepentant: U.S. television programs and local genres such as the *telenovela* had a functional equivalence: they were "practically identical" in that they had "the same purpose" within the structure of commercial television as a system. Furthermore, he argued, studies of the impact of particular programs on particular audiences does not provide evidence of the effect of "the total cultural package" (1991, pp. 22-24). This has meant that because cultural imperialism as "theory" can be neither proven nor refuted by empirical investigation, it never can be truly superseded.

Given that cultural imperialism discourse saw the cultural products circulated throughout the world by the United States as functionally homogeneous and assumed that they carried an intrinsic ideological effect for audiences, it followed logically that this effect would be the same everywhere—notwithstanding empirical evidence to the contrary (Liebes and Katz, 1993). This is perhaps the most persistent tenet of cultural imperialism, one that has leached into much popular discourse about cultural globalization today. However, as many cultural globalization theorists point out, there is a counter-tendency to heterogenization. The anthropologist Arjun Appadurai in his definitive essay on cultural globalization discerns international flows of people, technologies, and finance as well as the flows of media and ideologies familiar from cultural imperialism discourse, and furthermore observes that these flows are subject to what he calls "indigenization" (1990). He means that outside influences are not imposed in raw form upon receiving societies, and neither are they swallowed whole: rather, there is a process of selective adoption and adaptation. Similarly, Roland Robertson refers to such local transformation of global cultural forms as "glocalization" (1995). Thus, what appears as homogenization at one level in fact is generating "heterogenization" at another: within sameness is its dialectic counterpoint of differentiation.

GLOBALIZATION AND CULTURE

Although "globalization" might have become the ideological buzz-word of the present era and its all-purpose explanation, and as such requires some critical distance (Ferguson, 1992), the concept does mark certain significant changes in the structure of the world and how it works that have developed since the end of the Cold War. The world of the last two centuries, made for and by nation-states, formerly grouped together in a basic dichotomy of adversarial blocs, has disintegrated into a more fluid and diverse, but still conflicted, set of alignments, largely based on regional trade and security. At the same time, nation-states have seen the increased power and prominence of supranational organizations such as the United Nations and World Trade Organization emerge above them, and below them, the forces of social movements and civil society.

As already suggested, corporations have become deterritorialized in the sense that corporate interests no longer can be identified with those of the nation-states that have given rise to them, and capital investment also behaves independently of its nation of origin, particularly in the interpenetration of capital from different source nations, at national, regional, and global levels. This trend has its impact upon national media systems in particular, which have become more internationalized both in their content and in their ownership and control, due largely to the processes inherent in marketization, including the liberalization of trade, the deregulation of national markets, and the inroads made by foreign capital. Thus, although globalization at first blush is an economic phenomenon with political implications, its "complex connectivity" (Tomlinson, 1999) entails an intrinsic cultural dimension, insofar as communication media and information technology are deeply implicated.

Although it is easy to overstate the degree to which nation-states have had their economic and political, not to mention cultural, sovereignty overtaken both above and below by the forces of globalization, the trends just outlined have had their effect on the academic disciplines of the humanities and social sciences as much as on the real world that those disciplines seek to understand. In that sense, globalization represents a paradigm shift, a wider frame of reference that recognizes that the economic, political, and cultural systems of any nation-state cannot be understood in isolation, but only in the context of their manifold links to the world beyond. In that light, to the extent that the discourse of cultural imperialism was cast in terms of the influence of one nation-state upon others, it was appropriate to that older world of nation-states, but not adequate to make sense of the complex flows and counterflows of globalization. That said, it is important to see the notion of globalization not as a panacea but a problematic, a way of posing

and conceptualizing questions about global cultural influence, not a philoso-
pher's stone with all the answers.

One such question is, quite apart from its alleged decline as an economic and political force, how far and how long the nation-state can, or even
should, persist as a cultural force, particularly in its traditional role as
guardian of a "national culture." In the first place, labor as well as capital is
deterritorialized in the global era, albeit in much more restricted ways. Thus,
impelled by the global economic integration of recent decades, there has
been a massive increase in the movement of people across borders, from professionals and managers to laborers and domestic servants, resulting in much
more culturally and linguistically pluralistic populations in each nation-
state. Consequently, nation-states are much less culturally homogeneous
than they once were, or at least, liked to represent themselves to be.
Furthermore, these new populations of diverse origins are able to retain
much stronger ties to the culture and language of their original homeland
than was possible in the past, particularly where they are able to access satellite television and other media services from their home nations (Sinclair and
Cunningham, 2000). In this respect, global communications media are fostering heterogeneity rather than homogeneity.

So, in other words, many residents of contemporary nation-states are no
longer obliged to assimilate themselves to a national culture, but are able to
maintain the cultural identifications they have brought from outside that
nation, even if their culture of origin is likely to undergo considerable adaptation and assume hybrid forms in the process. This situation has enormous
implications for the very concept of culture itself, which, metaphorically and
historically, has been rooted in terms of the organic way of life of a given
people who were defined by their fixed place in a certain territory. For traditional anthropology, this place was the village: for modern sociology, it
was the nation-state. Yet now, "culture" seems to be more a process than a
given "way of life," more about people on the move than in their place, more
characterized by "routes" than roots (Clifford, 1992). It is a form of adaptation to displacement and changing circumstances, and always necessarily
"hybrid" rather than "pure" (Nederveen Pieterse, 1995). Indeed, even
before the global era, the notion of cultural purity had been discredited as a
misguided and often dangerous social ideal, masking the realities of population movement and contact in actual cultural development, such as through
trade, conquest, and miscegenation.

Along with the emergence of cultural, ethnic, and linguistic diversity
within the contemporary nation-state, there has been a crisis for the very
idea of national culture. The national cultures that progressive critical theorists such as Herb Schiller once sought to defend against being swamped by
cultural imperialism now stand exposed as the ideological constructions
through which the dominant forces in each nation-state legitimize and per-

petuate their domination, in terms of gender, ethnicity, and class (Tomlinson, 1991). That is, national culture now is revealed as that which serves the dominant groups, not the nation as a whole. Thus, along with the critiques of global social movements such as those based on gender and sexual preference, migration has brought to the fore social differences that once were concealed under the flagfolds of national culture.

Nation-states can thus be seen to be losing their cultural authority over their own populations at the same time as their economic and political sovereignty is being compromised by pressures from the supranational level. Cultural imperialism discourse saw such loss as due to imported cultural influence from the United States and sought to defend the integrity of national cultures against it: in the era of globalization, the question is, rather, what is there about national culture that is worth defending? This is not to imply that the global forces of today should simply be allowed to fill the vacuum left by the self-serving and unrepresentative national cultures of the past. On the contrary, the cultural challenge for the nation-state is to hold its ground against global influences while it builds new institutions that foster cultural diversity and citizenship.

One other key question that arises once the cultural pluralism and porous borders of the contemporary nation-state are taken into account concerns the kind of consciousness that develops as a result, particularly where cultural identity is concerned. Cultural imperialism discourse was inclined to regard cultural identity as one-dimensional, arguing in effect that local identity would be driven out by United States cultural influence— there was no consideration of the possibility that people could retain their local identity yet see themselves as cosmopolitans at the same time. Like the modernization theory that cultural imperialism discourse ostensibly had risen to oppose, such a conception of cultural identity shared the assumption that the traditional could not coexist with the modern, and the media's function was to drive out the former and install the latter.

Against this can be put the postmodern view that the individual subject is composed, not of one single and relatively constant identity, but rather, of multiple identities that become mobilized in response to different cultural cues. This perspective is consistent with understanding cultural identity in the kind of world described above, where people are on the move, where there are cultural affiliations at various levels, and in which the cultural ties of national belonging are becoming ever less credible and binding. The several criss-crossing levels of structural organization fostered by globalization could thus be seen to correspond to cultural identifications: local, municipal, micro-regional, national, macro-regional, international, and global (Nederveen Pieterse, 1995, p. 50). It is not difficult to see how a person might, without too much contradiction, and setting aside other key dimensions of identity such as ethnicity and gender, think of him or herself variously in different contexts as, for example, a resident of Brixton, a Londoner, English, British, European, Western, and a world traveller.

Furthermore, by thinking of the production, circulation, and consumption of media and cultural products as occurring at the interlocking series of levels just described, with cultural identities corresponding to each level, we are able to arrive at a plausible version of the concept of global culture favored by some early globalization theorists (Featherstone, 1990). Rather than a universal force for homogenization, global culture can be seen as a new level at which certain kinds of cultural forms circulate around the planet. For example, Boyd-Barrett refers to the "global popular" (1997, p. 15), meaning a globally marketed cultural product of a certain kind, such as a blockbuster movie from Hollywood like *The Matrix*, or the global release of the latest CD from Madonna.

These products receive maximum publicity and marketing support on a global scale and are distributed through complex hierarchies of channels, ensuring the products reach local cinemas and stores in much the same way that Coca-Cola is brought to some of the remotest villages of the world. Yet it is crucial to appreciate that although this material might assert its own level of cultural influence, there is no reason to believe that it thereby drives out other identities, especially those based on ethnicity and religion. Culture, and cultural identity in particular, is not a fixed, zero-sum quantum that must be either local *or* global. As Marjorie Ferguson, the late Canadian globalization theorist, once laconically remarked, global commercial popular culture— "jeans, theme parks, fast food, CNN"—is a "surface" phenomenon that does not reduce the "deep" realities of cultural difference, but just adds "another layer of complexity" to understanding the process of identity formation (1993, p. 4).

CULTURAL GLOBALIZATION AS 'AMERICANIZATION'

Even some of the most sophisticated theorists of cultural globalization still cling to the cultural imperialism theorists' item of faith, that international cultural influence is ultimately a process of "Americanization." Yet if we ask what that really means, the answer turns out to be more of a hindrance than a help in pinning down the workings of the process. If we take it literally, this belief is that American culture, as a national culture, is able to penetrate and dominate the national cultures of the rest of the world, because of U.S. pre-eminence in the world's media industries.

However, as was argued above, national cultures now stand revealed as pluralistic rather than unified, and furthermore, subject to capture by the dominant interests within each nation-state. Thus, the United States are not actually united, and what the United States exports as its culture is in fact a hegemonic version of American culture. Even where it incorporates the subversive and oppositional cultural forms of the subaltern, such as with the whole phenomenon of rap music, it does so on its own terms, both in the process of commodification itself, and "within the larger, overarching framework of what is essentially an American conception of the world" (Hall, 1997, p. 28). There is a selectiveness at work in what can and cannot become part of the mythic American culture that is promoted for foreign consumption, at the expense of its actual diversity: "McDonald's *is* American culture in a way that no New York clam house, pizza parlour, Jewish deli or chop suey restaurant can ever be" (Tomlinson, 1991, p. 75).

What constitutes this hegemonic version of America? The British sociologist of globalization, Leslie Sklair, asserts that "Americanization itself is a contingent form of a process that is necessary to global capitalism, the culture-ideology of consumerism" (cited in Tomlinson, 1997, p. 179). Leaving aside the inherent difficulties of the concept of consumerism and the circular functionalist explanation implied in this view, the point here is that Americanization is not about the imposition of a certain national culture on the rest of the world, but the propagation of fundamental capitalist processes such as commodification and the structures and practices in which they are embodied. There is no disagreement between Sklair's view and cultural imperialism discourse. In fact, in raising the case of sport and the media, Herb Schiller even acknowledged that commodification, conceived as "the corporate takeover of (popular) culture" was "not a patented American practice," but certainly was "carried to its fullest development in the United States" (1991, p. 23). In this sense, it has to be recognized that Americans are subjected to Americanization, too: that America is just the place where Americanization usually happens first.

Others have argued that, more than capitalism as such, Americanization has become a cipher for modernity itself, or at least the dominant version of it. At a trivial level, as British critic Christopher Bigsby once observed, "complaints about Americanisation have often amounted to little more than laments over a changing world" (cited in Webster, 1988, p. 179). More tellingly, however, Americanization refers to Schiller's "total cultural package," the American inflection of modernity constituted by the capitalist mode of production and consumption; certain ways of organizing space, including urbanism; the media's pride of place in social communication; and fundamental principles of social organization such as rationalization and individualism (Tomlinson, 1991, p. 27). In other words, Americanization denotes not just the commercial media culture of television and advertising, but the whole culture of freeways and franchises, suburbs and shopping malls which characterizes the contemporary world, and that includes not just the wealthy West, but also the developing nations, especially those of Eastern Europe, Southeast Asia, and Latin America.

To take one element of this capitalist modernity package, which is not a media example, yet deeply emblematic and analytically revealing, there is the case of "McDonaldization," as formulated by Ritzer (1993, 1998). This is not just another voguish critical metaphor for cultural imperialism, such as "Coca-Colonization" was in the past, but an attempt to grasp the logic at the heart of capitalist modernity. The classic 19th-century German sociologist Max Weber identified "rationalization" as the guiding principle of capitalist modernity, tracing it to its roots in capitalist industrialism and the state in Europe. Essentially, he was referring to the hierarchical social control and discipline, and the standardization and quantifiability of procedures and outcomes, with which organizations, whether public or private, structure themselves to achieve their goals. This organizational model is similar to what has been called "Fordism" in manufacturing, but Ritzer finds a more contemporary embodiment in service industries such as fast food and consumer credit. The point is that although McDonald's (and Hungry Jack's, KFC, Subway, etc.) have built their global presence upon this model, it is not intrinsically American.

This is not Ritzer's own view: against the globalization theorists, he argues that McDonald's and their ilk have brought "the American style of eating on the run" to the rest of the world (1998, p. 84). However, because many parts of the world actually have had traditional fast food cultures, such as the hawker stalls of Southeast Asia, it would be more accurate to say that McDonald's rationalized and commodified fast food consumption. Furthermore, they have disciplined consumers by redefining a restaurant as a place where you serve yourself, eat with your fingers, and clear your own table afterwards. Apart from the contentious fact that McDonald's, like several other global companies, have found that they have to adapt their product offerings in response to resistance from local cultures (such as no beef in India), there is the obverse phenomenon, that the local eating cultures adopt the rationalized model of consumption, but in an indigenized form. In Spain, for example, the Boccata and Pans franchised chains offer a range of traditional sandwiches and drinks in premises that are laid out and organized on the "American" model, but wholly assimilated as part of the urban culture of modern Spain.

The many such instances of local adaptation and indigenization suggest that to resolve the debate on this issue of Americanization, it might be useful to resurrect the old distinction between form and content. That is, although the globalizing culture of mass media, freeway, suburb, supermarket, and fast food restaurant might have its origins, or at least have reached its highest development in the United States, that global culture consists of a series of forms of commodification that do not so much carry an intrinsic American content as provide an abstract mode that is made concrete and meaningful only by being fused with local content. To return to media examples, it would be an absurd reductionism to insist that Latin American *telenovelas* are "really" just American soap operas in Spanish, or Hindi movies are "really" just MGM musicals in saris.

How do the peoples of the world come to accept or reject Americanization? Cultural imperialism discourse would have had us believe that it was the insidious, irresistible influence of the Trojan horse of U.S. advertising, news, television programs, and films that softened them all up, made them aspire to want to be American. Yet analysis of the reception of U.S. culture in specific national and regional settings not only refutes this hoary premise, but illustrates the vastly different range of responses there have been. In Britain, there has been a long tradition of cultural criticism, both from the left and from the right, against the inroads made by American popular culture. In some ways, this was a carryover from the early 20th-century critique of "mass culture" (Webster, 1988). Yet the embrace of Americanization can be seen to have a progressive and subversive side. Dick Hebdige (1988) has argued persuasively that not only did American popular culture present British youth with a diverse range of new cultural identities to appropriate, but provided the working class with an escape from a restrictive bourgeois national culture.

Again, Annabelle Sreberny (2000) suggests that in the Middle East, exposure to Western media might provide more democratic models of how life can be lived, especially for women. Although democracy is not intrinsic to capitalist modernity, what Sreberny sees as a progressive force is perceived as a serious threat to those seeking to defend or restore the traditions of their societies. At the most extreme, the Iranian revolution of 1979, the rise of the Taliban in Afghanistan, and the advent of al-Qaeda have all been, to a significant extent, responses to Americanization.

BROADCASTING AND BEYOND IN LATIN AMERICA

We have seen how cultural imperialism first emerged as an issue in Latin America. In the 1960s and 1970s, when U.S. television networks were investing in Latin American countries and selling them large amounts of programming, critics such as Herb Schiller denounced this as the height of cultural imperialism, assuming that such trends were going to be permanent structural features of Latin American television. It turned out that they were more the inevitable compromises of a transitional start-up stage, subsequently followed by local development of the industry. Indeed, in this respect, Latin America was showing to other developing television markets the image of their own future.

Nevertheless, the active role of U.S. influence in the development of Latin American broadcasting cannot be denied. As they had in the days of radio, U.S. officials and companies encouraged Latin American governments and media entrepreneurs to adhere to the U.S. commercial model of broadcasting. For their part, the entrepreneurs needed no encouragement, seeing this as their own interest, and were also active in lobbying their governments. Perhaps the real conclusion to be drawn is that U.S. influence was significant at this stage not because of the incidence of foreign ownership, nor the high levels of program imports, neither of which was to last, but because of the institutionalization of the commercial model itself throughout the region (McAnany, 1984, pp. 194-195).

Thus, unlike Europe and most of the rest of the world outside the United States, Latin American broadcasting developed, right from radio days, on a commercial model, and largely has operated in a regulatory environment in which governments traditionally have provided freedom and protection to the established media entrepreneurs. This mode of corporatization has fostered the growth of quasi-monopolies or duopolies in the major national markets, notwithstanding the wave of privatization, liberalization and re-regulation in the 1990s.

In each of the major national markets, there is one historically dominant corporation: in Brazil it is Organizações Globo and in Mexico, Grupo Televisa. They have a lot in common. Both commenced in their respective markets at an early, strategic stage and formed a mutually supportive relationship with the government of the day. Both have perpetuated themselves through a dynastic and patriarchal system of family control. Both have grown to become vertically integrated conglomerates; that is, they have been allowed to integrate production and distribution, thus enjoying the cost advantages of producing most of what they broadcast. This also means exported programs have already paid for themselves in the home market. Both are also horizontally integrated, owning companies across related media fields. This gives them synergies, such as promoting their recording artists on their television and radio stations and in their magazines. Each of them has known how to take advantage of its supremacy in the world's largest Portuguese-speaking and Spanish-speaking country respectively, to use that as a base for internationalization.

Globo has 70% of the broadcast television market in Brazil, equal to that of its competitors combined, and an only somewhat less decisive lead over its main competitor in cable and satellite subscription services. Globo's traditional dominance has been less affected by liberalization than by Brazil's currency crisis, reflecting the ultimate dependency of these regional giants on the fortunes of the national economies in which their strength is based (Cajueiro, 2002). Conversely, Televisa has weathered currency crises, but as a result of the state's embrace of liberalization and privatization, it now has to deal with a serious competitor in the form of TV Azteca, which has captured about a third of the audience (Tegel, 2003).

Argentina and Venezuela form the next tier in the region's hierarchy, both having much smaller national markets, but very dynamic ones. The historical absence of networks and the relative recency of deregulation in Argentina has given a special prominence to cable, and much more recently, satellite-to-cable and DTH (Direct-to-Home) modes of distribution. Argentina has nearly half the cabled homes in the entire region. Combined with a wave of pro-market re-regulation in the first half of the 1990s, the multiplicity of platforms has produced a volatile and much more competitive environment than in the bigger markets. Furthermore, the high incidence of cable links Argentinian television into the convergence of media and telecommunications technologies and their industries on a global scale, and this makes it attractive to international investment, mainly from Spain and the United States (Galperín, 2002).

Venezuela has by far the smallest market of the region's leading television nations. In spite of a series of new channels licensed in a wave of privatization during the 1990s, television broadcasting in this market today remains dominated by two strong and internationally active networks—an effective duopoly (Mayobre, 2002). The pre-eminent network is Venevisión, part of a conglomerate built on a similar model to Globo and Televisa, but facing a more substantial competitor, RCTV (Radio Caracas Televisión).

Even if a more competitive environment has emerged out of the wave of deregulation and privatization of the 1990s, the established market leaders have not suffered much erosion of their dominance as a result. What has changed is the degree of internationalization experienced by media in the region. This is seen in the interpenetration of local, regional, and global capital evident in the digital DTH ventures initiated in the 1990s, in which News Corporation and Liberty Media aligned themselves with Globo and Televisa, and DIRECTV partnered with these companies' domestic rivals. There is also the growth in the number of U.S.-based cable channels providing special Spanish and Portuguese-language services, such as HBO Olé, MTV Latino, CNN en Español, and Fox Latin America. However, neither of these developments could be characterized as cultural imperialism, because they both involve the U.S.-based corporations having to come to terms with the cultural and linguistic differences of the region through collaboration and customization of programming—in other words, cultural globalization. Furthermore, the market for these services is restricted to the elites of the region, so although the Latin companies are dependent on their global partners in DTH and must compete with programming from the United States (and Europe) on cable, they remain secure in their hold over mass audiences in the still lucrative free-to-air arena.

The metaphor of empire is showing signs of returning to intellectual fashion, but this time in an utterly abstracted, postmodern form (Hardt and Negri, 2000). Meanwhile, in the real world, the United States, as a nation-state, is pursuing its global objectives with pre-emptive force, much more significantly than by means of using commercial entertainment as a Trojan horse. In fact, these days, in their attempts to break down trade barriers and subdue piracy in foreign markets, the U.S. cultural industries are using U.S. economic strength and political clout as levers to achieve media market penetration and power, rather than the other way around, as was posited in the discourse of cultural imperialism. Although there can be no doubt as to their massive presence on a global scale, the influence of the U.S.–based producers and distributors of cultural products and services is much less self-evident, and much more complex, in the era of cultural globalization.

REFERENCES

Appadurai, Arjun (1990) "Disjunction and difference in the Global Cultural Economy." *Public Culture* 2(2): 1-24.
Boyd-Barrett, Oliver (1977) "Media imperialism: Towards an international framework for the analysis of media systems." In J. Curran, M. Gurevitch, and J. Woollacott (Eds.), *Mass Communication and Society* (pp. 116-135). London: Edward Arnold.
Boyd-Barrett, Oliver (1997) "International communication and globalization: contradictions and directions." In A. Mohammadi (Ed.), *International Communication and Globalization: A Critical Introduction* (pp. 11-26). London: Sage, .
Cajueiro, Marcelo (2002) "Marinho clan slaps sale sign on debt-hit Globo." *Variety*, December 2-8: 22.
Clifford, James (1992) "Traveling cultures." In L. Grossberg, C. Nelson, and P. Treichler (Eds.), *Cultural Studies* (pp. 96-116). London and New York: Routledge.
Collins, Richard (1990) *Television: Policy and Culture*. London: Unwin Hyman.
Curran, James (1990) "The New Revisionism in mass communication research: A reappraisal." *European Journal of Communication* 5(2-3): 135-164.
Dagnino, Evelina (1973) "Cultural and ideological dependence: Building a theoretical framework." In F. Bonilla and R. Girling (Eds.), *Structures of Dependency* (pp. 129-148). Stanford, CA: Stanford University Press.
Dorfman, Ariel and Mattelart, Armand (1975) *How to Read Donald Duck: Imperialist Ideology in the Disney Comic*. New York: International General.
Featherstone, Mike (Ed.) (1990) *Global Culture*. London: Sage.
Ferguson, Marjorie (1992) "The mythology about globalization." *European Journal of Communication* 7(1): 69-93.

Ferguson, Marjorie (1993) "Globalisation of cultural industries: Myths and realities." In M. Breen (Ed.), *Cultural Industries: National Policies and Global Markets*. Melbourne: Centre for International Research on Communication and Information Technologies.

Frew, Wendy (2003) "Murdoch stared down over options." *The Age* (Melbourne), 16 October: 1.

Galperín, Hernán (2002) "Transforming television in Argentina." In E. Fox and S. Waisbord (Eds.), *Latin Politics, Global Media* (pp. 22-37). Austin: University of Texas Press, .

Hall, Stuart (1997) "The local and the global: Globalization and ethnicity." In A. King (Ed.), *Culture, Globalization and the World System* (pp. 19-39). Minneapolis: University of Minnesota Press, .

Hamelink, Cees (1983) *Cultural Autonomy in Global Communications*. New York: Longman.

Hardt, Michael and Negri, Antonio (2000) *Empire*. Cambridge, MA and London: Harvard University Press.

Hebdige, Dick (1988) *Hiding in the Light*. London and New York: Comedia.

Iwabuchi, Koichi (2002) *Recentering Globalization: Popular Culture and Japanese Transnationalism*. Durham, NC and London: Duke University Press.

Lash, Scott and Urry, John (1994) *Economies of Signs and Space*. London: Sage.

Liebes, Tamar and Katz, Elihu (1993) *The Export of Meaning: Cross-Cultural Readings of "Dallas."* Cambridge: Polity Press.

Martín-Barbero, Jesús (1993) *Communication, Culture and Hegemony: From the Media to Mediations*. London: Sage.

Mattelart, Armand (1980) "Cultural imperialism, mass media and class struggle: An interview with Armand Mattelart." *The Insurgent Sociologist* IX(4): 69-79.

Mayobre, José (2002) "Venezuela and the media: The new paradigm." In E. Fox and S. Waisbord (Eds.), *Latin Politics, Global Media* (pp. 176-186). Austin: University of Texas Press.

McAnany, Emile (1984) "The logic of the cultural industries in Latin America: The television industry in Brazil." In V. Mosco and J. Wasko (Eds.), *The Critical Communications Review Volume II: Changing Patterns of Communications Control*, (pp. 185-208). Norwood, NJ: Ablex.

Nederveen Piertese, Jan (1995) "Globalization as hybridization." In M. Featherstone, S. Lash, and R. Robertson (Eds.), *Global Modernities* (pp. 45-68.). London: Sage

Ritzer, George (1993) *The McDonaldization of Society*. Thousand Oaks, CA: Pine Forge Press.

Ritzer, George (1999), *The McDonaldization Thesis*. London: Sage.

Robertson, Roland (1995) "Glocalization: Time-space and homogeneity-heterogeneity." In M. Featherstone, S. Lash, and R. Robertson (Eds.), *Global Modernities* (pp. 25-44). London: Sage.

Schiller, Herbert (1976) *Communication and Cultural Domination*. White Plains, NY: International Arts and Sciences Press.

Schiller, Herbert (1991) "Not yet the post-imperialist Era," *Critical Studies in Mass Communication* 8(1): 13-28.

Sinclair John (1999) *Latin American Television: A Global View*. Oxford and New York: Oxford University Press.

Sinclair, John, Elizabeth Jacka and Stuart Cunningham (Eds.) (1996) *New Patterns in Global Television: Peripheral Vision.* Oxford and New York: Oxford University Press.

Sinclair, John, and Cunningham, Stuart (2000) "Go with the flow: Diasporas and the media." *Television and New Media* 1(1): 11-31.

Sreberny, Annabelle (2000) "Television in the Middle East." In J. Curran and M-J. Park (Eds.), *De-Westernizing Media Studies* (pp. 63-78). London and New York: Routledge.

Tegel, Simeon (2003) "Battling billionaire powers Azteca." *Variety*, 26 May-1 June: 22.

Tomlinson, John (1991) *Cultural Imperialism: A Critical Introduction.* Baltimore, MD: Johns Hopkins University Press.

Tomlinson, John (1997) "Cultural globalization and cultural imperialism." In A. Mohammadi (Ed.), *International Communication and Globalization: A Critical Introduction* (pp. 170-190). London: Sage, London.

Tomlinson, John (1999), *Globalization and Culture.* Cambridge: Polity Press.

Tunstall, Jeremy (1997) *The Media Are American.* London: Constable.

Webster, Duncan (1988) *Looka Yonder! The Imaginary America of Populist Culture.* London: Comedia.

CHAPTER EIGHT

GLOBALIZATION OF CULTURAL POLICYMAKING AND THE HAZARDS OF LEGAL SEDUCTION

Jane Kelsey

The Adam Smith Institute's web page for Culture Media and Sport offers the following (highly contestable) insights into cultural policy prescriptions for a neoliberal world:

> **Managing the Media:** Government and regulatory control is out of date in today's multi-channel and Internet world. We don't have it in book publishing, so why do we for newspapers, TV and radio? Nor do we have a government-run publishing house: so why do we need the BBC?
>
> **Art of the State:** The arts have been nationalized. Not one of the UK's national opera, ballet or theatre companies turns a profit: they survive on taxpayer subsidies. But the arts do not have to depend on taxpayer support: it's better to boost sponsorship of the arts by businesses, individuals and charities.
>
> **Liberating Libraries:** Throughout the world, the free or near-free libraries provided by city or district governments are shabby and under-resourced. It need not be so. Some cities have started to contract out their library services—boosting stock, innovation, and services, and attracting larger numbers of users.

Who Owns the Past: Archaeology, our heritage, our museums—all are falling under the protection of a growing army of state-licensed "professionals." But that gives individuals no incentive or freedom to explore, conserve, or collect. Time to return the past to the people?[1]

Such propositions would have seemed absurd 30 years ago. Today they form part of a neoliberal orthodoxy whose foundational assumptions too often go unquestioned. Markets are premised on scarcity and excludability; cultural exchange is a shared enterprise that is embedded in communities whose understandings of life it shapes and provides a unique conduit for social communication and identity.[2] Culture is not a product that is capable of substitution by commercial exchange—showing *Harry Potter and the Sorcerer's Stone* cannot convey to young Mapuche in Chile or Maori in Aotearoa (New Zealand), the place of the shaman or the tohunga in their cultural world. Nor is culture a purely symbolic or aesthetic interaction. It has multiple dimensions. Canadian literary scholar Northrop Frye identified three aspects to (national) culture:

> Culture as popular lifestyle—the elementary level encompassing the way a society lives, eats, clothes itself and carries on its daily social rituals;
>
> Culture as traditional ideology—the middle level of a shared sense of historical experience, transmitted through a common language;
>
> Culture as creative powers—the upper level of intellectual output of a society through its arts, music, painting, stories, architecture, scholarship, etc. (Frye 1989; Kertzer 2004/5)

Leaving aside Frye's hierarchy, the distinction between these elements is useful for analytical purposes—this chapter focuses on the third—but only if they are then reintegrated and their shared material foundations are understood. It is equally important to see how the cultural landscape is shaped and reshaped as communities respond to internal and external influences, changes in the social order and shifts in economic paradigms (Negus and Roman-Velaquez 2000), and how the symbolic content, form and function of creative outputs are affected by the way that cultural production is financed, organized and regulated (Golding and Murdock 2000).

Since the 1980s, the broader cultural landscape, and within that creative outputs, have been transformed by an increasingly internationalized marketplace and people's variable place in relation to that market. Three interrelated factors have driven that transition. First, at the national level, Keynesian welfarism and state socialism have given way to neoliberal policies of commercialization, privatization, deregulation, liberalization, weak competition rules, and a limited state. Second, the ownership, financing, production, distribution, and exchange of cultural products have become consolidated, nationally and internationally, in a small number of mega-corporations. Third, new technologies have fundamentally changed the nature, form, and spaces of cultural production and interaction in ways that blur the distinction between carrier and content and create new opportunities for individuals and countries, while also deepening divides.

These transformations of policy, commerce, and technology have converged within a dominant paradigm of neoliberal globalization that appears invincible, yet is fraught with contradictions and vulnerability (Jessop, 2002). That paradigm has been legitimized, embedded, and extended by a new legal regime of binding international agreements that masquerade as "trade" under the mantle of the World Trade Organization (WTO). At the same time, agitation against these incursions on national "policy space" has intensified within and outside the WTO (Wallach and Woodall, 2004). This dissent has stymied attempts to expand its rules and strengthen the protections it provides for transnational firms. The United States and the European Commission as allies-cum-competitors, have turned to WTO-compatible regional and bilateral agreements to complement and leverage up the WTO process and create precedents that support their separate offensive and defensive interests in the multilateral arena.

Culture is one major site of dissension. The General Agreement on Trade in Services (GATS) and related regional and bilateral agreements have undermined national policies and regulatory techniques that were traditionally used to sustain local culture, as examples from New Zealand, Canada, Mexico, Australia, and South Korea show. In contrast to the historic accommodations between trade and culture that were reached in the General Agreement on Tariffs and Trade (GATT) in 1947, it has become politically and technically impossible to quarantine cultural policies from the new "trade" rules.

In response to this dilemma a number of mainly non-Anglophone governments sponsored a counter-Convention on Cultural Diversity, in collaboration with international organizations of creative artists and cultural professionals. The nongovernmental organizations (NGOs) envisaged an agreement that could act as an antidote to the GATS and promote a progressive form of globalization that enhanced cultural diversity. The major powers that supported the Convention were prepared to settle for a more limited tool that allowed them to promote their defensive cultural interests through UNESCO while pursuing their overriding offensive economic interests at the WTO. The document that was forwarded to the UNESCO General Conference in October 2005 was little more than a hortatory declaration. Its assertion of parity between the Convention and international treaties (such as the GATS) was a legal fiction that belied the institutional hierarchy of enforceable WTO agreements over an aspirational and unenforceable instrument from UNESCO.

Drawing on insights from the political economy of law, this chapter challenges the seductive belief that contradictions between culture and globalized capitalism can be resolved through technical exclusions and exceptions or a competition of legal texts. These texts are an artifice. When people treat them as real they lose sight of the underlying relations between capital and states, superpowers and minnows, and classes of cultural workers in the international division of labor. The economic and political practices that shape the texts remain unchallenged. As Frederick Engels astutely observed, this fetishises material reality: "[T]he juristic form is, in consequence, made everything and the economic content nothing" (quoted in Hunt, 1993, p. 19). Nor is the state a neutral player in international policymaking and regulation. The interests of cultural professionals and creative artists as workers and as guardians seeking to defend genuine cultural diversity from global market forces require a more sophisticated strategy where resistance to "trade" agreement is just one tactic in a broader counterhegemonic struggle against neoliberal globalization.

THE GLOBALIZATION OF CULTURAL POLICYMAKING

Western law can recognize and foster culture in all Frye's senses; equally, and often simultaneously, it can embody rules that undermine or negate cultural sustainability and diversity. Neither approach emerges or operates in a vacuum. The pillars of private property rights and contractual relations sustain capitalist economic relations, whereas the elasticity of legal instruments, judicial decisions and institutional arrangements respond to shifting political and economic conditions (Hunt, 1993).

During the twentieth century Western law operated through a complex array of social orders that were embedded in divergent economic paradigms: interventionist welfare states, state socialism, exploited colonies, newly independent one-party states, suppressed indigenous nations. Each was governed by unique policy and legal settings that were typically centralized in a nation-state and promoted an assumed, but commonly contested, national identity.

Post–World War II, the governments of wealthier industrialized democracies sought to reconcile the needs of capital with the maintenance of social stability and political legitimacy (Offe 1984). Cultural policies traversed a range of commercial, aesthetic, advocacy, propaganda and "nation building" dimensions. Laws mandated state ownership of radio and television, libraries, galleries, museums, and archives as public services to deliver public goods, while they limited private, foreign and cross-media ownership. Taxpayer subsidies represented a collective investment in orchestras, ballet, and writing. Media regulations required local content and "balanced" reporting (except in national emergencies) and restricted the intrusion of advertising and commercialism. Public telecommunications were regulated and subsidized to ensure access and affordability. Intellectual property law sought to blend the moral rights of authors, common access to creative works, and guarantees of commercial returns. Material support for culture workers, such as musicians, poets, artists, dancers, weavers, film makers, writers, and actors, was provided through direct employment in public services and protected local industries or via state subsidies, local community grants, and government procurement.

It is tempting, in retrospect and with nostalgia, to romanticize such interventions. This regulatory regime was far from benign. State intervention often stultified innovation and creativity and obstructed international cultural exchanges. Governments used law as a tool to promote hegemony, backed by coercive techniques such as censorship, sedition, and criminal libel, especially in times of crisis (Hall et al., 1978).

Western law's ideological and coercive roles were more overt in colonial regimes. Almost uniformly, culture was imported and imposed. Metropolitan identities and Western law were celebrated by the occupying powers as intrinsically superior manifestations of civilization by colonial administrators, settlers, and indigenous elites (Fitzpatrick, 1992). Media were vehicles for colonial propaganda. Indigenous cultures and identities were suppressed through practices that were often genocidal. In settler colonies, indigenous peoples became silenced minorities or exotic curiosities. Once former colonies gained their political independence, traditional cultures re-emerged in more hybridized forms (Sreberny, 2000). States often displayed a nationalist fervor that was itself culturally intolerant; in response, culture provided a vital organizing tool for political resistance against authoritarian regimes (Comfort 2002; Santiago 2003). Similar closures prevailed under state socialism. Paradoxically, the legacy of investment in skills and infrastructure created the potential for a vibrant cultural revival in these societies, if the flow of resources and political support could be sustained following democratization.

This was the heyday of the nation state. International exchanges were generally framed by historic and linguistic relationships. Discriminatory immigration laws circumscribed movement of creative artists. Trade (understood as the movement of tangible goods across borders) primarily involved books, movies, records, artefacts, and art works. Only films were considered to be so threatened by international competition that they required a special carve-out in Article IV of the General Agreement on Tariffs and Trade 1947.

The economic crises of the 1970s heralded a transition from Keynesian welfarism and state socialism to neoliberal globalization that privileged the interests of mobile finance capital and transnational corporations. This radically transformed economic relations, the social order, and the cultural landscape, and hence the direction and status of cultural policies. As the Adam Smith Institute shows, the new orthodoxy is intolerant of such notions as cultural sovereignty, national identity, and public service. Government agencies that fostered those values have been progressively corporatized, privatized or forced to compete on commercial terms. Regulatory regimes that privileged or protected local culture and practitioners gave way to light-handed regulations that could foster the newly liberated markets and international competition. Subsidies and government supports, along with procurement preferences, have suffered cuts or been made contestable among a wider group of private bidders (Murdock and Golding, 2002).

Governments became the authors of their own disempowerment through a new legal and policy regime, either as debt conditionalities or through voluntary liberalization (Kelsey, 1997). Privatization, outsourcing, and cuts to state support have made the livelihoods of many creative artists more precarious. Professionals, such as journalists, teachers, librarians, archivists, technicians, actors, musicians, and visual artists face added pressures from labor market deregulation and exposure to transnational corporate strategies and practices.

The liberalization of controls on foreign direct investment and movements of capital, combined with weak competition policy, has fostered vertical and horizontal integration through mergers and acquisitions. Mega-corporate holdings span an ever-widening range of activities: newspaper production, magazine and book publishing, music, film, and television production, pay television, information technology, software development, satellite transmission, e-commerce, retail, advertising, public relations, sports promotion, events management, star management, leisure facilities, museum franchising, intellectual property, brand marketing, financing, and much more. The increased level of intra-firm transactions facilitates tax evasion and impedes effective ownership and disclosure requirements. Meanwhile, corporations press governments to lower their regulatory thresholds, tax laws, and foreign investment rules to attract their commercial presence and prestigious productions.

Momentous technological changes in computers and telecommunications coincided with and enhanced the rise of neoliberalism. This has opened new opportunities for creators and professionals by fostering economies of scope and scale, lower-cost technologies, real-time co-production, and outsourcing of specialist services. Niche markets for technological innovations and cultural products targeted the young and affluent. However, these still exist within a terrain that has been laid by and for the mega-transnationals and are often absorbed by them when they become lucrative or too competitive.

A number of "developing" countries have the scale and investment capacity to dominate their own markets, such as India, Brazil, China and some Arabic states, and to create reverse flows of cultural products into the United States and Europe (Sreberny, 2000)—although they often mirror their corporate practices. But this is not a level playing field. Mobile capital allows mega-corporations to diversify their product range by exploiting what Harvey calls the "collective symbolic capital" of locations whose name, places, or events make them exotic and potentially profitable (Harvey, 2002). Hence, Hotel Rwanda can be hailed as evidence that liberalizing tourism and audiovisual sectors can benefit African countries, while control of the investment, profit and images remains with the mega-corporations. The historical international division of labor is still reflected in the Eurocentric bias of corporate ownership, customer base, language, cultural norms, and race and gender stereotypes. Even new forms of resistance through participation in "cyberdemocracy" and alternative media are uneven, reflecting barriers to participation in cultural exchange and deepening the digital divide (Lister, 2003; Murdock and Golding, 2002).

The mega-corporations have moved to secure control of content, plus carriage, plus delivery, free from both regulatory hurdles and the risk of being excluded from new markets (Murdock and Golding, 2002).[3] As the line between content and technology blurs, traditional modes of content regulation are less effective. Cross-border transmission and extraterrestrial technologies pose new regulatory challenges, especially given the permanent state of flux surrounding the new technology. Some governments have shifted their attention to regulating the use of or access to certain technologies (Street, 2001), often as a new way to censure content (Sreberny, 2000). Others have broadened the geographical scope of regulation to a regional level, most notably the European Union's *Television Without Frontiers*.[4]

This radical paradigm shift has reconfigured the relationship between capitalism and culture in almost every country in the world. Neoliberal globalization presents the flip side of the *Great Transformation* from laissez faire to Keynesian welfarism that was incisively chronicled by Karl Polanyi (Polanyi, 1957). Yet it embodies the same contradictions: faced with systemic market failures, economic disparity and social distress, governments will come under pressure to impose new constraints on capital, rebuild social and cultural cohesion and rescue the state's legitimacy.

SUBORDINATION OF CULTURAL POLICY TO TRADE RULES

This is where international treaties become such a critical, and yet destabilising, element of the neoliberal project. Because binding international agreements can be drafted outside the national political arena, survive changes of government, and be enforced by an extraterritorial body, they offer the prospect of long-term security. As normative rule-based regimes they also purport to depoliticize their substantive effects. Legal theorist Valerie Kerruish observes how embedding ideological premises in legal texts based on seemingly neutral rules and norms creates "a capacity to replace fact with fiction, to close the door on further inquiry and so to be that which we cannot go beyond in our legal understanding" (Kerruish, 1993, p. 124). At the same time, these agreements intensify the potential for instability and resistance precisely because they aim to render governments impotent to address such economic, social, and political crises.

The creation of the WTO in 1995 heralded a new generation of international "trade" treaties that confer a uniquely privileged position on international capital and increasingly usurp the regulatory functions of national governments. This pre-eminent legal domain operates beyond nation states, but is constructed by them. It constrains their "sovereign" authority at the domestic policy and regulatory level. Trade sanctions for breaches of WTO obligations also require member governments to act coherently when making commitments in other international forums whose subject matter falls within the ever-expanding ambit of the "trade" agreements.

This pre-eminence is also a weakness. Southern governments have been increasingly critical of the creeping hegemony of the WTO over vast areas of policy and regulation and have impeded moves led by the United States and European Commission to expand the number and scope of its agreements. The resulting semi-paralysis has been reinforced by popular protests over the WTO's antidemocratic process, the negative impacts of its neoliberal agenda, and its intrinsically partisan relationship with capital. The major powers and associated corporations have responded by using their leverage to advance and secure the same agenda through regional and bilateral agreements. These agreements are required to be both WTO-compatible and WTO-plus,[5] and so create precedents that can be used to try to break the deadlock at the multilateral level.

The impacts of these agreements on culture are most obvious from the General Agreement on Trade in Services (GATS) and related regional and bilateral treaties, although the analysis can be adapted to investment and government procurement.[6] The historical relationship between international trade agreements and culture dates back to the General Agreement on Tariffs and Trade (GATT) in 1947 and objections from the American motion picture industry to measures taken by European and other governments to protect their film industries.[7] Ivan Bernier explains:

> In 1947, a compromise solution appeared to have been reached with the inclusion of Article IV in the *General Agreement on Tariffs and Trade*

(GATT) that recognized the specificity of cultural products, at least in the case of films, without removing them from the disciplines of the agreement. However, in the early 1960s, the dispute resumed when the United States asked the GATT to investigate the restrictions imposed on its television programs by a number of countries, including Canada. A special group was constituted to look at the matter but was unable to reach an agreement. (Bernier, 2005, p. 5)

During the Tokyo round of GATT negotiations in the 1970s the United States objected that the use of television and cinema subsidies were "non-tariff barriers" to trade, to no avail.

This uneasy accommodation between trade and culture was possible within the ideological and economic paradigm of postwar Keynesianism. It helped that trade was defined simply as the cross-border import and export of tangible goods, and that disputes and demands for exemptions focused almost solely on audio-visual products.[8] By contrast, the Uruguay round of GATT negotiations that ran from 1986 to 1994 came to symbolize the omnipotence of neoliberal globalization and reached far beyond "trade" as traditionally defined. The U.S. administration threatened not to negotiate on matters of critical importance to struggling Third World economies if they blocked a consensus to include the "new issues" of services and intellectual property rights in the round (Raghavan, 2002). U.S. corporations wanted binding rules to reduce the restraints they faced on foreign investment, the transfer of capital, and temporary immigration of executives and skilled workers; but their primary objective was to pre-empt the regulation of new and largely unregulated technologies through which finance, information, commerce, and content would be transmitted in the future (Feketekuty 1988).

The idea was to apply generic trade rules to all services, using the analogy of trade in goods. The neoclassical model of trade says each country should play to its strength (comparative advantage) and ensure that its scarce resources are applied to those activities that it can undertake most efficiently within a competitive internationalized marketplace (which might not include cultural outputs) and rely on other countries to meet its remaining needs (including for cultural services). The pursuit of national self-sufficiency is intrinsically inefficient and a denial of consumer choice (Feketekuty 1988). This theory is problematic when applied to "trade in goods." It is untenable when applied to international services transactions, where unique cultural content is not amenable to simple substitution and where "trade" is defined as including foreign direct investment (van Welsum, 2003). Yet "free trade in services" is invested with a quasi-scientism that excludes any alternative perceptions — even the possibility that culture workers and producers who are inefficient in a market sense might legitimately receive state support

or preferential treatment to create enriching experiences for people, communities, and the society that would not otherwise occur.

Under the "trade" rubric cultural exchanges that involve foreign participants and have a commercial element are treated as "exports" and
"imports." The most favored nation rule (Article II) requires governments
to give exports and exporters of (cultural) services from all WTO members
the same treatment. The national treatment rule (Article XVII) prevents
governments from giving preference to local (cultural) service suppliers over
foreign ones. Market access obligations (Article XVI) open cultural services
to foreign competition.

Paradoxically, the "exporter" and "importer" must have different
national origins to trigger the trade rules; yet the uniqueness of those nation-
alities is irrelevant. Because the rules are premised on "free trade," measures
that seek to maintain or enhance the uniqueness of local culture in its symbolic or economic sense become "trade barriers" that need to be removed.
Examples of measures that discriminate against foreign firms include providing government subsidies only to locally owned theater companies or
museums; requirements that movie theaters show a proportion of local films
through domestic exhibition quotas; restrictions on foreign direct investment and cross-ownership in broadcasting or print media; labor market tests
that require local journalists to be hired first; country-specific coproduction
agreements that treat film-makers from some countries better than those
from others; or domestic regulation of licences that impose more burdens on
foreign firms than trade experts think is necessary to ensure quality—even
where other considerations, such as sensitivity to local cultural practices,
suggest a different regulatory approach is preferable.

Services are defined in terms of how foreign providers—mainly transnational firms—conduct their operations. Mode 1 (cross-border) involves provision of a service into a country from outside the national border, such as
satellite or the Internet. Under Mode 2 (consumption abroad) the service is
delivered to consumers who travel overseas to the provider, such as foreign
visitors to an event like the Edinburgh Fringe Festival. Mode 3 (establishing
a commercial presence) covers foreign direct investment, where media
barons like Murdoch or Packer buy up (but rarely create) businesses in the
"importing" country or a franchised Guggenheim museum is opened outside the United States. Mode 4 (presence of natural persons) applies to
providers of services who work temporarily in a foreign country, such as a
self-employed Australian rock band on an Asian tour, an Indian film crew
and actors working offshore on a "Bollywood" production, or U.S. journalists reporting from overseas for CNN.

This legal framework is protected by a closed neoliberal epistemology.
Culture has no value in itself: *Time Warner* remarked in 1990, "The cultural issue is appearing with alarming frequency in the international market-

place and must be roundly rejected" (quoted in Sreberny, 2000, p. 102). Because the only vantage point is that of the "exporter," the domestic implications of "imports" are almost totally irrelevant. Unlike the GATT, there is no provision in the GATS even to erect temporary safeguards when an unexpected flood of foreign imports endangers the survival of domestic "suppliers." The only actors that are recognized are the service suppliers and the governments that regulate their activities. Even consumers are invisible, except in describing the "modes of supply" by which services can be delivered. The real-life existence of culture workers, indigenous nations, or local communities is literally beyond the conception of the agreements.

The implied objectivity of a "rules-based" services regime obscures its ideological content and the substantive inequities that result from applying the same rules to grossly unequal players. These rules intrinsically advantage those mega-transnational enterprises that have scale, technology, research, and development capacity; access to capital, marketing, and brand recognition; control over intellectual property; and the patronage of major powers. They disadvantage countries that lack the capacity to compete, however culturally rich they may be. Hence, the horizontal and vertical integration of mega-corporations like Bertelsmann, AoL Time Warner, or Disney represent the legitimate pursuit of their "home" country's comparative advantage (provided that the oligopolies do not collude in inefficient anticompetitive practices). Far from questioning the dominant position of such "exporters," agreements on "trade in services" set out to ensure that they are not "unfairly" discriminated against.

The ultimate goal is a seamless, integrated global market across all sectors and modes. A transnational advertising firm, such as Saatchi and Saatchi, would be able to standardize its operations and products across a range of countries. Foreign firms that engage in diverse activities within one country, for example as cross-media owners of television, radio, and newspaper production, could integrate all elements of their operation. Corporations that specialize in one activity across a range of services, such as IT specialists or marketing agencies, could be confident that the same rules would apply across all services.

During the Uruguay round, the GATS only went part way to achieving the original ideal. Significant compromises were struck: partly to appease Third World governments who were nervous about a wholesale takeover of their services by transnational companies; partly because the United States wanted to protect some of its own services (especially maritime) and was not prepared to provide "most favored nation" access to countries that offered little in return; and partly because the European Commission and Francophone countries belatedly and unsuccessfully insisted on their ability to exclude "cultural services" from the rules (see further below).

As a result, at the end of the Uruguay round every WTO member was automatically a signatory to the GATS. However, it would lodge a country-specific schedule that stated which service sectors were subject to the national treatment and market access rules (known as a "positive list") and any limitations that would apply to those commitments (a "negative list"). It could also make (supposedly limited-term) exceptions to the "most favored nation" rule that required members to apply their commitments to all WTO countries equally. Articles VI, XV, and XVIII mandated further negotiations on rules to develop "disciplines" on domestic regulation, subsidies that allegedly distort trade, and government procurement. Part IV affirmed that this rule making was an ongoing process, with the next negotiations to extend sectoral commitments to begin in 2000.

The architecture of these schedules is Byzantine (Kelsey 2003a). Each country's complex matrix records separate market access, national treatment, and "additional" commitments in each of the four modes of supply across eleven main categories and some 160 subsectors.[9] The WTO's classification list was based mainly on an early iteration of the United Nations Central Product Classifications (CPCs). Each subcategory describes activities as the supplier engages in them. In this way, what people experience as a unitary and integrated service, such as a daily newspaper, becomes disaggregated across a range of CPCs that includes writing, editing, printing, publishing, photography, translation, news agencies, advertising, finance, retail, distribution, and transport. Paradoxically, that fragmentation has created an unevenness of liberalization and artificial boundaries for corporations whose activities span numerous classifications—just what the agreement was intended to overcome.

Defenders of these agreements deny that they undermine governments' sovereignty because of the voluntary and country-specific nature of commitments (WTO undated). Yet the notion of informed government choice is often illusory. The GATS "positive list" approach, combined with a "negative list" of limitations and reservations and a separate schedule for MFN exceptions, is complex enough. But many bilateral agreements use a "negative list," whereby every service and aspect of a service is covered unless it is explicitly excluded, and is supplemented by horizontal commitments and limitations. The matrix is only comprehensible to the initiated few. There are grave risks that governments do not understand the implications of the commitments when they make them or that changing technology and policy settings give commitments unanticipated new meanings. The secrecy that surrounds the negotiations commonly precludes input from people whose activities may be adversely affected, precisely to prevent such "vested interests" from influencing their government's decisions (Drake and Nicolaidis, 1992). Withdrawing or amending a commitment is very difficult, in line with the presumption of ongoing liberalization, and is generally only allowed where the government offers compensatory liberalization in another service sector to foreign countries whose firms might lose "trade" as a result.

Geopolitical realities deny some governments any real choice over what sectors they commit. This is especially so when schedules are drawn up as part of the WTO accession process, which potentially allows existing WTO members to veto accession if its demands have not been satisfied. The proposition that a country like Iraq, which began to negotiate accession under conditions of military occupation, could engage in genuine negotiations with the imperial occupying powers seems preposterous. Often acceding governments face demands for services commitments that are simply designed to create or avoid a precedent. Vanuatu, a small island in the South Pacific, began the process of accession to the WTO in 1996 and was supposed to be the first Least Developed Country to join at the Doha Ministerial Conference in 2001. Its negotiators were told that Vanuatu could only join if they agreed to the United States' GATS demands, including full commitments on audiovisual services. They capitulated. Remarkably, days before the Doha Ministerial, the Vanuatu government decided the price was too high and suspended its accession (Grynberg, 2000). In mid-2004 the government decided to reactivate the process, if it could withdraw its promised commitments on foreign investment (Mode 3) in health, education, audio-visual, environmental, and retail and wholesale distribution. A year later the U.S. Trade Representative (USTR) had still not replied to their formal request (Kelsey, 2005).

A paper prepared by the WTO Secretariat in 1998 expressed concern that only nineteen Members had made market-opening commitments in the audiovisual sector. There were four developed countries (the United States, Japan, New Zealand, and Israel) and fifteen developing countries, six of which had done so as part of their accession (WTO, 1998). Most commitments were subject to various limitations. Exemptions to MFN treatment had been lodged by 33 WTO members,[10] mostly in relation to coproduction agreements.

The second round of GATS negotiations that were designed to extend these commitments began in 2000 and moved very slowly, reflecting a growing nervousness about its implications. Ironically, that fuelled the rapid growth of GATS-plus regional and bilateral agreements. The result is a web of agreements on "trade in services" that increasingly require a market-driven approach to regulation of cultural services.

WHEN PARADIGMS CONFLICT, "TRADE" RULES

Agreements on "trade in services" rarely force governments to open their markets to foreign firms. That has usually been achieved via structural adjustment programs or domestic neoliberal policies. As the following examples show, their main purposes are to lock open those markets so future governments are unable to backtrack and to constrain the regulation of new activities and technologies.

Sometimes governments make commitments that tie the hands of their successors. New Zealand politicians and trade officials mainly viewed the GATS negotiations as a way to build collateral for agriculture negotiations, but they also served an ideological function. By 1994 New Zealand had experienced a decade of radical deregulation, corporatization, and privatization (Kelsey, 1997). Private sector media was largely foreign controlled. The radio spectrum was privatized and auctioned. Public television and most public radio was fully commercialized and required to compete with private channels on neutral terms, backed by repeated threats of privatization (Murdock, 1998). The GATS offered a means of entrenching this new market-driven broadcasting regime.

The first draft of New Zealand's offer on audiovisual services was prepared for the Labour government in 1990 when the new broadcasting regime was still evolving (Kelsey, 2003b). The proposed commitments were tentative and retained the possibility of reintroducing policies that were no longer being used. The accompanying reservations contained modest limits on foreign ownership in radio and television, restrictions on the use of the radio spectrum by foreign governments, and controls on short wave and satellite broadcasting. Subsidies for production, distribution, exhibition, and broadcasting were restricted to New Zealand persons and companies. Rights to discriminate by imposing local television and radio quotas were protected, as were 100% tax write-offs for investment in production of New Zealand films.

A revised draft was prepared following the change of government in late 1990. That draft reflected the deregulatory status quo. Officials suggested that the Minister of Communications might wish to consider protecting New Zealand's future options in areas such as local content quotas. The Minister chose not to do so. Trade officials subsequently pointed out to the Cabinet that the proposed wording on foreign investment "prevents us from making the regime more restrictive in the future, for example by reintroducing the recently removed restrictions on investment in broadcasting, without negotiating adequate compensatory adjustments elsewhere" (quoted in Kelsey, 2003b, p. 39-40). Their instructions were confirmed.

New Zealand's final schedule made full commitments to market access in Modes 1 (cross border supply), 2 (consumption abroad), and 3 (commercial presence) for production, distribution, exhibition, and broadcasting of audiovisual works, and more limited commitments in Mode 4. A broadly similar approach was taken to national treatment, with minor exceptions for funding of Maori broadcasting and the film industry. Not surprisingly, the United States hailed New Zealand's offer as exemplary.

In 1999 a new Labour-led "Third Way" government was elected that had campaigned on a policy of introducing compulsory local content quotas for radio and free-to air-television. The Prime Minister, as Minister of Culture, was advised that this would breach New Zealand's audio-visual commitments under the GATS and similar obligations under the Closer Economic Relations (CER) free trade agreement with Australia signed in 1988. After lengthy delays, the government backed down and announced there would be voluntary targets for New Zealand programming for free-to-air television networks, modeled on a voluntary Code of Practice that had recently been adopted by commercial radio.

The government subsequently insisted that the voluntary approach was proving effective and there was no need for compulsion.[11] However, the voluntary quotas applied only to state television and one private channel owned by CanWest. If the latter suffered a serious competitive disadvantage, it could withdraw from the arrangement. The government's only real leverage was over state-owned TVNZ, but that was required by law to be commercially competitive.

If the voluntary approach failed, the government had two options: to abandon its "nation building" approach to broadcasting or to regulate. Government ministers promised they would introduce legislation if necessary (NZLP, 2002). But doing so would bring the government into direct conflict with the GATS and CER. Legally, the government could amend New Zealand's services commitments in both agreements to allow for a compulsory quota scheme, in return for compensatory adjustments in other services (although there were relatively few options), but it had no inclination to do so. New Zealand's cultural policy was now hostage to the government's trade objectives. New Zealand politicians and trade officials were determined to protect the country's reputation as an exemplary WTO citizen. Amending the GATS schedule would undermine its demands for extensive and binding commitments from other countries on agriculture. Amending CER would send a similar message—compounded by the embarrassment that a previous New Zealand government had taken legal action in Australia to require Australian local content quotas to include material from New Zealand (Masterman & Williamson, 1998). Moreover, the USTR's "Trade Summary on New Zealand" in 2005 repeated previous objections that voluntary quotas were backed by threats to legislate, making it clear that the United States would demand a high price if New Zealand did so (USTR, 2005b).[12]

A related New Zealand example shows how a domestic policy decision, in this case privatization, could change the effect of a commitment. In an attempt to restore a "nation building" role to public television, the Television New Zealand Amendment Act 2001 removed the requirement for the broadcaster to operate exclusively on the basis of commercial considerations and changed its legal form. It also introduced a new charter that required the company to "feature programming across all genres that informs, entertains and educates New Zealand audiences"; "provide shared experiences that contribute to a sense of citizenship and national identity"; "ensure in its programmes and programme planning the participation of Maori and the presence of a significant Maori voice"; and "support and promote the talents and creative resources of New Zealanders and of the New Zealand film and television industry." The charter was supported by an explicit subsidy (TVNZ, 2003).

The new regime is arguably permissible under the GATS. Disciplines on "trade-distorting subsidies" have not yet been agreed upon, and the national treatment requirement to treat foreign channels the same as TVNZ applies to "like" services, whereas the charter imposes distinct obligations. However, if the previous government had proceeded with its plan to privatize TVNZ, any move to impose comparable charter-style requirements on the free-to-air private sector television channels would have been open to challenge from foreign owners as a breach of the rules on domestic regulation, in particular licensing. Article VI requires that a government that has committed a sector to the GATS rules must adopt the least trade burdensome approach to regulating for quality in that sector and carries the onus of proving that.

A second set of examples show how the United States is progressively achieving its movie industry's goal "to keep digital networks free of cultural protectionism" through commitments on new technologies (MPAA, quoted in Bernier, 2004, p. 235). Back in 1994 governments that wanted to protect the culture sector focused their attention on audiovisual services. Digital technologies were covered by commitments pertaining to "other telecommunications services." The original GATS also included a "state of the art" Annex on Telecommunications that guarantees foreign firms have "reasonable and non-discriminatory" access to, and use of, public telecommunications networks that are necessary for them to provide the services that a host government has committed in its schedule. However, measures affecting cable or broadcast distribution of radio or television programs were excluded.

The United States refused to extend MFN treatment to all countries partly because of the small number of initial commitments on telecommunications. Negotiations on "basic telecommunications" were extended to 1996 and culminated in the Fourth Protocol to the GATS. Some 72 governments submitted new schedules that covered voice telephone, data transmission, leased circuits, access for cellular/mobile telephone markets, and other areas such as satellite-related communications and domestic regulation. These complemented earlier sectoral commitments mainly with regard to value-added telecommunications. The Protocol was accompanied by a Reference

Paper on Regulatory Principles for Basic Telecommunications, which invited voluntary commitments on competition safeguards, interconnection guarantees, licensing, and independence of regulators. In May 1998, a further agreement on e-commerce was brokered by the U.S. administration (as a precondition for President Clinton attending the second WTO ministerial conference in Geneva) for a moratorium on customs duties on e-commerce transactions in goods and a working party to consider trade-related aspects of global economic commerce, including services.

Since then, the convergence of technology and content has intensified, opening a debate over whether cultural services are covered by commitments relating to content or carriage. In 1998, and again at the start of the 2000 round of GATS negotiations, the United States tabled papers that argued that new technologies were providing worldwide access for cultural consumers and stimulating new and cheaper distribution options for locally based content producers (USTR, 1998, 2000). Because those technologies were expensive to develop and producers needed to recoup the cost of production across all markets, it was essential to have predictable and defined international rules. The United States wanted more extensive commitments and a review of classifications to ensure a "principle of technological neutrality" applied to content commitments. Existing classifications were creating uncertainties about what services were covered and where. Some services were not covered by any CPC, such as satellite or digital networks, wireless cable systems, and "converged" transmission services that transmit other forms of data, voice, or communications services. In an attempt to recruit allies, the paper attached a list of firms from other countries "whose converging functions and technologies transport a wide range of content, including films, music, news, games, and other forms of entertainment and information to customers" (USTR, 2000).

Predictably, the United States made little progress on audiovisual services in the GATS. The European position was well known, and other countries chose not to engage on those questions. The discussion resurfaced in the context of telecommunications, where the EC and other advocates of a cultural exception had their own offensive interests. The Commission tabled a paper in February 2005 where it, too, expressed concern that legal uncertainties surrounded the meaning of existing and potential commitments. This could be solved by adopting the carrier-based definition used in the GATS Annex on Telecommunications: "all services consisting of the transmission and reception of signals by any electromagnetic means." Economic activities or services that required telecommunications for delivery would be better covered by other sectors and regulatory issues through the adoption of the reference paper on telecommunications (EC, 2005). In essence, the EC wanted a definition that allowed it to exclude cultural content while pursuing its own interests in telecommunications.

The U.S. counter-proposal insisted that "value-added" was an essential part of telecommunications and said it would have difficulty accepting otherwise. The Commission's proposal would limit the scope of the sector, increase uncertainty, and diminish existing telecommunications commitments that included value-added services. The United States proposed an alternative classification: "All services consisting of the transmission and reception of signals by any electromagnetic means, *alone or in combination with enhancing, storing, forwarding, retrieving, or processing functions added to the transmission and reception of signals*" (USTR, 2005a, original emphasis). Further, "the principle of technology neutrality with respect to market access should also apply to the value-added sector and include services provided through IP-based networks." If there was no consensus on the adoption of this classification, individual WTO members should still choose it for the purposes of their schedules. It remains to be seen how many will do so.

The third limb of the U.S. strategy was to secure such commitments and create precedents in the growing number of bilateral negotiations where it was able to exert more direct pressure. In the Chile-U.S. free trade agreement signed off in 2003 the United States was prepared accept the grandfathering of existing protections for cultural sectors (known as a "standstill"). But it demanded full guarantees of access, non-discrimination, and market-driven regulation for its companies in the rapidly expanding digital sphere. The e-commerce aspect of that agreement was drafted so broadly that all products traded or delivered digitally, including cultural services, were covered. The U.S. summary described the e-commerce chapter as "a breakthrough in achieving certainty and predictability in ensuring access for products such as computer programs, video images, sound recordings and other products that are digitally encoded" (USTR, 2003).

Similar proposals were strenuously opposed by the Australian culture sector in negotiations for an Australia-U.S. Free Trade Agreement (AUSFTA) that was signed in 2004. The Australian Coalition for Cultural Diversity objected, unsuccessfully, that agreeing to a Chilean-style standstill would tie the hands of Australian governments in adopting any innovative new policies, including strategies to promote digital cultural industries, and effectively outsource the creation of Australian cultural policies to Hollywood (ACCD, 2003b; Duffy, 2003).

The agreement imposed onerous standstill provisions, with some limited concessions. There was no exception for public broadcasting, aside from a general exclusion for grants and subsidies, as the standard exclusion for "services supplied in the exercise of governmental authority" only applies where there is no commercial element and no competitors in the market. In relation to new media, the United States argued that digital is a different product from analog; the Australian government insisted that it was the same product supplied through a different mode of delivery. In the words of the U.S. Trade Representative, the final agreement "calls for each government to adopt state-of-the-art protection for digital products such as software, music, text, and videos, and encourages adoption of measures to promote trade through electronic commerce" (USTR, 2004).

A third set of examples show the complex interplay of agreements on trade in goods, trade in services, and investment at the multilateral, regional, and bilateral levels. In 1987 the Canadian government secured an "exemption" (Article 2005) for national cultural industries in its free trade agreement with the United States. However, this still allowed the U.S. to retaliate to an equal commercial value if the Canadian measures would otherwise have been inconsistent with the Agreement. That "exemption" was carried through into the North American Free Trade Agreement (NAFTA) 1993 (Acheson and Maule, 1998).

The Mexican government did not seek a similar provision under NAFTA, arguing it was not necessary to do more than list the measures that Mexico wanted to maintain. It had already begun to privatize the network of state cinemas that had guaranteed Mexican people access to Mexican films. In the next few years many theaters closed and were replaced by Canadian and U.S. multiplexes. With U.S. firms dominating both distribution and exhibition, the two state-supported distribution chains went into bankruptcy. After an initial burst, U.S. firms virtually stopped producing films in Mexico. Backed by strong guarantees in the investment and services chapters of NAFTA, they pushed the Mexican government to make further cuts to cultural regulation. In 1992, half of the movies shown in Mexican theaters had to be Mexican, with a price ceiling on ticket prices of 3 pesos; by 1997 the required quota of Mexican movies would be down to 10% and the price ceiling raised (Johnson, 1996). In 2003, when U.S. studios had captured 80% of the film market, the Mexican government announced plans to sell the national news agency, the National Cinematographic Institute, and various studios and workshops (Tuckman, 2003). The combination of NAFTA and a neoliberal government effectively undercut support to the Mexican film industry, and Mexican productions were marginalized (McIntosh, undated).

The United States and Canada had their own prolonged dispute over "Canadian" editions of U.S. titles, such as Time Warner's *Sports Illustrated Canada*, which contained mostly U.S. content but with Canadian advertising. Concerns that split-run magazines were capturing the Canadian advertising dollar and reducing the viability of local publications prompted the Canadian federal government to impose a tax on magazines that originated abroad. The government apparently assumed this was permissible because of the grandfathering of protections for cultural industries under NAFTA, and Canada had no commitments on advertising services under the GATS (WTO, 1997).[13]

The United States successfully complained to the WTO that the measure breached the rules against discrimination on trade in *goods*, as the magazines themselves were treated as directly competing or substitutable products. The WTO Appellate Body Decision said neither the GATT nor the GATS took precedence: "a periodical is a good comprised of two components: editorial content and advertising content. Both components can be viewed as having services attributes, but they combine to form a physical product—the periodical itself"'(WTO/AB, 1997, p. 17). Specific aspects of each transaction could be assessed under different rules. Hence activities that were permitted by one WTO agreement could be struck down through another.[14] Even if Canada had won that dispute at the WTO, it could then have been caught by its commitment of advertising services under NAFTA.

The Canadian government responded in 1999 with the Foreign Publishers Advertising Services Act. That prohibited Canadian advertisers from placing advertisements in foreign magazines, with fines for any foreign publisher that breached the rule. The law imposing the tax on split run periodicals was repealed. Other support measures were also removed, notably the tariff on imported split run magazines and a postal subsidy that reduced the distribution costs for Canadian periodicals. In response to continued U.S. objections, the Act was limited to publications that contained a level of Canadian advertising that would almost never be reached. Split-run magazines from the United States secured a virtual free rein.

Investment agreements can have equal, or greater, impact on culture as the GATS. The United States initiated a bilateral investment treaty with South Korea in the shadow of the 1998 financial crisis. It insisted that the clause designed for general commodities should also be applied to audiovisual products, despite the exemption in the GATT. This would have endangered the Korean screen quota system that required local theaters to screen Korean movies at least 146 days a year. Between the introduction of quotas in 1993 and 2002 the market share for domestic films had grown from 15% to 40%, attendance had risen from 48 million to 105 million, and export earnings had dramatically increased.

The South Korean film industry mounted a successful protest campaign of lobbying, public education, and street protests, including a 63-day sit-down strike. Negotiations on the U.S. Korea investment treaty stalled, and legislation to promote the active opening of the culture sector was defeated in 2001. The Korean government remained under intense pressure from the United States. In a communication to the WTO Council on Trade in Services in November 2001 it reportedly promised to abolish measures that conflicted with the MFN principle. Consistent with this, the government terminated a co-production agreement between South Korea and France. The United States (and other countries) launched a renewed attack on the screen quotas in June 2002 with an initial request for liberalization of the Korean cultural sector as part of the second round of GATS negotiations (KCCD, 2002).

By 2004 South Korea's cultural policy had become a major obstacle to its government's trade and investment strategy, which included securing the bilateral investment treaty. The United States said that was impossible without including movies. Frustrated South Korean officials said the quotas, which by then accounted for over 50% of local screenings, should be sacrificed for the benefit of the country; the industry was robust enough to compete openly with Hollywood films and allow movie patrons to choose what to view and theaters what to show. Korean filmmakers maintained their opposition, fearing that loss of the quota and strong U.S. control over distribution networks (which is covered by a separate CPC under the GATS) could see Hollywood secure over 90% of screenings and devastate the Korean industry. Supported by a broad base of supporters among students, farmers, educationists, and trade unions, they insisted that movies and other cultural products were not mere commodities to be governed by free trade rules, as the GATT had recognized many years before (Sung-jin, 2004). In mid-2005 the standoff remained unresolved.

THE ILLUSION OF A CULTURAL CARVE-OUT

The instinctive response to situations where "trade trumps culture" is to quarantine culture from the coverage of the trade rules. The most obvious strategy is for a government not to make sectoral commitments or to list explicit reservations in its schedule. Before a government can do that, however, it must be able to define the scope of "cultural services" and identify the relevant CPC headings. New technologies and transnational corporate practices make that virtually impossible. Governments and lobbyists have traditionally focused on *audio-visual services*, with its subheadings of production, distribution, exhibition, and broadcasting. Yet *recreational, cultural, and sporting services* apply to entertainment, news agency, libraries, museums, archives, sporting and recreational, and other cultural services. *Professional services* includes architecture, urban planning, and landscape. *Research and development* has a subcategory for social sciences and humanities. *Other business services* include advertising, photography, printing and publishing, and translation.

Targeting even this wider range of CPCs offers false security because it ignores the spectrum of financing, production, distribution, and exchange through which transnational corporations and investors now dominate the cultural domain. Generic service sectors such as retail, franchising, distribution, information technology, real estate, consultancy, financial services, telecommunications, and e-commerce increasingly determine production and consumption within the culture sector. Wal-Mart, for example, chooses what music, books, magazines, and videos it wants to sell. By dominating market share in the United States it can effectively dictate the content of those products. An EMI music executive quoted in *BusinessWeek* (6 October 2003) claimed it is impossible to take an artist to a mainstream audience without having the biggest retail player on board. Major music companies supply Wal-Mart with sanitized versions of the raunchy CDs that they provide to radio stations, and magazines and book titles are vetted to meet the corporation's self-defined ethical code. Wal-Mart's international reach, including inroads into China, gives it enormous global market power. Yet the most relevant CPCs for Wal-Mart are *distribution services*: retail and ancillary services, which according to its submission on the 2000 GATS negotiations include "information technology services, consolidation and deconsolidation of merchandise, marketing, advertising, telecommunications, financial services and insurance" ("Wal-Mart", 2002).

As previous examples show, it has also become difficult to predict the future implications and applications of any commitments that are made. Convergence of technology and content opens a whole new arena of confusion and potential dispute. In 2005 the WTO Appellate Body found that the United States had made market access commitments on Internet gambling, which it said it had never intended to commit (USTR, 2005c). Moreover, general obligations and disciplines in Part II of the GATS, such as those on competition and state enterprises, apply whether or not a sectoral commitment has been made.

A broader defensive strategy is to include a carve out for cultural services in the texts of an agreement. According to Ivan Bernier, Canada initially proposed a (partial) cultural carve-out during the Uruguay round on similar lines to its NAFTA exemption, but received no support. Then

> [i]n 1990, a working group was set up in the context of the negotiations on services to consider the feasibility of having a specific annex on audiovisual services. Two conflicting views characterized the discussions, that of the United States and some other countries completely opposed to any kind of exception for audiovisual services, and that of the EEC, willing to make a commitment itself in that area only if a cultural exemption clause, more or less along the lines of what Canada had obtained in the (US-Canada) FTA, was included. After a few sessions, the group discontinued its activities for lack of agreement on the content of the proposed annex. (Bernier, 2005, p. 6)

The issue resurfaced in 1993. This was prompted by a mobilization of European artists, who published a declaration in favor of a cultural exception in five of Europe's most prominent newspapers. The Commission then proposed a cultural specificity clause that would have

> accommodated exemptions from the m.f.n. clause for audiovisual industry assistance programmes, permitted the continuance and extension of public aid and operational subsidies, allowed screen time to be reserved for indigenous production of films and TV programmes, and permitted the regulation of existing and future broadcasting technologies and transmission techniques. (WTO, 1998, fn 27)

When that failed to get support, the Commission announced that it would make no specific commitments with regard to the *audiovisual* sector. Switzerland again floated the possibility of an annex of cultural services during the second round of GATS negotiations, but there is no evidence of any enthusiasm, even from the Europeans (Switzerland, 2001).

Campaigns for legal carve-outs have been more successful in bilateral and regional agreements. In an Annex to the Australia-Singapore Free Trade Agreement, where coverage of services is by a negative list, the Australian government reserved the right to "adopt or maintain any measure relating to the creative arts, cultural heritage or other cultural industries, including audio-visual services, entertainment services and libraries, archives, museums and other cultural services; broadcasting and audio-visual services, including measures relating to planning, licensing and spectrum management, and including services offered in Australia [and] international services originating from Australia". "Creative arts" and "culture heritage" are both extensively defined, with the former including "digital interactive media and hybrid arts work which uses new technologies to transcend art-form divisions."

However, this innovation proved largely symbolic. It could not override Australia's existing or future commitments under the GATS, even between the two parties. So it was only relevant to the extent that the particular bilateral agreement contained more extensive commitments than existed (for the time being) under the WTO—which it did, especially given the use of a negative list. However, that was rapidly over-ridden by the Australia- U.S. Free Trade Agreement that lacked equivalent protections.

A third option is to expand the General Exceptions provisions in the services agreements. Article XX of the GATT allows "necessary" measures to be taken for the protection of "national treasures of artistic, historic or archaeological value"; but the corresponding GATS Article XIV does not contain even that limited exception, reflecting the assumption that governments could protect these interests by not scheduling commitments. To broaden these exceptions would require a formal amendment. In theory, amendments can be approved by a two-thirds of WTO Members. In practice, the United States (and others) could be expected to oppose both the substance and precedent of such changes and threaten to withdraw from the WTO if it was approved. The United States could also decline to adopt the amendment, largely defeating the purpose of the change.[15] Again, there is more flexibility in bilateral agreements. Article 71 on General Exceptions in the Singapore New Zealand Closer Economic Partnership 2001 (which has a positive list for services) uses similar, but slightly less extensive, wording to the annex in the Australia-Singapore FTA. But again this cannot override the GATS and is subject to requirements that it not be a disguised trade barrier and satisfies a trade-centered "necessity" test.

One further, limited, option is to strengthen the provision that excludes from the agreement "services supplied in the exercise of governmental authority" (Article 1.3 in the GATS). At present these services must have neither a commercial dimension nor be offered in competition with private firms.[16] Television, radio, and almost every other cultural activity in almost every country—such as public service broadcasters competing with commercial stations or museums that charge an entrance fee—automatically fall outside that protection. When the WTO and governments insist that public services are protected (WTO undated) they can only be referring to the dwindling number of noncommercial monopoly services that are owned or provided directly by the state, not those on which the public depends. A much broader definition of "social rights" or "public goods" would be needed for an exclusion to have any real meaning. Securing agreement on those terms would be difficult enough among their advocates, let alone the two thirds of WTO members required to amend the agreement.

Paradoxically, the pursuit of carve-outs has tended to reinforce the commodification of culture by promoting reservations and exemptions that fragment and fetishize aspects of the cultural domain, and leave the broader threat of neoliberal globalization to go unchallenged. This was epitomized by an early statement from the Australian Coalition for Cultural Diversity (ACCD) on the proposed free trade agreement between the United States and Australia: "The ACCD is not opposed to a free trade agreement with the United States—just one that sells out our local culture" (ACCD, 2003a). As the campaign intensified, alliances with others fighting for their own sectors meant opposition to the entire agreement became critically important and their perspective broadened. But once the campaign was over, the limited concessions they gained and fears of a retributive backlash from the government prompted many cultural practitioners to argue that they should retreat from politics and focus on their work.

A COUNTER CONVENTION ON CULTURAL DIVERSITY

The flurry of new WTO-compatible agreements and the effective closure of options in the "trade" arena prompted an alliance of culture ministers, professionals, and activists to pursue a more ambitious strategy. The rhetoric broadened: this was no longer about protecting cultural goods and services, but about protecting and promoting cultural diversity (although culture was still limited to Frye's third sense of creative outputs). The new discourse eschewed protectionism of national interests in favor of a progressive form of globalization that could harness new era technologies to foster cross-border "trade and exchange" in creative works from all corners of the world. In practice, this remained a largely nationalist project to defend the capacity for state policies and regulatory regimes to sustain the local cultural landscape and the livelihoods of culture workers and industries. Redressing the structural inequalities that hindered genuine international diversity and promoting development in the global south were at best secondary concerns, and at worst, hypocritical on the part of some northern governments.

The political impetus came from an International Network on Cultural Policy (INCP). This was created in 1998 when ministers responsible for culture from 47 countries gathered in Ottawa to address the challenge posed by the GATS and the OECD's ill-fated Multilateral Agreement on Investment. The following year they commissioned a paper on International Responses to the Challenges Facing Cultural Diversity, which developed the idea of a new international convention to defend cultural diversity (INCP, 2000). The proposal was endorsed in 2000 by the INCP and the first international meeting of cultural activists and nongovernment organizations that gathered under the umbrella of the International Network for Cultural Diversity (INCD), which produced the first draft of a potential convention. Meanwhile, national coalitions for cultural diversity were being formed, modeled on the Canadian coalition that was created in Quebec in 1998 in response to the MAI and in preparation for the WTO ministerial conference in Seattle. An International Steering Committee of Coalitions for Cultural Diversity (ICCD) was established in 2001 to promote the establishment of country-based chapters of professional cultural organizations that would advocate for the convention and cultural diversity in their home countries.[17]

A gap soon emerged between the idealism of the NGOs and the political pragmatism of sponsoring governments. The INCP mandated its working group to develop a draft Declaration on Cultural Diversity, which was produced at a joint meeting in South Africa in late 2002. That text would oblige parties to pay particular attention to sustaining cultural diversity in other international forums where it may be called into question. When governments were asked to make such commitments, they would consult to develop a common approach and refrain from making commitments that were contrary to the objectives of the Convention. The INCD urged the ministers to go further. Their draft provided that

> nothing in this Convention, or any other International Agreement to which it may be a Party, shall be construed to prevent a Party from adopting, maintaining or enforcing measures that accord special, preferential or more favourable treatment to indigenous or national goods and services for the purpose of achieving the objectives of the Convention. (INCD, 2003)

Either text would have given willing governments a tool to help them resist new "trade" commitments; the INCD wording would also have deliberately provoked a conflict with existing "trade" commitments. However, these initial drafts would inevitably be compromised once negotiations with hostile governments began.

The initiative gained momentum from intergovernmental endorsements at the Francophone Summit in Beirut and the Brixen Declaration of European Regional Ministers for Culture and Education, both in October 2002. The Convention now needed an institutional sponsor. The United Nations Educational, Scientific and Cultural Organization (UNESCO) was the obvious location, given its cultural mandate. In 1998 UNESCO had hosted an Intergovernmental Conference on Cultural Policies for Development. In 2001 it adopted a Universal Declaration on Cultural Diversity, accompanied by an Action Plan, which described the preservation of cultural diversity as a moral obligation that is inseparable from the dignity of humankind, and urged each country to establish and implement policies to suit its unique situation. Consecutive meetings of ministers and culture activists in Paris in February 2003 resolved to approach UNESCO to sponsor the initiative. The resolution to develop a binding standard setting Convention on the protection of cultural contents and artistic expressions was adopted at UNESCO's ministerial meeting in October 2003 (INCP, 2003).

A group of independent experts prepared a preliminary draft Convention that was released for comment in July 2004 (UNESCO, 2004). Article 19 on Relationship to Other Instruments offered two options. Option A affirmed the primacy of existing agreements on intellectual property rights, including the WTO TRIPS agreement. The Convention would not affect the rights and obligations of any state party deriving from any other existing international instrument (such as GATS or bilateral trade in services agreements) "except where the exercise of those rights and obligations would cause serious damage or threat to the diversity of cultural expressions." Notably, this wording provided a limited support for parties to the Convention to adopt measures that contravened current and future commitments and rules under the existing WTO and bilateral agreements. Option B was a blanket statement that the Convention shall not affect the rights and obligations of parties under other existing international instruments. That was the worst conceivable outcome. Far from an antidote to the GATS, the United States and its allies would have reinforced its legitimacy and supremacy over culture.

That draft was refined by a group of intergovernmental experts with help from a drafting subcommittee, taking into account submissions from governments and international organizations, including the WTO. Initially, the WTO Secretariat advised UNESCO's Director General that they would hold formal discussions at the relevant councils (on services and intellectual property) and then the General Council. Subsequently the WTO opted simply to hold an informal seminar in November 2004, convened by the WTO Director General, at which views were aired but no position taken; Member governments would make their interventions at UNESCO. Prior to that session, the United States had convened a meeting of Chile, India, China-Hong Kong, China-Taiwan, Japan, and Mexico (dubbed the "Friends of Cultural Diversity") to discuss their strategy. Discussions held by the author with WTO representatives of governments on all sides revealed a mutual concern that a full-blown formal discussion would have put cultural services explicitly on the WTO agenda at a time when they were seeking to defuse mounting criticisms that "trade" was invading other policy arenas and undermining state sovereignty. They all preferred to isolate the discussion within UNESCO.

Political compromises set in as INCP governments pushed to conclude a final a text in time for UNESCO's biennial General Conference in October 2005, rather than the "preliminary draft Convention" mandated by the 2003 resolution. In March 2005, a composite text was released that maintained the standoff on Article 19, but indicated support to find a third way in which no international instrument took precedence (UNESCO, 2005a). A composite Chairman's text then proposed a cosmetic solution whereby the Convention and the trade agreements would be "complementary and mutually supportive." That satisfied neither the United States and its allies, who wanted WTO agreements to prevail, nor INCP governments, who wanted a more explicit assertion of parity. The final text (UNESCO, 2005b) contained a more detailed variation on the Chairman's theme:

Article 20: Relationship to other treaties: mutual supportiveness, complementarity and non-subordination

1. The parties recognize that they shall perform in good faith their obligations under this Convention and all other treaties to which they are parties. Accordingly, without subordinating this Convention to any other treaty, they:

  (a) shall foster mutual supportiveness between this Convention and
      the other treaties to which they are parties; and
  (b) when interpreting and applying the other treaties to which they
      are parties or when entering into other international obligations,
      Parties shall take into account the relevant provisions of this
      Convention. Nothing in this Convention shall be interpreted as
      modifying the rights and obligations of the Parties under any
      other treaties to which they are parties.

The Article 21 obliged parties to "promote the principles and objectives
of this Convention in other international forums," but stopped short of
requiring cooperation or solidarity among its parties.

An already weak draft text had been gutted. The affirmation in Article
20(2) that the Convention does not modify existing rights and obligations
means it could not be invoked by a signatory even as a moral justification
for withdrawing or amending a "trade in services" commitment or arguing
that it should not have to offer compensatory redress, even to other parties
to the Convention.[18] The "obligations" and "relevant provisions" in the rest
of the Convention that provided the reference points for Article 20(1) had
become purely aspirational. The requirement that parties "take into
account" those provisions would allow more powerful governments to
invoke the Convention in defence of their own narrow cultural exception, if
they were willing to use it. (Even the European Commission was not in
agreement that the "cultural exception" should extend to music, let alone to
the broader range of culture-related services in which they also have offensive interests.) At best, Articles 20 and 21 might inhibit the lodging of
"trade" disputes by one INCP government against another, such as the
European Commission's challenge to Canada over film distribution in 1998,
and favor conciliation. But those major powers were already able to look
after themselves.

Some tenacious advocates of a strong Convention, such as Senegal and
Cuba, might try to talk up its provisions to justify holding the line. Other
larger players, such as Brazil and South Africa, would face internal pressure
to subordinate cultural policies to broader trade priorities. Ultimately, the
Convention offered nothing to the most vulnerable countries that face a
gross inequality of power in the "trade" arena, as in accessions or bilateral
and regional negotiations. In the unlikely event that the United States
became a party, the USTR would hardly be swayed by an obligation to "take
into account" the Convention's aspirational provisions.

The "mirror" solution in Article 20(1) was a mirage. Despite the rhetoric of nonsubordination, the UNESCO Convention was always going to
occupy a subordinate legal space to the WTO, even if it had binding obligations and a strong enforcement mechanism, which it did not. Complaints
that a WTO member's policy or regulations have breached the GATS are

judged solely by trade rules before a panel of WTO-appointed trade experts and backed by economic sanctions. The obligations of those governments under other international instruments are irrelevant. The real power lies in the WTO's enforcement mechanism, which is not replicated in any other international agreement or forum—except for regional and bilateral trade and investment agreements. Given that hierarchy of potency, the obligation in Article 20(1)(a) to "foster mutual supportiveness" will in practice require the Convention to operate within the WTO's neoliberal paradigm and conform to its rules.

Institutional factors reinforce this. UNESCO was a post–World War II creation of a now displaced historical compromise. It survives tenuously in an international regulatory arena that is driven by and for the interests of international capital. Its marginality is reflected at the national level. The UNESCO Convention was primarily the responsibility of culture ministers and ministries. Responsibility for the GATS and related agreements rests with the more powerful trade ministers, ministries, and Geneva-based negotiators. Cultural services are one small part of their multifaceted "trade" negotiations, where tradeoffs are made with other services and with agriculture, industrial products and intellectual property. It is hard to imagine that governments that strongly supported the Convention would privilege cultural concerns over their strategic trade objectives at a "whole of government" level.

The politics of intergovernmental negotiations also ensured that UNESCO was never going to deliver a strong convention. The United States would never have allowed that to happen. The Convention provided a major motivation for the U.S. government to reaffiliate to UNESCO, sealed by Hillary Clinton's attendance in 2003. Constant and vigorous interventions throughout the drafting process were designed to subvert the original objectives, even though the United States would probably never accede to the instrument.[19] The rapporteur's report on the final negotiating session recorded a stream of formal objections from the United States to the text and an unsuccessful demand that two texts be forwarded to the General Conference (Wilczynski, 2005).

The final statement from the U.S. delegation described the document as "deeply flawed and fundamentally incompatible with UNESCO's Constitutional obligation to promote the free flow of ideas by word and image" (Martin, 2005). The process, including voting, had undermined "the spirit of consensus" that normally characterizes UNESCO and "would weaken its reputation as a responsible, thoughtful international organisation"—which was ironic, given the travesty of "consensus" that pervades decision making at the WTO (Jawara and Kwa, 2003). The United States also objected that the Convention was not about culture, but about trade— as evidenced by provision for the participation of the European Commission, which had competency for trade, not culture. "Because it is about trade, this convention clearly exceeds the mandate of UNESCO" (Martin, 2005). Yet cultural policy had become a "trade" issue at U.S. insistence through agreements that intruded deeply into areas of cultural and social policy regulation. The United States was now using that redefinition to disqualify an international organization whose constitutional mandate is to "preserve the fruitful diversity of cultures" from seeking to neutralize the negative impacts of those agreements on culture.

At the same time, it is vital to understand that the weak outcome also reflected the interests of its powerful patrons, notably France, Canada/Quebec, and Spain. They have their own offensive interests in the WTO. The last thing they wanted was to inflame attacks on the "trade" agreements for subordinating culture, human rights, social policy, and democracy, and were eager to quarantine the issue to UNESCO. The weak outcome suited their needs for a pragmatic balance of cultural and economic self-interest within the neoliberal paradigm.

The NGOs have struggled to respond. They sought a high-quality agreement that would provide some justification for governments (such as New Zealand's) to amend their existing schedules; strengthen the resolve of governments (such as Vanuatu or South Korea) to resist making trade or investment commitments that would endanger their culture sectors and cultural diversity; legitimize the cultural exceptions insisted on by Canada and the EC; and offer competing enforcement mechanisms in disputes over measures that were consistent with the culture convention but inconsistent with the trade agreements, so as to induce a stalemate. Only the third of these was partially achieved. The Canadian Coalition on Cultural Diversity, whose raison d'etre was to secure the Convention, pragmatically hailed the text as a success and urged its adoption. The International Network on Cultural Diversity was more ambivalent:

> If the objective of the new Treaty is to declare the right of States to implement cultural policies and to establish a new foundation for future cooperation, the Treaty has succeeded. If the objective is to carve out cultural goods and services from the trade agreements, the Treaty is inadequate, at least in the short term. (INCD, 2005)

BUILDING A COUNTER-HEGEMONY

The experience of the Convention provides important points for reflection. First, it illustrates the dangers of being seduced by legalism. The Convention was a strategy for raising awareness and building support to resist and delegitimize the "trade" agreements. The NGOs lost sight of that and believed they could find a legal solution. Law is not abstract, and international institutions do not exist in a vacuum. The WTO and UNESCO are creatures of different conceptual paradigms. In the era of neoliberal globalization the WTO's paradigm rules. It does not provide any space for "balance" or for the equality of cultural and economic considerations. The challenge posed to culture by neoliberal globalization cannot be resolved within the legal terrain established by agreements that are instruments of that paradigm. That is not to suggest that campaigns to oppose commitments or promote counter-instruments should be abandoned; quite the opposite. But rather than ends in themselves, they must be seen as one tactic in a strategy to heighten and expose the contradictions that are intrinsic to neoliberal globalization.

Nor can the state be treated as a neutral player in national and international policymaking and regulation. The primacy of its relationship with capital means that attempts to change the current dynamic, especially in the current era, cannot rely on state patronage. Yet the state remains the primary, if imperfect, vehicle through which progressive cultural policy and regulation can be secured. It is not simply an enemy or ally, but a contested zone. There is a challenge to find ways to harness technology as a genuinely empowering and liberating tool and conceive of cultural policy and regulation in the 21st century that allow that to occur.

Second, this experience confirms the indivisibility of the three elements of Frye's typology and their shared material foundations. The interests of cultural professionals and creative artists are inextricably entwined with culture as ideology and culture as lifestyle. The Director of South Korea's Coalition for Cultural Diversity, Gi Hwan Yang, described losing one's culture as "tantamount to losing one's language and soul. . . . No culture should disappear from the face of this earth because it lacked market competitiveness" (Hwan, 2003). The struggle, he says, is to open borders, not close them. The goal is to stop market-led cultural invasion and secure a truly balanced exchange among cultures, so that diversity and self-determination are able to thrive.

To achieve this means recognizing that the ideologies, geopolitics, and social relations that currently shape the cultural landscape are embedded in global capitalism. The postmodernist pluralism of "cultural diversity" implies a depoliticized form of globalization, but in practice accepts the hierarchies of wealth, power, and culture that are endemic to neoliberalism. Culture professionals and creative artists rarely see themselves as culture workers who are direct or indirect captives of international capitalism or locate themselves within an international division of labor where those in the global south, north, and indigenous peoples occupy different economic and social orders. Solidarity that recognizes the widespread alienation and exploitation of culture workers can, as David Harvey urges, use the validation of particularity, uniqueness, authenticity, culture and aesthetic meanings in ways that open up new possibilities and alternatives. . . . It also entails trying to persuade contemporary cultural producers to redirect their anger towards commodification, market domination and the capitalistic system more generally. (Harvey, 2002, p. 108)

This deeper conception of cultural diversity cannot be separated from the struggle for sustainable agriculture, education, and health care, rights to land and water, decent work and living conditions, a safe environment, debt cancellation, decolonization, and self-determination. This implies alliances with workers, students, farmers, indigenous peoples, and other communities that are also threatened by the neoliberal model of globalization, and recognition that the lived realities of those who sustain the integrity of culture and community expose the lie of neoliberal hegemony.

NOTES

1. www.adamsmith.org/cissues/media-culture-sport/home.htm. Accessed 10 June 2005
2. Arguments about the uniqueness of culture can be overplayed; similar claims are made, for example, for education or water.
3. Once dismantled it is almost impossible to restore. Likewise, governments cannot easily maintain or restore cultural policies that are incompatible with the neoliberal paradigm and will need to balance demands for such measures with their offensive interests in securing the best possible advantages in the global economy.
4. Directive 89/552/EEC adopted 3 October 1989 by the European Council, amended 30 June 1997 by the European Parliament and Council Director 97/36/EC, allows Community coordination of national legislation to provide for the free movement of television broadcasting services in the European Union to promote the development of a European market in broadcasting and related services, such as television advertising and production of audiovisual programs.
5. Article XXIV of the GATT and Article V of the GATS require that economic integration agreements provide more extensive liberalization than exists under the WTO and do not raise overall the barriers to other WTO members.
6. The agreements on intellectual property rights raise additional complex issues that are beyond the scope of this chapter.
7. Article XX(f) of the GATT also permits measures related to the protection of national treasures of "artistic, historic and archaeological value" provided they are not a means of arbitrary or unjustifiable discrimination between countries where like conditions prevail or disguised trade barriers, and are judged "necessary" to achieve the objective.
8. Bernier notes that U.S. officials have retrospectively attempted to explain Article IV as motivated by economic, rather than cultural, considerations. Communi-

cation on Audio-visual and Related Services from the United States to the WTO Council for Trade in Services of 18 December 2000 said: "In 1947, in recognition of the difficulty that domestic film producers faced in finding adequate screen time to exhibit their films in the immediate post–World War II period, GATT founders authorized continuation of existing screen-time quotas." That view is not shared by other independent and partisan commentators.

9. Set out in MTN.GNS/W/120 of 10 July 1991

10. The EC counts as one.

11. Hon Steve Maharey, Minister of Broadcasting, in response to a Parliamentary question from Sue Kedgely MP (Green Party) 18 May 2005. www.greens. org.nz/searchdocs/other8679.html

12. However, Bernier notes that the U.S. has not carried through its threats to lodge complaints under the GATT against quotas under the EU's *Television Without Frontiers* or in Canada or France (Bernier, 2004, p. 226)

13. Canada explicitly excluded musical scores, audio and video recordings, books, magazines, newspapers, journals, and periodicals from its commitments in the sector of wholesale trade services; see GATS/SC/16: 47

14. Bernier notes that the U.S. complaint against Turkey on taxation of foreign film revenues in 1996 was based on Article III of the GATT (*Turkey—Taxation of Foreign Film Revenues*, Doc. WT/DS43 [1996]), but the EC complaint against Canada on measures affecting film distribution services in 1998 was based on Articles II and III of the GATS: *Canada-Measures Affecting Film Distribution Services* WT/DS117/1 (1998). The latter complaint was dropped a few months later when the company at the origin of the case, Polygram, was bought by a Canadian company (Bernier, 2005, p. 35).

15. Article X.5 of the Agreement Establishing the World Trade Organization allows individual Members not to accept an amendment to most of the substantive provisions of the GATS. For exceptional amendments, a Member that declines to accept that amendment can be required to elect to leave the WTO or seek permission to remain as a Member.

16. Likewise, the temporary exclusion of government procurement under Article XIII does not extend to services that are purchased with a view to commercial resale, such as documentaries or dramas sold to another media or on video.

17. These NGOs had overlapping memberships and mandates, but sometimes competing organizational imperatives. The INCD has a broad-based membership that operates loosely on a regional and international level. The coalitions organize cultural professionals on a national basis and tend to have a narrower industry focus and closer relationship with individual governments. Both groups have members from the north and south with divergent political perspectives and perceptions of the problems and solutions.

18. This obligation only arises under GATS Article XXI where one WTO Member objects to a proposed amendment of another Member's schedule of commitments.

19. The United States had used this tactic with considerable success on numerous environmental and human rights treaties, such as the Kyoto Protocol, Persistent Organic Pollutants Treaty, Basel Convention, Biosafety Protocol, Convention on the Rights of the Child, Protocol to the Biological Weapons Convention, and the Landmine Ban Treaty.

REFERENCES

Acheson, Keith and Christopher Maule (1998) "The culture of protection and the protection of culture—A Canadian perspective in 1998." www.carleton.ca/economics/cioru/cioru98-01.pdf

Australian Coalition for Cultural Diversity (ACCD) (2003a) Media release: "Australians say don't trade off our culture." www.accd.org.au

Australian Coalition for Cultural Diversity (ACCD) (2003b) "Australia-United States free trade agreement briefing: Cultural services & trade." www.accd.org.au

Bernier, Ivan (2004) "Content regulation in the audio-visual sector and the WTO." In Damien Gaeradin and David Luff (Eds.), *The WTO and Global Convergence in Telecommunications and Audio-Visual Services.* Cambridge: Cambridge University Press.

Bernier, Ivan (2005) "Trade and culture." In Patrick Macrory et al. (Eds.), *The World Trade Organization: Legal, Economic and Political Analysis.* New York: Springer International.

Comfort, Susan (2002) "Struggle in Ogoniland: Ken Saro-Wiwa and the cultural politics of environmental justice." In Joni Adamson et al. (Eds.), *The Environmental Justice Reader. Politics, Poetics and Pedagogy.* Phoenix: University of Arizona Press.

Drake, William and Kalypso Nicolaidis (1992) "Ideas, Interests and Institutionalization: Trade in services and the Uruguay round." *International Organization:* 37.

Duffy, Greg (2003) "Australian television content. The new culture vultures." Sydney: Evatt Foundation. http://evatt.labor.net.au/publications/papers/127.html

European Commission (2005) "Communication to the CSC and CTS-SS on classification in the Telecom sector under the WTO-GATS framework." TN/S/W/27, S/CSC/W/44, 9 February 2005.

Feketekuty, Geza (1988) *International Trade in Services. An Overview and Blueprint for Negotiations.* Cambridge, MA: Ballinger.

Fitzpatrick, Peter (1992) *The Mythology of Modern Law.* London: Routledge.

Frye, Northrop (2003) "Speech at the new Canadian embassy, Washington (14 Sept 1989)." Tn Jean O'Grady and David Staines (Eds.), *Northrop Frye on Canada* (p. 639.). Toronto: University of Toronto Press.

Golding, Peter and Graham Murdock (2000) "Culture, communications and political economy," In James Curran (Ed.), *Mass Media and Society.* London: Edward Arnold.

Grynberg, Roman et al. (2000) "The accession of Vanuatu to the WTO: Lessons for the multilateral trading system." *Journal of World Trade* 34(6): 159.

Hall, Stuart et al. (1978) *Policing the Crisis. Mugging, the State and Law and Order.* London: Macmillan.

Harvey, David (2002) "The art of rent: Globalization, monopoly and the commodification of culture." In Leo Panitch and Colin Leys (Eds.), *A World of Contradictions. Socialist Register 2002.* London: Merlin Press.

Hunt, Alan (1993) *Explorations in Law and Society. Toward a Constitutive Theory of Law*. London: Routledge.

Hwan, Gi Yang, (2003) "Why UNESCO should adopt a convention on cultural diversity." International Liaison Committee of Coalitions for Cultural Diversity, Paris, September 2003. www.comitedevigilance.org/unesco/Yang.pdf

International Network on Cultural Diversity (INCD) (2003) "Proposed convention on cultural diversity, prepared for the international network for cultural diversity 2003." www.incd.net

International Network on Cultural Diversity (INCD) (2005) "INCD Position on New UNESCO Treaty," 3 June 2005. http://www.incd.net/docs/INCD Position.htm

INCP Working Group on Cultural Diversity and Globalization (INCP) (2000) "Discussion paper for ministerial consideration: International responses to the challenges facing cultural diversity", 29 September 2000. http://206.191.7.19/meetings/2000/santorini2/consid_e.shtml

International Network for Cultural Policy (INCP) (2003) "Draft international convention on cultural diversity by the working group on cultural diversity and globalization to be presented to ministers at the 6th annual ministerial meeting of the International Network on Cultural Policy in Opatija, Croatia, October 16-18 2003" July 2003. www.incp-ripc.org

Jawara, Fatoumata and Aileen Kwa (2003) *Behind the Scenes at the WTO: The Real World of Trade Negotiations*. London: Zed Books.

Jessop, Bob (2002) *The Future of the Capitalist State*. Cambridge: Polity Press.

Johnson, Randel (1996) "Latin American film policy." In Albert Mora (Ed.), *Film Policy: International, Regional And National Perspectives*. New York: Routledge.

Kelsey, Jane (1997) *The New Zealand Experiment. A World Model for Structural Adjustment?* (2nd ed.). Wellington: Bridget Williams Books.

Kelsey, Jane (2003a) "Legal fettishism and the contradictions of the GATS." *Globalization, Societies and Education* 1(3): 267.

Kelsey, Jane (2003b) *Serving Whose Interests? A Guide to New Zealand's Commitments under the WTO General Agreement on Trade in Services*. Christchurch: ARENA.

Kelsey, Jane (2005) "World trade and small nations in the South Pacific region." *Kansas Journal of Law and Policy* XIV(II): 247.

Kerruish, Valerie (1993) *Jurisprudence as Ideology*. London: Routledge

Kertzer, Jonathan (2004/5) "Northrop Frye on Canada (review)." *University of Toronto Quarterly* 74(1): 569.

Korean Coalition for Cultural Diversity (KCCD) (2002) "Recommendation to the Minister of Culture and Tourism, Korea, 30 June 2002." www.screenquota.org/epage/Board/kccd_view.asp?

Lister, Martin et al. (2003) *New Media: A Critical Introduction*. London: Routledge.

Martin, Robert (2005) "Final statement of the US delegation; The Hon Robert S. Martin," 3 June 2005. Washington, DC: Department of State.

Masterman, Asa and Dugald Williamson (1998) "What is the historical background to the current controversy over Australian commercial television content standards?" www.ins.gu.edu.au/shr/sr05/mod5/sr05m05t03.htm

McIntosh, David (undated) "The rise and fall of Mexican cinema in the 20th century. From the production of a revolutionary national imaginary to the consumption of globalised cultural industrial products." http://www.umanitoba.ca/faculties/arts/english/media/workshop/papers/mcintosh/mcintosh_paper.pdf

Murdock, Graham (1998) "Public broadcasting in privatised times: Rethinking the New Zealand experiment." In Paul Norris and John Farnsworth (Eds.), *Keeping It Ours: Issues of Television Broadcasting in New Zealand.* Christchurch: New Zealand Broadcasting School.

Murdock, Graham and Peter Golding (2002) "Digital possibilities, market realities: The contradictions of communications convergence." In Leo Panitch and Colin Leys (Eds.), *A World of Contradictions. Socialist Register 2002.* London: Merlin Press.

Negus, Keith and Patria Roman-Velazquez (2000) "Globalization and cultural identities." In James Curran (Ed.), *Mass Media and Society.* London: Edward Arnold.

New Zealand Labour Party (NZLP) (2002) *Broadcasting Policy 2002.* http://labour.org.nz/policy/arts_and_culture/broadcasting_policy_2002/index.html

Offe, Claus (1984) *Contradictions of the Welfare State.* London: Hutchinson.

Polanyi, Karl (1957) *The Great Transformation.* Boston: Beacon Press.

Raghavan, Chakravarthi (2002) *Developing Countries and Services Trade: Chasing a Black Cat in a Dark Room, Blindfolded.* Penang: Third World Network

Santiago, Lilia Quindoza (2003) "Art and culture as peacekeepers." *Cultures and Development* 43-44. http://www.networkcultures.net/publications.html

Street, John (2001) *Mass Media, Politics and Democracy.* Houndmills: Palgrave.

Sreberny, Annabelle (2000) "The global and the local in international communications." In James Curran (Ed.), *Mass Media and Society.* London: Edward Arnold.

Switzerland, Government of (2001) "Communication from Switzerland: GATS 2000 Audio-visual Services." S/CSS/W/74, 4 May 2001

Sung-jin, Yang (2004) "Screen quota system in dispute again." *Korean Herald* (Seoul). www.bilterals.org/article.php3?id_article=853.

Tuckman, Jo (2003) "Mexico: Film studio sell off." *Guardian (London),* 14 November 2003.

TVNZ (2003) "TVNZ charter." http://corporate.tvnz.co.nz/tvnz_detail/0,2406,111535-244-257,00.html

UNESCO (2004) "Preliminary draft of a convention on the protection of the diversity of cultural contents and artistic expressions." CLT/CPD/2004/CONF-201/2, July 2004.

UNESCO (2005a) "Preliminary report of the Director-General containing two preliminary drafts of a convention on the protection of the diversity of cultural contents and artistic expressions." CLT/CPD/2005/CONF.203/6, 3 March 2005.

UNESCO (2005b) "Preliminary draft convention on the protection and promotion of the diversity of cultural expressions." Revised text, 2 June 2005.

U.S. Trade Representative (1998) "Communication from the United States. Audio-visual services." S/C/W/78 8 December 1998.

U.S. Trade Representative (2000) "Communication from the United States. Audio-visual and related services." S/CSS/W/21, 18 December 2000

U.S. Trade Representative (2003) "Statement of Regina KK. Vargo, Assistant U.S. Trade Representative for the Americas, Senate Committee on the Judiciary, 14 July 2003" .www.ustr.gov/assets/Document_Library/USTR_Deputy_Testimony /2003/asset_upload_file803_6641.pdf

U.S. Trade Representative (2004) "Press release: US and Australia Complete Free Trade Agreement," August 2. www.ustr.gov/Document_Library/Press_ Releases/2004/February/U.S._Australia_Complete_Free_Trade_Agreement.ht ml

U.S. Trade Representative (2005a) "Communication from the United States: Classification in the telecommunications section of the WTO-GATS frame-work." TN/S/W/35 S/CSC/W/45 22 February.

U.S. Trade Representative (2005b) "Trade summary on New Zealand." www.ustr.gov/assets/Document_Library/Reports_Publications/ 2005/2005_NTE_Report/asset_upload_file435_7485.pdf

U.S. Trade Representative (2005c) "US internet gambling restrictions can stand as US wins key issues in WTO Dispute," 7 April 2005. www.ustr.gov/Document_ Library/Press_Releases/2005/April/U.S._Internet_Gambling_Restrictions_Ca n_St_as_U.S._Wins_Key_Issues_in_WTO_Dispute.html

van Welsum, Desirée (2003) "International Trade in Services: Issues and Concepts" (mimeo). London: Birkbeck College.

Wallach, Lori and Patrick Woodall (2004) *Whose Trade Organization? A Comprehensive Guide to the WTO.* New York: The New Press.

Wal-Mart to USTR (2002). "Comments with respect to Doha multilateral negotia-tions and agenda in the World Trade Organization," Public Document, 1 May 2002.

Wilczynski, Artur (2005) 'Oral report of the Rapporteur Mr Artur Wilczynski at the closing of the third session of the intergovernmental meeting of experts on the draft convention on the protection and promotion of the diversity of cultural expressions", UNESCO, 25 May-3 June 2004.

World Trade Organization (WTO) (1997) "Canada—Certain measures concerning Periodicals" (97-3220). www.wto.org/english/tratop_e/dispu_e/distab_e.htm

World Trade Organization (WTO) (1998) "Audio-visual services: Background note by the Secretariat." S/C/W/40, 15 June.

World Trade Organization (WTO) (undated) "GATS fact and fiction: misunder-standings and scare stories." www.wto.org/english/tratop_e/serv_e/gats_fact-fictionfalse_e.htm

World Trade Organization Appellate Body (1997) "Canada—Certain measures con-cerning periodicals" (AB-1997-2) WT/DS31/AB/R. www.worldtradelaw.net/ reports/wtoab/canada-periodicals(ab).pdf

CHAPTER NINE

MARKETIZING THE "INFORMATION REVOLUTION" IN CHINA

Yuezhi Zhao

China is setting a world record in its "great leap forward" into the information age. Information and communication industries have been the fastest growing economic sector in China since the early 1990s, with an average annual growth rate of more than 30%—three times faster than China's overall economic growth. The population is becoming "wired" at an unprecedented rate, through television, telephone, and the Internet. China's information revolution, in the context of market reforms and the country's accelerated integration with the global market system, is widely heralded in mainstream domestic and international discourse, as the most positive revolution that has happened in that country to date, with neither the bloodshed of the Communist Revolution nor the madness of its aftermath, the Cultural Revolution. And, if one believes the Chinese media, the democratic features of this emerging Chinese information society are already taking shape. During the National People's Congress meeting in March 2002, for example, at least 20 delegates held Internet forums with Chinese citizens on topics concerning the governance of the country. Xinhua news, the state news agency, teamed up with China Mobile to offer the public the chance to send their suggestions, desires, and wishes to the country's lawmakers through short message services. Nor have farmers in remote villages been left behind:

they were said to have become rich through using the Internet to market their fruit and livestock.

Although the Chinese media continue to herald informatization and digitalization and embrace the information society utopia with almost the same enthusiasm as it once did the communist utopia, the actual political and social dimensions of the Chinese "information revolution" are much darker. Moreover, the situation is much more complicated than ongoing Western news flashes about the Chinese state's jailing of yet another Internet activist or the promulgation of yet another draconian piece of Internet regulation. In this chapter, I argue that China's information revolution in the age of marketization and globalization is profoundly antidemocratic in its very making. This state-controlled and market-driven revolution, I will argue, is inspired by a deep-rooted technocratic rationality and driven primarily by the convergent interests of domestic bureaucratic and international corporate capital, along with the consumption priorities of China's urban middle classes. Although this "revolution" has empowered a super-wired elite, it has been premised upon the exclusion of the majority of the population from meaningful political participation in shaping the direction of the country's reform process, and is intrinsically connected to the deepening economic inequality and pervasive social injustice facing millions across China. The resulting explosive social tensions, rather than the continued aggregation of television sets, mobile phones, and Internet accounts, are likely to shape the course of Chinese history in the 21st century. I begin by outlining the political economy of the Chinese "information revolution" and then move on to discuss the social communication patterns that this revolution has engendered. I conclude this chapter with a discussion of the political and social implications of this process.

INFORMATIZATION AS THE MOTHER OF ALL MODERNIZATIONS: ALL-OUT MOBILIZATION, ALL-OUT CONTROL

Lost in both the popular and scholarly literature's emphasis on the Chinese state's relentless efforts to maintain control over information is a single important fact: it is the Chinese state itself that has been the chief instigator of this "great leap forward" into the information age. This analogy to the "great leap forward" is not invoked here lightly. Just like the first "great leap forward," in which Mao aimed for China to catch up with the West through indigenous forms of industrialization, the current leadership aims to catch up with the West by "leapfrogging" into the digital age. It is worthwhile recalling that China's economic reforms began with the leadership's embrace of the "four modernizations": agriculture, industry, national defense, and science and technology. However, because the post-Mao technocratic elite's pursuit of modernization via the acquisition of advanced Western technologies and deeper integration into global capitalism was undertaken just as the global market system itself was reconstituting its operations around transnational networks, the Chinese leadership soon realized the critical importance of a network infrastructure for China's modernization program and elevated "informatization" into the mother of all modernizations. Mesmerized by "information age" rhetoric from the West, top leaders embraced the view that, as former Party General Secretary Jiang Zemin declared, "None of the four modernizations would be possible without informatization" (Y. Zhao and Schiller, 2001). Informatization, then, became the highest developmental priority of the Chinese state. The strategy of "using informatization to carry forward industrialization, taking advantage of late development, and achieving leapfrogged development in the society's productive force," was written into the Chinese state's Tenth Five-Year-Plan (2001-2005), announced in 2001. In another unprecedented move in 2001, the Chinese state become the first—and so far only—state to officially establish an "Informatization Index," with 20 statistical indicators that include: household penetration rates for computers, television sets, and Internet accounts; number of broadcast hours per 1,000 population; amount of bandwidth per capita; length of long distance trunk lines; number of satellite ground stations; volume of e-commerce; number of college graduates per 100 population; percentage of investment in R&D; rate of contribution to growth of GDP by the IT sector; and so forth. The sixteenth Party Congress in November 2002 further entrenched this information technology focus by positing IT application as the "logical choice" for accelerated industrialization and modernization. As Jiang Zemin stated in his report to the Party Congress, "It is . . . necessary to persist in using IT to propel industrialization," consequently, "[w]e must give priority to the development of information industry and apply IT in all areas of economic and social development" (Jiang, 2002).

The Chinese state, precisely because of its authoritarian nature, has been able to achieve the optimal mobilization of organizational and financial resources to carry out a top-down informatization drive. At the policy level, the past two decades have witnessed the accelerated integration and the political escalation of policymaking in the information sector. The first supra-ministry body, the Leading Group for the Revitalization of the Electronic Industries, was established in 1982. Its scope, as indicated by its name, was limited to the electronic manufacturing sector. In 1993, the State Council established the National Joint Conference on the Informatization of the National Economy, an ad hoc policymaking body consisting of the heads of more than 20 relevant government ministries and large state enterprises in the electronics and telecommunication industries. The single objective of this supra-ministry body was to promote and coordinate the state's informatization efforts in the overall economy, with a special focus on reform in the telecommunications service sector and the development of information systems in both the economy and in the state's macro-economic management structures. The formation of this group marked the official beginning of the Chinese state's orchestrated effort to promote the informatization of the national economy. In 1996, this body took a more solid institutional form and evolved into the State Council Leadership Group on Informatization. By then, overall economic and societal informatization and the development of an information economy, or knowledge economy, had become the all-encompassing state objective, and the state's informatization drive had taken an organized and planned form. Plans for informatization were drafted, and government offices for promoting informatization were established at both national and local levels. Broadcasting and cable, which had traditionally been foregrounded for its ideological and cultural significance, was for the first time being recognized for its network functions and emphasized as part of the national information infrastructure. In 1998, in a major government overhaul and at a time when other industry-based government ministries were dismantled, the government established a super ministry, the Ministry of Information Industries (MII), to promote, coordinate, and regulate the development of China's information sector. However the MII, with a strong power base in the old Ministry of Post and Telecommunications, quickly proved to be inadequate and ineffectual in macro-managing an increasingly converged information sector in the context of China's WTO membership and accelerated integration with the global market system. Consequently, in December 2001, the Chinese leadership created the State Leadership Group on Informatization. Premier Zhu Rongji, and now his successor, Wen Jiabao, assumed the leadership of this supra-ministry policymaking body. Other members include the heads of relevant state commissions, ministries, party departments, and government agencies responsible for the print and broadcasting media, as well as state security apparatuses. In effect, this created a separate cabinet above the State Council, a de facto "information cabinet," to ensure the highest and broadest possible state stewardship in the unfolding informatization drive. The objective is two-fold: "to further strengthen leadership over the promotion of our country's informatization build up and over the maintenance of the state's information security" (He, 2001). The Chinese state is trying to have the "cake" of information revolution and eat it too.

In tandem with ongoing bureaucratic reorganization and coordination around information technologies, the Chinese state, through a series of administrative and financial policies, has for the last 25 years pursued a high-investment and high-accumulation policy in the information industries. The result has been a network build-up unprecedented in the history of world communications. Various government ministries, in an attempt to claim a stake in the informatization drive, competed against each other in network build-up efforts. Following Deng's dictum that "development is an irrefutable argument," these ministries realized that their bureaucratic powers are inextricably linked to the length of fiber-optical trunks that each respectively manage to install. Metropolis and municipalities, meanwhile, are competing to establish info-ports and claim the status of China's most advanced informational city. Although competition for the right to wire China has been fierce, and bloody battles for control of China's information superhighway have literally been fought out in China's neighborhoods (see especially the conflicts between some local telecommunications and broadcasting authorities over the construction of cable networks [Y. Zhao, 2000a]), state-regulated bureaucratic competition created a powerful dynamic for network expansion (Lovelock, 1999).

State mobilization has expanded from network construction to network applications in the past decade. Beginning in 1993, the Chinese state launched a series of network and information systems projects in the Chinese economy and government administration. These included the various "golden projects," where the term "golden" connotes a special importance and state backing, and "project" (*gongcheng*) connotes technocratic and social engineering. There were at least 20 of these projects by the end of the 1990s (Mueller and Tan, 1996). They included the "Golden Bridge Project," a nationwide data network that aims to provide an information infrastructure for macro-economic management by the state; the Golden Card Project for debt cards; the Golden Gate Project for customs; the Golden Tax Project, a special-purpose network introduced by the State Administration of Taxation that aims to control and eliminate tax evasion by computerizing the collection process; the Golden Enterprise Project, focusing on China's then 12,000 large- and medium-sized state-owned enterprises; and the Golden Shield Project in the area of public security. With the popularity of the Internet, the Chinese state quickly expanded its informatization drive to cyberspace. Thus, 1999 was declared the year for "government on the net," with the aim of establishing Web sites by governments at various levels. "Enterprise on the Net" and "Family on the Net" projects have been announced in subsequent years.

Although there is no question that the latest telecommunication devices and information systems have created a highly dynamic state-dominated economic sector amid a massive retreat of the state sector in general, the social benefits of these projects are far from clear. If one of the purposes of the implementation of information and computer technologies was to monitor transactions, increase transparency, and combat corruption, then the continued plunder of state assets by government officials and state enterprise managers, and the exposure of cases of massive smuggling and fraud in the country's major ports are telling evidence that information technologies are of limited use in this regard. Similarly, continuing problems with the reliability of data demonstrate that information systems cannot solve problems of human activity. As Ure notes, a reliance on technology to solve problems of human activity and motivation is naïve unless accompanied by a process of transparency and accountability (Ure, 2001). The "government on the net" or "e-government" project is particularly ironic in the context of the state's ongoing repression and refusal to permit any meaningful public participation in the political process through the establishment of basic democratic institutions such as independent trade unions and farmers associations. And, in the context of massive corruption and a bureaucratic culture in which officials spend billions on meetings and dining, the objective of promoting the paperless office as a way to cut government costs sounds, at best, ridiculous. Still, each of these state-engineered efforts at constructing a networked economy and society means shopping sprees for information hardware and software and the direction of resources—mostly public resources—toward the information industries. With the further entrenchment of informatization as a state policy and the state's policy of deficit spending, investment in the information industries is positioned to accelerate.

MARKET-DRIVEN DEVELOPMENT: WINNERS AND LOSERS OF THE CHINESE "INFORMATION REVOLUTION"

Contrary to arguments about the inherently subversive power of the market, the inherent social biases of the market are ensuring differentiated access to information, something that has always been pursued as a political goal by the Chinese state. The massive build-up in the Chinese communication industries is occurring at a time when the Chinese state is progressively liberalizing the Chinese economy and promoting market forces. With the deepening of market reforms and the state's embrace of the "information revolution," the information sector is no longer seen as a technological and ideological infrastructure to be subsidized by the state. Information is recognized as a commodity, and the information industries have been reorganized according to market logic and themselves turned into platforms of state capitalism. Market logic, or in the official language an "insistence on market orientation," is listed as the most important consideration in a set of guiding principles announced at the inaugural meeting of the state's "information cabinet" in December 2001 (J. He, 2001). Although the state's leading role in promoting informatization is presented as the second principle, there is no reference to any concept of public service. This is a very significant development; although there has been an acceleration in market-oriented development both in theory and practice, this is the first time that the Chinese state has publicly set market orientation as the most important principle for informatization.

At the same time, because of the political nature of the information sector, the Chinese state, prior to the WTO accession in 2001, restricted investment from both domestic and foreign private capital in the core areas of the information industries. This left government departments and their affiliated businesses as the titans of the Chinese information revolution. These government departments and their affiliated communication operators, in turn, become the "most spoiled households" in China's "socialist market economy." On the one hand, they were given preferential policies to pursue limitless expansion; on the other hand, these operations are unaccountable to the public. Under a localized and decentralized financial rewarding system, executives and employees in the state's monopolized information industries were part of the group that became rich first. Meanwhile, corruption—from journalists receiving bribes from sources to Party media bosses plundering the riches accumulated by their business operations—becomes rampant. This is epitomized by corruption cases involving a top entertainment executive at China Central Television and the top management of the Guangzhou Daily Press Group, the Party's flagship press conglomerate. Although Mao once famously said that a revolution is not a dinner party, China's reform-era "information revolution" had become an extravagant dinner party for the Party's privileged bureaucrats and workers.

The urban middle class at large, the favored customers of an increasingly market-driven communication system, have received a disproportionate slice of the pie in China's information revolution. As part of the state's liberalization and marketization strategy, the 1990s witnessed a series of major reforms in the media and telecommunications sectors that aimed to implement market logic in state-owned enterprises in the communication industries. Such reforms extended from the liberalization of value added telecommunication service in 1993 to the corporatization and partial privatization of the state's telecommunication operations. In the area of telecommunication service, market-oriented reforms lead to the vertical and geographical break-ups of China Telecom, the dominant telecommunication carrier, and the creation of new telecom operators—China Unicom, China Mobile, China Netcom and others—for purposes of promoting market competition and global integration.[1] Increased market competition and intensified profit orientation in the communications industries in turn played a crucial role in shaping the social orientation of communication services provision.

To be sure, the traditional statist objective of network expansion, not business efficiency, continues to play an important role in shaping the development of China's information infrastructure. In both broadcasting and telecommunications, for example, the "wiring the villages" projects have been instrumental in expanding network coverage. Population coverage for radio and television, for example, had reached 92.47% and 93.65%, respectively, by 2001. In telecommunications, although the state's strategic policy to direct investment toward urban and coastal areas has led to much faster growth in these areas than in the interior and rural areas, the old Ministry of Post and Telecommunication, and later the MII, continued to set general network expansion as a priority, despite the disfavor of market-oriented telecommunication strategists. Like the country's broadcasting authorities, the MPT/MII announced an ambitious objective of "wiring every village" by 2000 in its Ninth Five Year Plan (1995-2000). Although the MII was way behind its target, there is no question that the gains in network expansion have been substantial. Indeed, in some places, telecommunication authorities and local governments, eager to drive up their informatization indicators, have consistently managed to oversell telephone subscriptions. In some provinces, "telephone counties" and "telephone villages" were prematurely established, and some farmers, after having been lured into installing a telephone line at attractive rates, found that it is not only not of much use, but also a financial burden.

Still, it is important to underscore the social bias of China's network build-up. In the telecommunications sector, the explosive growth of the mobile phone market and the business trajectory of China Unicom are illustrative of this bias. China Unicom was formed in 1994 as a result of bureaucratic rivalry—a means by which government ministries other than the then Ministry of Post and Telecommunications, which had monopolized telecommunication services, secured entry into the lucrative telecommunication service market. Not surprisingly, China Unicom's initial point of entry was in the highly profitable area of mobile phone service. China Unicom brought competition to the mobile phone industry and played an instrumental role in the spectacular growth of the Chinese mobile phone market. Between 1995 and 2000, the annual average growth rate for fixed line telephones was 29%, compared to 88% for mobile phones (Li, 2002). By the first half of 2003, China Mobile and China Unicom's combined revenue from mobile phone had accounted for 46.2% of overall telecommunication services revenue of 219.97 billion Yuan in China, by far the largest revenue stream in all telecommunication services (PRC Ministry of Information Industry [MII], 2003).

It is useful to provide some social contextualization for China's present status as the world's number one phone market in terms of the number of subscribers, with 312,443 million fixed line and 334,824 million mobile phone subscribers respectively by the end of September 2004 (MII, 2005). Although both fixed line telephone and mobile phone are defined as basic telephone services, a mobile phone is typically the second or third phone in a super-wired affluent urban household. Thus, although the Chinese state officials and the media celebrated a telephone penetration rate of close to 50% by the end of 2004 (Zhang and Wang, 2005), the national average actually concealed the concentration of telephone access in a strata of super-wired families. The explosive growth of mobile phones is as much a symbol of the achievements of China's economic reforms as a statement about the magic rise of China's "middle class" as the champion consumers of the nation.

Telecommunication service prices are still disproportionately high in China. An average user in urban China spent 10% of his or her monthly income on telephone fees in the early 2000s, perhaps the highest among all countries in the world. In economically prosperous Shenzhen, the average monthly mobile phone bill was 323.5 Yuan at the end of 2001, compared with an average monthly income of 3,240 Yuan in the city (D. Zhang, 2001), and the state's 250 Yuan monthly handout for laid off workers. Although the mobile phone continues to attract new customers, analysts predicted in early 2002 that the purchase of new handsets by existing mobile phone customers looking for an update would soon overshadow first-time buyers in China's mobile phone market (Hou, 2002). China Mobile and China Unicom are engaged in intense competition to furnish high-end customers with the most up-to-date mobile phone sets and services.

Not surprisingly, an increasingly market-driven Chinese mass media system has made mobile phones an obsessive topic, to the point of celebrating the power of mobile phone consumers as something almost divine. In fact, the media sector itself, especially the print media, is also strongly oriented toward affluent urban consumers. On the one hand, television, which has always been more mass propaganda– and mass entertainment–oriented, expanded rapidly to every corner of the country, thus enfranchising the Chinese mass consumers, whose aggregated numbers compensate for the lack of individual purchasing power. The story of the development of the print media in the past two decades, however, is more about redistribution and fragmentation than about expansion. Between 1980 and 2000, the number of newspapers increased more than tenfold, but the overall size of the Chinese press, measured by issues of newspapers published, only doubled. The Chinese state's control of newspaper licences, prices, and the shift from state subsidies to business subsidy through advertisement have been mainly responsible for this development. In particular, state-controlled commercialization has been responsible for the rise of urban mass-appeal media outlets, the proliferation of specialized business and consumer publications, and the marginalization of media outlets and content catering to social groups that are the majority in numbers, but marginal in political and economic power—namely Chinese workers and farmers (Y. Zhao, 2000b). Although there is considerable gain in the expansion and diversification of the print media, the history of 25 years of media reform can be seen primarily as a process of (re)-allocating discursive power in an increasingly stratified Chinese society. The proliferation of media outlets specializing in stock analysis and the availability of Chinese versions of Western consumer magazines such as the *Elle* and the *Esquire* (selling for 20 Yuan per issue in 2003, the equivalent of one day's salary for an unskilled worker), is as at least as much a concrete development of the class orientation of the print media system as it is about the unfolding of some abstract principle of media liberalization. As is often noted in Chinese media studies literature, the Party maintains tight political control, but is loose in nonpolitical business and lifestyle areas. For this reason, the Chinese media system is often seen as bifurcated and schizophrenic (Z. He, 2000; Lee, 2000; Y. Zhang, 2000). However, it can be argued that the persistence of control in the political domain and liberalization in the economic and lifestyle spheres are two sides of the same coin in a communication system that serves the interests of the political and economic elite.

Alongside privileged state bureaucrats, communication sector workers, and affluent urban consumers, transnational communications firms—especially telecommunications equipment makers—have been the other principal winners in the Chinese information revolution. Foreign telecommunication equipment makers have become the primary suppliers for China's network build-up under the Chinese state's leapfrog policy. With the burst of the digital bubble in the West, the continuing expansion of the Chinese market has assumed critical importance for transnational IT corporations. In 2001, profits from the China market made up for losses in other markets for Motorola, which is the largest foreign investor in China. Similarly, China Unicom's massive investment in its CDMA network was good news not only for Qualcomm, which lobbied tirelessly to ensure the Chinese state's decision to purchase its technology for China Unicom, but was also crucial for Lucent Technologies, which won one-fourth of China Unicom's contracts for its CDMA network buildup, at a time when Lucent's overall business plunged. "Lucent's salvation lies in China, China's business hinges on CDMA," Lucent executives reportedly said. Thanks to China Unicom, Lucent's revenue in the Chinese market increased by 150% in 2001, with a projected 50% increase for 2002 (J. Zhao, 2002). In this context, the Chinese state's intensified network build-up drive meshes perfectly with the business interests of transnational communication corporations. As Dan Schiller (2005) has observed, China's reintegration with the global market system and the rapid expansion of communication and information technologies are two poles of market growth for transnational capitalism.

In the telecommunication services sector, back-door foreign capital—foreign capital invested in China illegally through joint ventures set up between a Chinese firm and a pre-established joint venture between a Chinese and a foreign firm—played a crucial role in China Unicom's initial funding—US$1.4 billion, or 70% of its total funding (G. Chang, 2001). Most of this back-door foreign capital came from the world's largest telecom operators, which were eager to get a foot into the Chinese market. With China's WTO entry, foreign capital has secured its right to participate in the Chinese telecommunications service market—up to 49% ownership in basic services and 50% in value-added services. And if China Unicom, indirectly backed by back-door foreign capital, spurred the growth of the high-end mobile phone market, foreign capital from the front door in the post–WTO China has initiated a process of further "cream-skimming" in the Chinese telecommunication services market; the profitable "cream" this time being large business users, especially transnational corporate users. In March 2002, the first foreign-invested telecommunications firm, Shanghai Symphony Telecommunications, went into business in Shanghai's Pudong District, a special administrative zone where the headquarters of many transnational corporations are located. This company, a joint venture between AT&T, Shanghai Telecom, and the Information Investment Corp. of the Shanghai government, started to provide broadband Internet Protocol value-added services to transnational corporations operating out of Pudong (T. Chang, 2002). Competition for high-end consumers and major business users is the new rule of the game in the Chinese telecommunications market.

The tendency of foreign capital to move rapidly into lucrative elite markets is also evident in the Chinese mass media sector (Y. Zhao, 2003a). In the print media, areas of operation for foreign capital have included publications in technical information for China's rising information elite, as well as consumer and lifestyle magazines for the affluent urban consumers. Given the state's informatization agenda, it is perhaps not surprising that the most significant foreign investor in the Chinese press has been the Boston-based information technology publisher, the International Data Group (IDG). As the *South China Morning Post* put it, the joint venture between IDG and the Chinese government is "arguably one of the quietest foreign investor success stories in the mainland" (Mitchell, 2000). Despite the Chinese state's longstanding ban on foreign capital in the Chinese media sector, *China Computerworld*, the Chinese version of the IDG's worldwide weekly publication, launched in 1980, was in fact the first Sino-U.S. joint venture business, and its ideological role in the making of China's "information revolution" cannot be overestimated. Today, *China Computerworld* is the most voluminous computer newspaper in the world. It sells 10,000 pages of advertisements a year and is among China's highest advertisement-revenue-earning newspapers, rivaling mass circulation papers in Beijing, Guangzhou, and Shanghai. With *China Computerworld* as the flagship, IDG's publishing empire in China encompasses highly influential and popular titles such as *Network World, PC World China, CEO & CIO World,* and *Home PC World.* More recently, many other foreign publishers have managed to publish Chinese editions of their lifestyle and consumer magazines: *Cosmopolitan, Esquire, Popular Mechanics, Motor China, Electronics Products China, Elle, Madame Figaro . . .* the list goes on.

In the broadcasting sector, Phoenix TV, a Hong Kong-based satellite television joint venture between Rupert Murdoch's Star TV, Liu Changle (an overseas Chinese entrepreneur well connected to the Chinese state), and the Bank of China, claimed to reach 44.98 million households in China, or 15.9% of total Chinese television households in the late 1990s. As with the aforementioned foreign-invested joint venture publications, Phoenix TV is primarily oriented towards an elite audience in China. Although state regulations prohibited the reception of foreign satellite television by private households, the Chinese elite has never been constrained by such regulations. According to state regulations, Chinese hotels that rank three stars and above and luxurious apartment complexes catering to foreigners and affluent domestic customers are allowed to install satellite dishes to receive foreign satellite transmissions. In addition, major government departments, media, academic, and financial institutions are allowed to install their own satellite receiving dishes. As most of these institutions have internal cable television systems that wire their offices and living quarters, residents in these exclusive neighbourhoods receive Phoenix TV legally. Compared with the average Chinese television audience, the Phoenix viewers are characterized by "three highs and one low"—high official rank, high income, high education level, and low age. Indeed, as the *Wall Street Journal* wrote, "Phoenix's stylish shows are a must-see for a growing middle class fed on, and fed up with, a diet of state-run television" (L. Chang, 1999).

The collective will and the political power of transnational capital were brought to bear through the demands of major Western states during negotiations for China's WTO concession agreements. U.S.–based transnational communications capital, in particular, mounted a major lobbying effort in the U.S.–China WTO negotiations. Although China did not open up direct foreign investment in its core media operations, transnational media secured significant market entry gains, including increased film import quotas, reduced tariffs on Chinese audiovisual imports, the opening up of China's consumer markets for audiovisual products to foreign distributors, and permission for foreign ownership in movie theaters and Internet operations (Y. Zhao and Schiller, 2001). In late 2001, Time/Warner and News Corporation achieved major breakthroughs in their long pursuit of the Chinese satellite broadcasting market by securing cable-landing rights for their respective satellite television operations in the affluent Pearl River Delta. As transnational communications corporations have conglomerated and converged, so have their investments in the Chinese market. News Corporation, for example, has a stake in China Netcom, one of China's four basic telecommunications carriers, and AOL/Time Warner has allied itself with Chinese computer maker Legend in an attempt to enter the Chinese Internet service market.

IMPLICATIONS OF A MARKET–DRIVEN INFORMATIZATION POLICY

The cumulative social impact of a market-driven informatization policy under China's authoritarian political system has been profound. First, this policy has enabled the Chinese state, and through it, a small elite, to dominate communications. Second, this policy has ensured the formation of a pattern of social communication that encourages horizontal linkages among a super-wired elite and discourages communication between social movements and oppositional forces. Third, this policy has led to an atrophy of any notion of public service in the country's information infrastructure and thus undermined the formation of a democratic polity. Finally, and viewed in a broader context, China's information revolution has contributed to extreme forms of uneven social development and profound social injustice.

Elite Orientation of Communications: Access and Beyond

Elite control of communications in today's China needs to be understood in two dimensions: uneven access to means of communication, and hegemonic control of social signification. On the one hand, as mentioned previously, access to television is no longer a problem for a majority of the population. The creation of a mass audience fits with both state and market objectives. On the other hand, limited expansion has meant that access to the print media, arguably a more important means of political communication, remains elite-oriented; there were still fewer than 50 copies of daily newspapers per 1,000 people by the end of 2004 (Wu, 2005). Even the most successful "mass appeal papers" reach only a small percentage of the urban population. Regional disparity in newspaper consumption is staggering: the average adult in Shanghai spent 139.12 Yuan on newspapers in 1999, compared with 10.48 Yuan in Nanchang, the capital city of the largely rural Jiangxi Province (China Publishing Science Research Institute, 1999). Although the number of Internet users has grown exponentially over the past few years, from 620,000 at the end of October 1997 to 94 million by the end of 2004

(MII, 2005), Internet users still constitute only 8% of the population. The country's communication resources are disproportionately concentrated in the hands of a minority in the metropolis.[2] In Beijing, for example, 2001 saw television set ownership reach 150 per 100 families, computer ownership 30 per 100 families, and fixed line and mobile phone penetration rate both exceeded 50%. Beijing's Internet users accounted for 10% of the China's total (30.8 million) by the end of 2001 (L. Wang, 2001).

The problem of uneven access to the means of communication, however, pales in comparison with an elitist orientation of media content. Media coverage of China's WTO entry is illustrative (Y. Zhao, 2003b). To be sure, membership in the WTO has been one of the most sustained news stories in the Chinese media, and thousands of news stories and books have been published on the topic. But it is how the story is covered that matters most. The media played no role in the public sphere other than to serve as cheerleader for China's WTO membership. In the coverage of the crucial U.S.–China WTO deal signed in November 1999, for example, the national press, although applauding the signing of the deal, provided virtually no content of the actual agreement, perhaps because any detailed coverage of the specific Chinese concessions could raise uncomfortable questions about economic and social costs of the WTO membership. Indeed, the elite's monopoly over information regarding the details of the WTO deal with the United States was so tight that even the Party's media bosses and state bureaucrats complained of being shut out and left in the dark. Party control and the middle-class bias of the media ensure that government officials, spokespeople of transnational corporations, pro-market economists, stock owners, and urban consumers dominated the discourse on the impact of WTO membership on China. There was virtually no discussion of the potential negative impact of the WTO membership for China's workers and farmers, who have largely disappeared in the Chinese press as discursive objects, much less as speaking subjects. In a typical hegemonic fashion, elite interest is represented as national interest, and Chinese workers and farmers were called upon to endure "short-term" pains for the "long-term" interest of the nation. The "ordinary folks" that newspapers speak on behalf of, meanwhile, turn out to be stockholders and affluent urban consumers.

Exclusionary Patterns of Social Communication

State control and economic marginalization have helped facilitate horizontal communication among the elites, but not among disenfranchised social groups or between different social classes. It is worthwhile in this context to revisit the patterns of social communication in 1989 and see how these patterns have changed after more than a decade of informatization and digitalization. Urban/rural, and intellectual/worker chasms were already rather acute in 1989, when social stratification was not as pronounced as it was by the late 1990s. As China scholar Mark Selden observes in the context of the 1989 pro-democracy uprising, city dwellers, notably students and intellectuals, established intra- and interurban networks, were well tuned in to international trends, ideas, and symbols, and even forged communications and economic links with overseas supporters, but they failed to establish, indeed never seriously contemplated establishing, organic ties with the countryside (Selden, 1993). Indeed, China's 800 million farmers were virtually absent from the Chinese political stage in 1989 and the urban middle class made no attempt to communicate with them. Even among the urban population, divisions between the educated elite and the urban industrial working class were acute. Whereas students and liberal reformers, both during and after Tiananmen, demanded liberal democracy and accelerated integration with global capitalism—two processes assumed to be interconnected—China's industrial workers had different concerns and agendas (Y. Zhao and Schiller, 2001). One recalls that during the height of the student demonstrations, students used their bodies to form a human chain to fend off workers and other protesting social groups from entering their ranks and thus affecting the purity of their movement. Rather than fighting for popular democracy, they wanted to negotiate a better deal with the Party elite. Not surprisingly, China's symbolic workers in the mass media, being themselves part of the urban and educated elite, displayed a considerable degree of opposition to the Party state, as demonstrated by their struggles for press freedom. Their ideological mobilization and their sympathetic coverage of the student demonstrations played an important role in the movement (D. Zhao, 2001).

Now, after more than a decade of state-engineered push toward integration with informational capitalism, the social chasms that were already highly visible in 1989 have further widened. Students and the educated strata now have their Internet connections, but most of them are careful with their newly gained privilege of being able to express themselves more freely in cyberspace. The intellectual elite, in particular, have gone through a process of upwardly mobile social stratification, and the majority are well integrated into the information economy (Q. He, 2000). Today, few have the intention, nor the practical possibility, to take advantage of the country's rapidly expanding communications network to give a voice to the voiceless. To be sure, there are exceptions. For example, in 2003, the combined effort of a rural family, urban middle-class social networks, and a few exceptionally brave journalists at the *Nanfang Metropolis News*, a market-oriented newspaper, led to the exposure of the death of Sun Zhigang, a young university graduate who was beaten to death while in the custody of policy authorities in Guangzhou. Subsequent media and Internet-based elite intellectual and popular mobilization led the government to abolish its draconian detention system that allowed the urban police to detain, fine, and often torture rural migrants simply because they failed to carry an identification card, a job permit, or a temporary residence permit. Nevertheless, most Chinese media outlets, operating under the double pressures of state censorship and profit maximization, are busy reporting on the rich and powerful and popularizing the rhetoric of information society, leaving their super-wired urban consumers uninformed about the conditions experienced by China's under classes of farmers, migrant laborers, and laid off workers.

Horizontal communication between social movements and vertical communication between organic intellectuals and social movements has been rendered almost impossible by the repression of a powerful state and as a result of a deep social division. A similarly stratified access to communication is paralleled in the realm of international communication. On the one hand, the middle-class elite is well connected to their transnational middle-class counterparts through international long-distance calls, the Internet, and special interests niche-market satellite channels and magazines. They are well furnished with the latest stock market quotes, the latest entertainment reports from Hollywood, and the latest fashion trends from Paris. On the other hand, China's protesting workers and farmers have been cut off from parallel social struggles in the rest of the world. In exile, political activists such as Han Dongfang and Wei Jingsheng are effectively isolated from domestic social movements. Though there have been noble attempts by overseas political activists to send information through the Internet to receivers inside China, the reality is that those who have access to the Internet are not necessarily the ones with a material interest in acting on this critical information.

Atrophy of the Public Information System

Historically, the expansion of public communication networks in China has been the responsibility of the Party state, and driven by its imperative of spreading propaganda to every corner of the country. It is in this spirit, for example, that loudspeakers and newspaper-reading boards were installed in both rural and urban public settings. Even today, the state's propagandist imperative continues to serve as a rationale for network expansion both in broadcasting and telecommunication. Increasingly, however, the commercial imperative, which has assumed an instrumental role in network expansion in the past decade, manifests its social biases and threatens to create a highly stratified system of access to means of public communication. In the media field, cable television, which developed more or less as a low-cost public service out of the womb of state socialism, is taking on an increasingly commercial character as the industry is re-organized around market principles.

A major, profit-oriented redefinition of the operational principle of the country's television and cable networks is underway, with focus on the development of pay-TV platforms. Reversing the network expansion model, the new thinking champions the concept of "channel efficiency," defined by the amount of income per channel per subscriber. The following journalistic summary of major industrial, policy, and conceptual developments in the Chinese media industry in March 2002 is illustrative:

> Our country must gradually get rid of the notion of "television viewing for free," Xu Guangchun [Director of the State Administration for Radio, Film, and Television] said in the No 3 issue of *Television Research*. The whole country has 350 million television sets, with a pay-TV market of 15 billion Yuan. Yet CCTV only garnered a mere 380 million Yuan in subscription fees. An article by deputy editor-in-chief of CCTV Sun Yusheng in the same issue [of *Television Research*] noted that the further development of television depends on the end of the conventional model of singular dependence on advertising revenue (95% of domestic television stations' revenue derives from advertising). [We] must not only pick on the pockets of enterprises [for advertising revenue], but also on the pockets of audiences [for reception fees]. . . . (Sun and Liu, 2003)

In telecommunications, the objective of wiring every village by Year 2000 in the Ninth Five Year Plan (1996-2000) was abandoned and reset to a more modest goal of wiring 95% of all villages by the end of 2005 in the Tenth Five-Year Plan (2001-2005). Given that actual universal coverage (defined as telephone access for every administrative village) was 89.8% by the end of 2003 (Huang, 2005), the MII faced a daunting task. The original cross-subsidy structure has been destabilized through the vertical and geographical break-up of China Telecom, and new mechanisms of universal service provision have not yet been established. Increased domestic and international competition and falling profits mean that universal service is not an easy sell in China today. Even before the breakup of China Telecom, the Chinese business press was full of rhetoric about the lack of efficiency considerations in reckless network expansion and complaints about the business burden of valueless telephone users in the countryside—especially those who only receive calls. Even the MII has made an official acknowledgement that "telecom reform . . . has to some extent weakened the incentive of service providers to invest and pursue development in rural and remote areas" (Fen, 2003). In 2004, the MMI, in the context of the Hu Juntao leadership's newly articulated agenda of addressing the long-neglected problem of rural poverty, launched a highly politicized top-down administrative campaign to speed up the fulfillment of its Tenth Five-Year Plan universal service objective. Although the project was declared a success by the end of 2005, as I have demonstrated elsewhere, the continuing expansion of universal service and the development of any notion of public service telecommunications remains a formidable challenge in the post-WTO accession industrial and policy environment (Y. Zhao, in press).

Perhaps the most telling case here, however, is the atrophy in a more basic public information infrastructure: China's public library system. After a brief spurt of growth in the early and mid-1980s, the country's public library system slid into a period of steep and devastating decline that persists until the present. Ongoing government underinvestment has been compounded by the accelerated commercialization of book publishing. Recent state investment in the public library system has been minimal, and increases in state allocation for book purchases by the country's public libraries have been miniscule. In the mid-1990s, the average amount available for book purchases at the country's more than 2,500 county- and above-level public libraries was only 41,000 Yuan. Of this, provincial level libraries averaged 960,000 Yuan, regional level libraries averaged 65,000 Yuan, and county-level libraries, accounting for 85.3% of China's total libraries, received an average 8,000 Yuan. 1212 libraries—nearly half of the national total—had a book budget of less than 5000 Yuan (M. Yang and Li, 1995).

At the same time, market prices for newspapers, periodicals, and books have increased dramatically and far outpaced any limited increases in public subsidies to libraries. Of China's more than 2,500 medium and large size public libraries, 351 did not purchase a single book in 1999 due to the lack of public funding. Despite an average annual increase of 5 million Yuan in book purchases by the country's public libraries, the number of books purchased is declining by about 1 million per year (Z. Yang, 2001). Many public libraries, therefore, fall into a vicious circle: reduced number of books decreases the number of readers, and with fewer readers, there is even less support for funding. Nanjing Public Library, for example, boasted an annual record of more than 600,000 readers between 1983 and 1988. By 1994, the number of readers had dropped to merely 90,000 (C. Wang, 1995). Public libraries in the economically backward areas have been the most devastated. The case of Shi Zhuishan Library in Ningxia Autonomous Region, held up as a model library during the 1980s, is illustrative. Between 1991 and 1996, the number of newspaper subscriptions held by the library dropped from 127 to 60, and periodical holdings from more than 900 titles down to 424. By 1997, the number of newspapers had been reduced to only 17, periodicals to a mere 44 (Xi, 1996).

However, it is Guangdong, one of the country's most economically prosperous provinces, that provides perhaps the best evidence of the lack of any state commitment to a public information infrastructure. Despite the province's economic prosperity, investment in Guangdong's public library system was proportionately well below the national average. In 2001, there was one public library for every 600,000 people in this province, compared to the national average of one library for every 440,000. Although national per capita spending on public library book purchases was 0.077 Yuan, the number for Guangdong was 0.068 Yuan. Four of the province's prefectural level cities, five of its counties, and 22 municipalities had no public library. At least ten county libraries had no special fund for books, and the special economic zones of Shantou and Zhuhai had only shell libraries with no books at all (Lin, Lin, Huang, and Liu, 2002). Clearly, China's drive for economic development does not automatically translate into increased investment in essential public information infrastructure.

Instead of providing funding for local libraries and promoting the use of public libraries, the state is mobilizing resources in pursuit of the massive China Digital Library Project, a centralized, state-sponsored project aimed at providing online access to library resources and increasing the volume of Chinese-language information on the Internet. The initiative was reportedly spearheaded through the nationalistic ambition of a cultural bureaucrat. While surfing the Internet one day in the summer of 1998, Xu Wenbo, then a deputy minister of culture, discovered with regret that almost all Web sites were in English. Determined to change the situation, Xu conceptualized the idea of a digital library project in China. In August 1998, Xu formed a feasibility study group, and by December of that year had submitted the project to the State Council for endorsement ("National Library", 2000). After more than a year of preparation, the Ministry of Culture, together with 21 government ministries and commissions, formed the China Digital Library consortium in April 2000 to coordinate the development of the project. With high-level endorsement and the mobilization of the country's leading experts in fields ranging from computer software development to copyright, the project was quickly recognized as a key component of the national digital information infrastructure, and its construction has proceeded at an astonishing rate. Within a year of the consortium's establishment, China Digital Library began to offer service to individual readers. By June 2001, the Library boasted 60 million online book pages, or the equivalent of 200,000 book volumes. The collection is said to expand at the rate of 200,000 pages per day ("China Digital Library", 2001). "Those who frown at the thought of facing howling winds and freezing temperatures on their way to the library will now be able to peruse books from the National Library of China's collection while sipping hot coffee in front of their personal computers," wrote the *China Daily* in a report ("National Library", 2000). In practice however, the utopian vision of high technology access to information embodied in discourse around the Digital Library project provides an all too convenient rationale for continued underfunding of public libraries; in essence, the message is "who needs local public libraries in this digital age?" Although the public service principle was underscored in the project's founding documents, a market orientation is evident. A corporation, the China Digital Library Corporation, is the organizational form of this project. User fees are the norm, with a one-year membership costing 100 Yuan. Corporate leaders are already calculating the project's market potentials and its contribution to the digital economy.

Uneven Social Development

The issue, however, is not just unequal access to public information. A membership card for the China Digital Library is not a top priority for the majority of the Chinese population, but the Chinese state's overriding prioritization of high technology in its development and social policies has had a direct impact on all of China's citizens. Indeed, the entire informatization initiative is elite controlled and special-interest driven. Unwittingly, Liu Ji, Vice-President of the Chinese Academy of Social Sciences, perhaps gave the most lucid articulation of the profoundly elitist nature of the Chinese "information revolution." As a top adviser to former President Jiang Zemin and arguably China's most powerful establishment intellectual, Liu saw the relationship between "socialist democracy" and the "information superhighway" in the following way:

> The goal of political system reform is clearly to build socialist, democratic politics. . . . But how do we reach this goal? We have to start from China's reality. For example, we now have about 200 million illiterates. . . . Do you give such a person the right to vote? Of course you should. But is his vote worth as much as the vote of a PhD who has returned from America? Or of a university professor? Or of a government official? They are not equal. Someone who is illiterate does not have the ability to choose. . . . If we gave everybody a vote, when their votes are of different value, then a lot of good resolutions put forward by intellectuals would never pass, because intellectuals are in a minority. . . . To build an information superhighway costs a lot of money. Intellectuals would immediately pass such a resolution unanimously. But the attitude of the 200 million illiterates would be: "What is an information superhighway? What has it got to do with me? My first demand is hurry up and give me food to eat. And then let me study at the primary-school level." As for the vote, he'd be likely to vote against the information superhighway, and want to solve poverty first. (Lawrence, 1998)

Liu used the term "intellectuals" liberally for "the educated elite" and he apparently confused universal suffrage with direct referenda on particular issues. Still, Liu's thinking is typical of the elite mentality and the social bias of the emerging digital economy in China. Moreover, Liu's remarks stand in stark contrast to those who believe in the magic of information-led development and the virtue of using the information superhighway to deliver the latest books and best classroom instructions in Beijing to remote villages. To invest in the information superhighway and to deliver basic education to the 200 million illiterates are different policy priorities. Massive build-up in telecommunications has been in sharp contrast with severe underinvestment in primary education and a steady decline of the state's education budget as percentage of GDP between 1991 and 1996. China's investment in public education as a proportion of GDP was consistently below the average of developing countries during the reform period—a mere 2.55% in 1998 (which was already an improvement over previous years), compared with 5% for Brazil, 4.9% for Malaysia, and 4.6% for Mexico. Moreover, higher education, which disproportionately serves the urban population (70% of the university student body are of urban origin, whereas 70% of the overall population are rural) accounts for a disproportionate share of the educational budget. The enfranchisement of a small minority of highly educated Chinese netizens has gone hand in hand with an increased dropout rate for school children in poor rural areas; in the Ningxia Autonomous Region, for example, 25% of students drop out after one year and less than 50% finish sixth grade (Rosenthal, 1999). Although the central state has the capacity to mobilize the entire society to launch its informatization drive, it has quite simply failed to take up responsibility for financing elementary education in the countryside.

Similarly, whereas the country's super-connected elite may be able to access government services online and participate in governance through the Internet, local governance is in a state of bankruptcy throughout the countryside, and for some rural residents access to a local government has become a luxury. If unpaid salaries to school teachers is no longer news in China, the latest news is that even local government officials are owed back salaries. Of the country's 31 administrative regions, 26 are afflicted with this problem ("Serious Problem," 2002). Although the central state can quickly mobilize resources to put a digital library into operation, it is apparently unwilling to provide centralized funding for basic services such as primary education in the rural areas and maintain the operation of local administrations at the township level—the closest level of government to tens of millions of Chinese farmers. With declining rural income and an expanding bureaucracy, rural government debts have ballooned in the past few years, leading to local officials' ruthless extraction of fees from farmers and the resultant growth of widespread rural unrest. Although the state is trying out a "tax-for fee" reform whereby farmers will pay a tax to provincial governments, which in turn will finance lower level rural administrations, the results of the reform have been mixed. Many local governments have ended up even poorer and less well equipped to provide essential services—in one

case reported in *The Economist*, local administrations were simply dismantled to save cost ("And There Is Another Country," 2001). But for rural residents, the retraction of the state is not necessarily a blessing. A government
farther from where they live means a government farther removed from
their daily concerns. As *The Economist* put it, "there's another country"
within China.

But this urban and rural divide is not the only problem. Urban poverty
has been on the rise as tens of millions of industrial workers are rendered
redundant in the new digital economy. About 10% of the urban population
live under the state's official poverty line, and urban poverty will only
increase with layoffs resulting from China's WTO accession. Although the
official unemployment rate was 4.2% for 2004 (Qi and Liu, 2005), some estimates put actual unemployment as high as 20%. Most important, however,
the same macro-economic policies that sustained high growth and high consumption in IT is the same process that further deprived the poor in both the
rural and urban areas. Massive investment in telecommunications not only
provided the infrastructure, but also the very platforms, that created an
export and foreign investment-dependent prosperity in the urban areas in
the coastal regions. Today, the dominant forces in Chinese society—state
officials, bureaucratic capital, and the urban middle class—are heavily
dependent on foreign investments and foreign trade for maintaining their
privileged positions within China's globally integrated political economy (Y.
Zhao, 2004). It is not a coincidence that while China-based IT industries
achieved the highest rate of growth in the economy and the Chinese digital
bubble created instant riches for some in the 1990s, the rate of growth in net
income for rural residents steadily declined from 9% to 2.1% between 1996
and 2000, with a net reduction in income from agriculture between 1998 and
2000 for the 77.5% of rural households whose main source of income is
from agriculture ("How to Solve," 2002).

PERILS OF A MARKET AUTHORITARIAN "INFORMATION REVOLUTION"

So far, political control and economic marginalization have enabled China's
elite to enjoy the cake of information revolution and eat it too. But how far
they can continue the feast remains an open question. Thanks partly to the
Chinese's state relentless informatization drive, the burst of the Chinese digital bubble is not as dramatic as that in the United States, and the Chinese
telecommunication sector has not experienced the same recession that has
afflicted the global telecommunications market in the past few years. But
there are signs that China's information-driven development has reached a

critical point. There are many manifestations. The problem of "hot installation and cold usage" has become a serious issue in telephone services. As the telecommunications network expands to include low-end users, revenue growth lags behind the increase in the number of users. Although the number of fixed line subscribers increased by 13.6% in 2001, and there was a slight increase in local fixed line fees, overall increase in the local network's revenue was only 10.8% (Liu, 2002). The same is the case in the more robust mobile phone market. The lukewarm reception to China's Unicom's CDMA network further testifies to the weak market situation. A similar pattern is emerging in Internet usage. While the growth rate for the number of Internet users was as high as 200% in the earlier years, growth dropped to about 83% between June 2001 and June 2002, and 41% between June 2002 and June 2003 (China Internet Network Information Centre, 2003). Moreover, the total online time logged by China's netizens in 2002 was 2% lower than it was in 2001 (Qing, 2002).

In the urban areas, telephone service has reached a point of near saturation—not because every household has a telephone, but because many families cannot afford a telephone. Growth rate for fixed line telephones in the major metropolitans of Shanghai and Beijing, for example, was only 3% in 2001. With the end of installation fees in July 2001, there has been an expansion of telephone subscribers in the countryside, but the addition of lower-end users is not necessarily good news from the point view of economic efficiency for telecommunications operators. New services, despite much hype, had not been a promising point of growth. Although state telecommunications and cable operators rolled out broadband networks at an unprecedented rate in the past few years, demands for broadband services have not been as robust as expected. In Shanghai, although the capacity of Shanghai Telecom's ADSL network potentially covered 4 million households, only 6000 households had wired up by late 2001—a utilization rate of 0.15% (Jing and Chen, 2001). In addition to overcapacity, uneven development between urban and rural areas has become a major problem. As the MII stated in an overview of the Chinese telecommunications service market in the first half of 2003: "Investment in rural telecommunications development decreases by the year, the number of new subscribers has declines by the year; while operational losses remain high" (MII, 2003).

Although China's "information revolution" has fattened some bureaucrats and created a strata of wealthy Internet entrepreneur "heroes," the capacity of this sector to create jobs is also beginning to decelerate. Major state telecommunications operators have begun to freeze their workforces, and some have even started to lay off workers as they strive to make themselves competitive in the international market. China Telecom announced the freeze of its workforce in 2000, and China Unicom reduced its workforce by 39% in 2001, with much of this accomplished through the transformation of permanent positions into contract positions (Shu, 2002). With the burst of the Chinese Internet bubble, many dot.com startups have disappeared—though buses carrying their ads are still running on the streets. Those that survived have laid off many workers, and the explosion in the number of Web sites since 2000 has not translated into jobs. For example, of the 238,249 Web sites established by 2001, more than 65% employed fewer than 3 people, and 31.6% have only one employee ("30% of Websites," 2001). In short, the growth of an information elite and middle class serving the information economy might not happen as quickly as the "great helmsmen" of the Chinese information revolution had initially hoped. Moreover, the digital economy has so far demonstrated very little capacity to enfranchise the rest of the Chinese population. Inhabitants of rural and industrial China, however, can no longer afford to wait for the benefits of the digital economy to trickle down. Under the pretext of national development and prosperity for all, these people are being asked to endure disproportionate sacrifices for an "information revolution" that has so far provided them no material or social benefits. Growing rural and industrial unrest suggests that China's workers and peasants may be reaching the limits of their tolerance.

Increasingly, the Chinese political elite is counting on the middle class to sustain its dominance. If the Party once championed the working class as a social force that would build a communist paradise, it is now relying on the middle class to sustain a consumer society. Whereas many in the West are celebrating the rising phoenix of the Chinese middle class as the agent of Chinese democracy, the Party is championing it as a force for social stability, thus essentially turning Communist ideology on its head. The Chinese press is also fascinated with the middle class (or "the middle strata," as this class is officially called) as a source of social stability: that is, a force in complicity with the Chinese ruling elite. According to a survey by the Chinese Academy of Social Sciences, this class accounts for 15% of the working population. China's chief WTO negotiator, Long Yongtu, meanwhile, boasted that within 10 years China's middle class will be 400 million to 500 million strong, making China's market much bigger than that of the United States. An official at the State Council Information Center estimated a middle-class consumer market of 200 million by 2005, and a CASS researcher argued that the middle class would remain closer to 100 million in five year's time ("China's Middle Class," 2002). Regardless of its size, there is no question that this "middle" class is still the "upper" class in China, and that the party state does seem to have its complicity.

Whereas the state focuses on furnishing the middle classes with the latest digital gear, and even improving communications and services provisions for this class through "e-government," those displaced and disenfranchised by the digital economy have stepped up their protests and intensified their struggles for economical survival and social justice. Previously localized worker protests have to some extent overcome their narrow isolation, although these struggles must overcome formidable communication blockages before one can realistically claim that working-class struggles are circulating nationally (Zhao and Duffy, forthcoming). Nonetheless, protests like those at the Daqing oil complex in March 2002 have grown both in scale and duration. In Daqing, once socialist China's most glorified oilfield, tens of thousands of laid-off workers, charging official deceit and betrayal, staged protracted protests between March and May 2002 (Eckholm, 2002). On some days as many as 50,000 workers took part. In the northeast industrial city of Liaoyang, 5,000 workers from six bankrupt factories in different industrial sectors overcame their sectoral isolation and staged a series of joint protests, apparently timed to coincide with the March 2002 session of China's National People's Congress. In addition to economic demands for unpaid wages and pensions, these workers have also put forward political demands, including calls for the investigation of corrupt officials suspected of embezzling funds, the sacking of the city legislature's Chairman, and dialogue with central and provincial political leaders ("Laid Off Chinese," 2002). By March 18, 2002, the Liaoyang protests had grown to include an estimated 30,000 participants from 20 different factories, and demands centred on the release of an arrested leader (Eckholm, 2002). In both Daqing and Liaoyang, workers have been able to sustain large-scale protests for weeks, despite vigorous state repression. There have also been reports of workers traveling to other urban centers to organize and coordinate protests. Meanwhile, the rapid spread of Falun Gong and its determined struggles to communicate its messages in the face of massive state repression (which have included successful hacking of state controlled satellite and cable networks) have demonstrated the cultural and ideological bankruptcy of the leadership's technocratic rationality and its top-down "information revolution." Clearly, increases in the information index as defined by technological standards do not necessarily translate into more communication between China's leadership and China's people. Nor, apparently, has it fostered a greater sense of community, or the widespread sense of a more meaningful social existence. Falun Gong's successful diffusion of a radically alternative symbolic universe amid a tightly controlled information system is also illustrative of the potentials for oppositional appropriation of information technologies—from audio and video tapes to emails—and the subversive power of these technologies, when they are connected with a social movement and integrated into effective organizational and interpersonal networks (Y. Zhao, 2003c).

Elite division, meanwhile, remains acute. For example, the Party's traditional leftist ideologists, who no longer have access to major state media outlets to articulate their critiques of the reform program for its revisionism and its betrayal of Chinese workers and farmers, have tried to disseminate their

views in the traditional forms of one thousand character essays and through
personal networks, and more recently through the Internet. As the Party's
closure of two marginal Marxist theoretical journals in the summer of 2001
testifies, the stakes are very high. Just as the battle for market share among
communication companies is intensifying, so too are elite and popular struggles for control of China's communication networks, and more importantly, for different stakes in and competing visions of China's "information revolution." These struggles, as I have demonstrated elsewhere (Zhao, forthcoming), have already forced the Hu Jintao leadership to start to undertake
the task of re-embedding the social in China's digital, or "information revolution." In the end, it may well turn out that the Chinese state, which came
to power through a social revolution in the first place, cannot have the
"cake" of "information revolution" and eat it too.

NOTES

1. The first break-up, announced in February 1999, involved the divestment of
    China's Telecom's mobile phone, satellite, and paging services, and the formation
    of a new China Telecom, China Mobile, and China Satellite, responsible for fixed
    line, mobile, and satellite communications respectively, and a strengthened China
    Unicom, which absorbed the original China Telecom's paging business; the sec-
    ond restructuring, announced in November 2001, involved the break-up of
    China Telecom along geographic lines and the formation of two new telecom
    corporations: yet another new China Telecom, which operates fixed line and data
    businesses in 21 provinces and autonomous regions in South and West China,
    and a new China Netcom, which combines the original China Netcom, Jitong,
    and pre-break-up China Telecom's fixed line and other business in ten provinces
    and regions in North China.
2. A single rural and urban dichotomy, of course, does not tell the whole story
    about uneven access to communications in China. The rich in the rural area, in
    fact, have a very high rate of access to information technologies. Rich farmers in
    coastal provinces (defined by those with a twice than the normal per capita
    income, at 6583.11 Yuan in 2000, for example, own 12 computers, 96 fixed line
    telephones, and 47.1 mobile phones per 100 households. See, "Most Rich
    Farmers in Mainland China No Longer Work in Agriculture," *The World
    Journal*, March 30, 2002, p. A2.

REFERENCES

"And there is another country: China's rural governments are bust" (2001) *The Economist*, 15 December: 36.

Chang, Gordon (2001) *The Coming Collapse of China*. New York: Random House.

Chang, Leslie (1999) "A phoenix rises in China: Rupert Murdoch's satellite TV thrives, legalities notwithstanding." *Wall Street Journal*, 26 May: B4.

Chang, Tianle (2002) "AT&T in Phone Venture." *China Daily*, 23 March.

"China Digital Library aims to be biggest DCP" (2001) *People's Daily*, 19 April. Retrieved 15 December 2006, from http://english.peopledaily.com.cn/english/200104/19/eng20010419_68046.html

China Internet Network Information Center (2003) *12th Statistical Survey on the Internet Development in China* (July 2003). Retrieved 16 December 2006, from http://www.cnnic.net.cn/download/manual/en-reports/12.pdf

China Publishing Science Research Institute (1999) Report on a Sample Survey of National Readership and Purchasing Orientations. Beijing: Zhonggou chuban kexue yanjiu suo.

"China's middle class: To get rich is glorious (2002) *The Economist*, 19 January: 33-34.

Eckholm, Erick (2002) "Leaner factories, fewer workers bring more labor unrest to China." *The New York Times*, 19 March.

Fen, Xiaofang (2003) "Ministry of information industry: Must meet rural telecom needs to the greatest extent." *Xinhua*, 2 September. Retrieved October 27, 2003, from ID=4255.

He, Jingsong (2001) "Zhu Rongji chaired first meeting of state informatization leading group meeting." *Xinhua*, 27 December.

He, Qinglian (2000) "China's listing social structur.e." *New Left Review* 5: 69-99.

He, Zhou (2000) "Working with a dying ideology: Dissonance and its reduction in Chinese journalism." *Journalism Studies* 1(4): 599-616.

Hou, Mingjuan (2002) "Upgrades spur mobile mania." *China Daily*, 11 February.

"How to solve the premier's most headache problem?" (2002) *Nanfang Weekend*, 28 March.

Huang, Ling (2005) "Telecommunications ensuring 95% village installation rate." *Sichuan Daily*, 19 May. Retrieved 24 June 2005, from http://www.sc.xinhuanet.com/content/2005-05/19/content_4258890.htm

"IT industry profit dropped last year in the country" (2002) *Jinghua Times*, 8 January: 12.

Jiang, Zemin (2002) Report at the 16th Party Congress: Full text of Jiang Zemin's report at the 16th Party Congress. Retrieved 15 October 2003, from http://www.china.org.cn/English/features/49007.htm.

Jing, Ren, and Wu Chen (2001) "Look Back at 10 Hot Spots in IT in 2001." *China Business Times*, 29 December. Retrieved 29 December 2001, from http://www.people.com.cn.

"Laid off chinese protest en masse" (2002) *The Associated Press*, 18 March.

Lawrence, Susan (1998) "False dawn." *Far Eastern Economic Review*, 1 October: 26, 28.

Lee, Chin-Chuan (2000) "China's journalism: The emancipatory potential of social theory." *Journalism Studies* 1: 559-575.

Lei, Zhufang (2002) "Flat opening exposes three potential problems in telecommunication services sector." *Telecommunications News*, 8 March: 1.

Li, Xuenong (2002) "The restructured Chinese telecom industry urgently needs to improve its competitive capacity," *People's Daily*, 8 March. Retrieved 10 March 2002, from http://people.com.cn.

Lin, Yanping, Lin, Yaming, Huang, Qin, and Liu, Guoxian (2002) "NPC members proposed to bring development of public library under urban plan." *Nanfang Weekend*, 28 January.

Liu, Weiqing (2002) "Telecom operators try to find new points of growth in the mobile market." *Beijing Morning Post*, 6 March. Retrieved 27 March 2002 from http://www.people.com.cn.

Lovelock, Peter (1999) *The Evolution of China's National Information Infrastructure (NII) Initiative: A Policy-Making Analysis.* Unpublished doctoral dissertation, University of Hong Kong.

Ministry of Information Industry (MII) PRC (2003) "Upholding the two-hand-grasp policy, sustaining huge development." Retrieved 27 October 2003 from http://www.mii.gov.cn/Mii/homepage.nsf/documentview/2003-07-25-01-AC1.

Ministry of Information Industry (MII), PRC (2005) "The operation status of the telecommunication industry from January to December 2004," Retrieved 24 June 2005, from http://www.mii.gov.cn/mii/hyzw/tongji%5Ctongjifenxil-12.htm.

Mitchell, Tom (2000) "Mainland ties bind pioneer publisher." *South China Morning Post*, 12 July.

"Most rich farmers in mainland China no longer work in agriculture" (2002) *The World Journal* 30 March: A2.

Mueller, Milton and Tan, Zixiang (1996) *China in the Information Age: Telecommunications and the Dilemmas of Reform*, Washington, DC: The Centre for Strategic and International Studies.

"National library puts collection on the web" (2000) *The China Daily*, 30 November.

Qi, Zhongyi, and Liu Zheng (2005) "Still hard to determine whether the .1% drop in employment rate is a turning point." Retrieved 24 June 2005, from http://news.xinhuanet.com/zhengfu/2005-01/26/content_2508479.htm

Qing, Haibo (2002) "A NPPCC member takes the pulse for the telecom industry." *The Economy Daily*, 28 February. Retrieved 2 March 2002, from http://www.people.com.cn.

Rosenthal, Elisabeth (1999) "School a rare luxury for rural Chinese girls." *The New York Times*, 1 November: A1, A9.

Schiller, Dan (2005) "Poles of market growth? Open questions about China, information, and the world economy." *Global Media and Communication* 1(1): 79-103.

Selden, Mark (1993) *The Political Economy of Chinese Development.* Armonk, NY: M. E. Sharpe.

"Serious problem in overdue salary payments to rural officials due to low rural taxes revenue" (2002) *World Journal*, 3 March: A8.

Shu, Xing (2002) "A tale of three kingdoms by China Telecom, China Mobile and China Unicom: Hard to tell who wins." *Telecommunications News*, 27 March: 9.

Sun, Zhengyi and Liu, Tingting (2003) "A retrospect view of the Chinese media industry in 2002, Part II." *Eastday*, 1 August. Retrieved 15 February 2003, from http://xwjz.eastday.con/epublish/gb/paper159/200301/class015900002/hw.

"30% of websites have only one employee" (2001) *Oriental Times* (Vancouver), 21 September: B2.

Ure, John (2001) "China's information and (tele)communications technologies: Planning, the WTO, and market liberalization." Paper presented at The Political and Economic Reforms of Mainland China Symposium, The College of Social Sciences, National Taiwan University, 25-27 April. Retrieved 15 March 2003, from www.mfcinsight.come/article/020312/oped4.html.

Wang, Chaohui (1995) "Can't we moderate the rise in book prices a bit?" *The People's Daily*, 6 November: 9.

Wang, Luifang (2001) "Beijing's level of informatization reached that of middle-level developed countries, and is highest in the country." *Sina*, 25 December. Retrieved 25 February 2002 from http://www.sina.com.cn.

Wu, Changliang (2005) "Experts examine list of 100 largest circulation newspapers." Retrieved 24 June 2005, from http://medianet.qianlong.com/7692/2005/06/03/33@2661583.htm

Xi, Xiangjun (1996) "Public library in Shizuishan City in trouble." *The People's Daily*, 13, November: 9.

Yang, Mingfang, and Li, Xinyan (1995) "Explorations into the problem with public libraries I." *The People's Daily*, 18 February: 5.

Yang, Zhongyang (2001) "Who are the victims of high book prices?" *Xinhua*, 27 July.

Zhang, Dongchao (2001) "What practical benefits have telecom restructuring brought to the ordinary people?" *China Youth News*, 5 December. Retrieved 5 April 2002, from http://www.people.com.cn.

Zhang, Ying, and Baoping Wang (2005) "Targeting the needs of the information society: Outstanding achievements of our country's information industries in 2004." *People's Post and Telecommunications News*, 12 January. Retrieved 24 June 2005, from http://www.cnii.com.cn/20050104/ca276950.htm

Zhang, Yong (2000) "From masses to audience: Changing media ideologies and practices in reformed China." *Journalism Studies* 1(4): 617-635.

Zhao, Dingxin (2001) *The Power of Tiananmen: State-Society Relations and the 1989 Beijing Student Movement*. Chicago: University of Chicago Press.

Zhao, Jing (2002) "Why does China let transnational IT corporations so excited?" *Economic Daily*, 28 March.

Zhao, Yuezhi (2000a) "Caught in the web: The public interest and the battle for control of china's information superhighway." *Info* 2(1): 41-66.

Zhao, Yuezhi (2000b) "From commercialization to conglomeration: Transformation of the Chinese press within the orbit of party state." *Journal of Communication* 50(2): 3-26.

Zhao, Yuezhi (2002) "The state, the market, and media control in China. In Pradip N. Thomas and Zaharom Nain (Eds.), *Who Owns the Media: Global Trends and Local Resistance* (pp. 179-212). Penang: Southbound Press & New York: Zed Books,

Zhao, Yuezhi (2003a) "Transnational capital, the state, and China's communication industries in a fractured society." *Javnost/The Public 10*(4): 53-74.

Zhao, Yuezhi (2003b) "Enter the world: Neo-liberal globalization, the dream for a strong nation, and chinese press discourse on the WTO." In Chin-Chuan Lee (Ed.), *Chinese Media, Global Contexts* (pp. 32-56). London & New York: RoutledgeCurzon.

Zhao, Yuezhi (2003c) "Falun Gong, identity, and the struggle over meaning inside and outside China." In Nick Couldry and James Curran (Eds.), *Contesting Media Power: Alternative Media in a Networked Society* (pp. 209-224). Lanham: Rowman & Littlefield.

Zhao, Yuezhi (2004) "The media matrix: China's integration into global capitalism." In Leo Pantich & Colin Leys (Eds.), *Socialist Register 2005: Empire Reloaded* (pp. 197-217), London: Merlin Press.

Zhao, Yuezhi (forthcoming) "After mobile phones, what? Re-embedding the social in China's 'digital revolution'." *International Journal of Communication* 1(1), http://ijoc.org

Zhao, Yuezhi (in press) "'Universal service' and China's telecommunications miracle: Discourses, practices, and post-WTO challenges. *Info* 9(/3)

Zhao, Yuezhi and Robert Duffy (forthcoming) "Short-circuited: Communication and labor struggles in China." In Catherine McKercher and Vincent Mosco (Eds.), *Knowledge Workers in the Information Age,* Lanham, MD: Lexington Books.

Zhao, Yuezhi and Schiller, Dan (2001) "Dances with wolves: China's integration into digital capitalism." *Info* 3(2): 137-152.

SECTION FOUR

RESISTANCES

Rebuilding The Commons

CHAPTER TEN

THE GLOBALIZATION OF RESISTANCE TO CAPITALIST COMMUNICATION

Sasha Costanza–Chock

The first years of the new millennium saw the continuous and seemingly unstoppable onslaught of capitalist globalization, greater consolidation of the cultural industries in the hands of ever fewer multinational conglomerates, and a blanket of information warfare, perpetrated by those conglomerates in conjunction with the Bush administration, intended to mask the horror of that administration's repeated, criminal, unilateral deployment of deadly military force. Yet these same years also saw extraordinary growth in the size, sophistication, and coordination of various progressive tendencies that aim to block further commodification of, and seize control over, communication and cultural production. These tendencies are globalizing in several senses: first, there is the rapid, self-organized, worldwide explosion of freely distributed audiovisual materials and software, which implicitly or explicitly undermines the so-called "intellectual property rights" regime; second, there are growing links between mass movements that resist the enclosure of the knowledge commons; third, workers and unions in the knowledge, culture, and communications industries are adopting a more progressive internationalist stance; fourth, reformist organizations that aim to change state or corporate communications practice and policy are forging stronger international ties; fifth, local autonomous media production is increasingly linked in global networks.[1] Across the spectrum, there is an increase in awareness of and actions targeting the trade regimes and supranational institutions that affect communication systems, and a corresponding recognition that alternatives must be developed, supported, and extended.

Of course, these tendencies do not advance unopposed. Capital does everything in its power to promote splits between them and to crush the growth of real alternatives to profit-driven communication systems. The key to the successful advance of alternatives will be for reformers and autonomists to sidestep the "in/out" dichotomy and to develop solidarity between those who seek to hold state or corporate media accountable, produce structural policy changes, and create fully autonomous communication. The battle for structural change must take place both in the arena of naked confrontation with capital, such as the so-called "free trade" deals (the WTO/GATS/TRIPS), and in the convoluted venues where capital now seeks to mask and legitimate the logic of the market by providing symbolic seats at the table, such as the World Summit on the Information Society (WSIS).

In this chapter I provide a brief theoretical orientation, then illustrate each of these tendencies with examples, and conclude by considering the serious threats to the globalization of movements for control of communication posed both by organized capital and by internal tensions between reformist and autonomist camps. Despite these threats, I argue that there are clear signs of the growth of a transnational movement around popular control of communication, and that this movement must be nurtured as a key element in the struggle to establish alternatives to neoliberal adjustment, imperialist war, and other manifestations of capitalist globalization.

BACKGROUND

Media, communications, and the entire cultural sector are now more highly concentrated in the hands of a few powerful multinational conglomerates than at any time in human history. Never has the sector been so profitable; never has it represented a greater proportion of capitalist accumulation; never has it extended so far into every corner of life. For progressives who hope for greater democratization of communications, lobbying in the halls of power appears to be less effective with each passing moment. Structural solutions to the extreme power held by corporate communications conglomerates over representation, public discourse, and the political process are hamstrung at the starting gate by the corporate media lobby: in the

United States, these companies spend millions each year wining and dining Congress and the Federal Communications Commission in order to assure an ever more favorable regulatory climate (Williams and Jindrich, 2004). Capital is consolidating control over communications at every level: production, distribution, regulatory environment, access to globalized markets through removal of "barriers" such as public broadcasting, screen quotas, and monopoly limits, and the commodification of previously personal or collective forms of knowledge, information, and communication in the form of so-called "Intellectual Property Rights" (IPRs). The only coherent response is the development of a movement that combines concrete demands for reappropriation of the public resources that enable communication (the public domain, the electromagnetic spectrum, the geosynchronous satellite orbits) with the active construction of radical communication networks and practices.

This is not a pipe dream. In every facet of communication that has been penetrated by capital, or caught in the straightjacket of neoliberal policies adopted by local elites or imposed from above, we find the reflection of myriad bottom-up resistances and concrete existing alternatives. This is true for the production and distribution of cultural goods and services via a range of alternative and autonomous spaces, sites, and networks, as well as for the hacking, altering, and reconfiguration of hardware, software, infrastructure, and sociotechnical practices. It is also true in terms of mass resistance, both organized in social movements and replicated widely in everyday practices, to the IPR regime, the commodification of previously common public knowledge, and the growth of the market for personal information. It is also true for those international governance institutions that bear on communications, which face increasing pressure to implement transparency and democratic reforms, and for U.S. designs to consolidate control over cultural industries by extending the "free trade" regime to audiovisual services, a process that currently faces the largest coordinated opposition since the New World Information and Communication Order debates of the 1980s.

The year 2003 alone saw the continued breakneck expansion of autonomous media systems, including the spread of the Independent Media Center network to more than 130 local nodes in over 60 countries. In the United States, 2003 was the year of a massive popular outcry against the Federal Communication Commission's relaxation of ownership caps and cross-ownership rules, which mobilized groups across the political spectrum to decry corporate media consolidation and transformed a seemingly arcane policy battle into one of the most important issues in Washington. Although this particular battle was a defensive action to maintain minimal antimonopoly limits within a regulatory status quo already favoring the corporate sector, it has without a doubt strengthened local and national advocacy networks and organizations. Also in 2003, the office of the United States Trade Representative (USTR) was thwarted not once but twice in its efforts to bring "audiovisual services" fully into the General Agreement on Trade in Services (GATS) regime, first at the World Trade Organization (WTO) Ministerial in Cancun and then at the Free Trade Area of the Americas (FTAA) Ministerial in Miami (Costanza-Chock, 2003a; Khor, 2003; Neil, 2003). Widespread resistance to the inclusion of the cultural sector in "free trade" deals also received a powerful boost in 2005 when the Convention on Cultural Diversity (CCD), which potentially allows each country to maintain public funding, local content quotas, national ownership requirements, limits on consolidation and cross-ownership, and subsidies for cultural production against the mandates of GATS, received the near-unanimous approval of the UNESCO General Conference over the objections of the United States.

2003 saw what may have been the first and also the second street mobilizations against the Geneva headquarters of the World Intellectual Property Organization (WIPO). The first such mobilization was part of the opening salvo against the May meeting of the G8: 3,000 to 4,000 people marched from the WTO to the International Organization of Migration to WIPO, to link the demand for freedom of information to the demand for freedom of movement (Indymedia UK, 2003). The second such mobilization took place in December, when autonomous media activists and progressive NGOs stood together against the implicit endorsement of the existing IPR regime by the World Summit on the Information Society (geneva03, 2003).[2] This second action against WIPO took place in the context of a great deal of activity around the WSIS, which, although a problematic process that will be discussed in more detail below, did provide a focal point around which communication reformers and autonomists from around the world were able to strengthen their networks.

Infocapitalism Sets the Stage

These resistances have not erupted spontaneously. If infocapitalism requires the wider distribution of information and communication technologies (ICTs) and associated skills among certain groups of workers, then at the same time that those workers are trained to increase their productivity through the use of ICTs, they also become prepared for new forms of nonwaged activity—including innovative types of cultural production, active resistance to capital, and self-valorized information work. Marxian thinkers have long pointed out that infocapitalism produces technologies and sociotechnical skills that, though initially designed in the service of capital, can be and have been appropriated for resistance (Mosco, 1996; Dyer-Witheford, 1999).

This process of reappropriation is not new, and is of course not specific to information and communication technologies and skills, let alone to "new" ICTs. Yet it is possible to specify that infocapitalism, at the same time as it broadens the base of ICT-literate workers in order to staff the growing cultural, knowledge, information service, telework, and back-office industries, actively produces the conditions for a shift in the strategies, tools, and tactics of the resistance movements. As ICT skills become mainstreamed throughout the population, existing movements are able to take up these new tools and skills and add to their capabilities; simultaneously, the increased capitalist emphasis on immaterial, symbolic, and communicative labor reveals new pressure points for resistance and sets the stage for the emergence of movements focused explicitly on democratizing control of communication.

Inequality of Access

This process is deeply constrained by the radically unequal distribution of ICTs and sociotechnical skills both between and within nations. Although the development establishment, including national telecom policymakers and multilateral bodies including the G8 Dot Force, the New Partnership for African Development (NEPAD), the WSIS, and others frame this inequality in terms of a so-called "digital divide," the phrase is a thin scrim: ICT-access inequalities, for the most part, replicate other existing disparities (Noronha, 2004). The "digital divide" is the good old economic divide, which is deeply gendered, as well as constituted by massive inequality according to ethnicity, caste, age, and other vectors of oppression (Breathnach, 2002; Di Martino, 2001; Skinner, 1998; Wilson, 1998). Nevertheless, it would be a mistake to dismiss either the potential or actually existing significance of ICTs to social movements even among the most excluded populations. In fact, it is clear that the diffusion of ICTs has been significant not only for NGOs and professionalized advocacy organizations but also for many social movements. ICTs developed or even embedded in the service of capital have repeatedly been taken up, reconfigured, and redeployed by resistant forces.

ICT Use by Social Movements

The "new" ICTs are not so new, and neither is the process of their (re)appropriation by social movements. Almost from the earliest days of the fledgling Internet, activists of all stripes recognized its potential to amplify and strengthen their work. In the late 1980s, when ftp and e-mail were the primary capabilities of the nascent Net, already groups such as GreenNet,

PeaceNet, LaborNet, and WomensNet seized on these tools for rapid global information distribution and action alerts (Association for Progressive
Communication, 1997; Banks et. al., 2000; León, Burch and Tamanyo, 2001;
Surman and Reilly, 2003). The effective use of the Net by solidarity networks in support of the Zapatista uprising against NAFTA and neoliberalism should barely need repeating here since it has become a paradigmatic
tale of the use of the Net by social movements, narrated in depth and detail.
The attention of global civil society, generated in part by the wide distribution of Subcomandante Marcos' poetic communiques from the Lacondan
jungle, produced the necessary "boomerang effect:" international pressure
raised the stakes until the Mexican government was forced to abandon its
initial plan to repress the uprising with overwhelming military force (Keck
and Sikkink, 1998; Ronfeldt and Arquilla, 2001; Smith, 2001).

It is not my aim here to develop a case study of a particular social movement or organization's use of "new" communications technologies, or to
rehearse in more sweeping strokes the history of social movement use of the
internet or older communication technologies. Many well-written case
studies now proliferate rapidly across scholarly fields, including social
movement studies, political science, and communications, as well as within
literature and documentation produced by radical communicators and by
movement organizations themselves (Rodriguez, 2001; Halleck, 2002; Kidd,
2002).[3] There is a growing body of work that aims to further analyze, theo-
rize, categorize, or map movement use of new communication technologies;
for example, in terms of the relation to the shifting nature of capitalism
(Mosco, 1996; Dyer-Witheford, 1999), by distinguishing among various
forms of electronic contention (Costanza-Chock, 2003b), or in other ways.
There is a growing body of self-reflection by independent media movement
participants, as well as by external observers, drawing attention to persistent
problems, including north/south inequalities, gender dynamics, lack of connection to labor, need for race analysis, and so on (Halleck, 2003; Indymedia
Documentation Project, 2004; Kidd, 2003; Milberry, 2003). The Social
Science Research Council (SSRC) has recently created a set of "state of the
knowledge" reports examining the ways in which social movements are
using ICTs, and in which changing global governance of ICTs might impact
social movements' continued ability to utilize these technologies to organize for social change (O'Siochru with Costanza-Chock, 2003; Surman and
Reilly, 2003). In broader strokes, there have long been detailed descriptions
of social movement use of other communications technologies including
radio, video, and of course the printing press. In other words, the recent
interest in social movement use of the Internet reflects only the latest stage
in the broader cycle of the appropriation of communication technologies by
social movements.[4]

Given this burgeoning discussion of the adoption, deployment, and
innovation in the use of ICTs by social movements, my goal here is to use a

broad brush to distinguish between various types of movement activity aimed at restructuring communication control. This is crucial, because it is increasingly evident that neoliberal states and global media firms are aware of these tendencies and are already taking steps to exploit them, to drive in wedges, to split the emergent movements around communication control between "good" reformers who are willing to sit at the table and "bad" radicals who, their numbers diminished once the policy advocates have been siphoned off, professionalized, and given a (back)seat at the table, can be actively crushed or marginalized into near invisibility. As the movements around control of communication gain steam, it is important to develop our own analysis of their composition. The next section, the main body of this chapter, is an attempt to understand recent instances of resistance in this light.

GLOBALIZING RESISTANCE

At the risk of caricature or reductionism, and always recognizing that boundaries between categories are blurry and contingent, there are several broad tendencies in the globalization of the movements for control of communication. These include the following ideal-types: unorganized resistance, mass movements, communication/knowledge/cultural workers, media monitors, reformist policy organizations, and autonomists. Of course, it is easy to find examples of organizations or networks that crosscut each tendency. For example, the global networks of programmers, hackers, and users who develop and spread Free/Libre Open Source Software (F/LOSS) span all categories, from anarchists who deploy F/LOSS to support radical horizontal communication during street protests against meetings of international financial institutions, to policymakers who mandate the use of F/LOSS by government agencies and schools. In the final section of this chapter I emphasize that linkage, crossing, and solidarity within and between all tendencies is not only desirable but crucial to their mutual advance. Here, I will ground each category with concrete examples.

Unorganized Resistance: File Sharing

First, there is the rapid, unorganized, worldwide explosion of freely distributed audiovisual materials and software, which implicitly or explicitly undermines the so-called "intellectual property rights" regime.

It would be a mistake to look for resistance to capitalist communication only where it manifests in formally structured organizations or movements. Perhaps the most widespread opposition actually exists in the unorganized forms of increased popular distrust of both state and corporate media, as well as in the practical rejection of so-called "intellectual property rights" regimes.

File Sharing

Arguably, one of the largest threats to capitalist control of communication is the massive everyday undermining of the IPR regime by millions of Net users who upload, download, and otherwise freely share texts, music, audio-visual materials, and software. It is true that a majority of users may not necessarily engage in so-called "pirate" practices with the conscious purpose of undermining IPR, an artificial form of resource scarcity that serves as the linchpin of capitalist control of culture and knowledge (Martin, 1998). It is also true that technolibertarians who assert that "information wants to be free," quite aside from their mistaken assignment of agency to the dead product of living human creative processes, are naive to assume that illicit information flows cannot be regulated or controlled. To the contrary, vast technical, legal, and discursive resources have been deployed by both the corporate sector and the state in their attempts to reign in the hemorrhage of IPR through fiber optic arteries. These efforts have met with varying degrees of success, and there is every reason to believe that recuperation of profits can be reimposed through various layers of control, including technological, legal, and normative (Lessig, 1999).[5] Nevertheless, the seriousness of the threat to the cultural industries, and to the very principle of information scarcity they impose as a precondition to squeezing profits from their imposed monopolies on cultural material, can hardly be overstated.

One indication of the severity of the crisis for the information and cultural industries are the figures disseminated by those industries themselves. The International Intellectual Property Association (IIPA) estimates profits lost to intellectual "piracy" in 2002-2003 at 1.7 billion in the Americas, 5 billion in Asia, 3.1 billion in Europe, and 894 million in Africa and the Middle East. The IIPA country-by-country "piracy level" estimates for 2003 find, for example, that in the People's Republic of China, 95% of motion pictures, 90% of records and music, and 92% of business software were pirated product. In India, these figures were 60%, 40%, and 69%, respectively, and in the Russian Federation, they were 75%, 64%, and 93% (IIPA, 2004). Tellingly, all these figures are only for "hard" piracy, or production of material copies for sale; profits lost to the free distribution of material through filesharing are so vast that IIPA refuses to even publicly release estimates.

Domestically, the industry and the state have attempted triage in the form of lawsuits against individual filesharers, including now infamous lawsuits against senior citizens and Brianna LaHara, a 12-year-old girl living with her mother in New York City public housing (BBC, 2003). It remains to be seen whether this strategy will backfire on the industry; there are already signs of organized resistance to the crackdown (Werde, 2004). For example, groups such as downhillbattle.org have begun sophisticated campaigns to mobilize filesharers to take political action, sponsoring nationwide call-ins to block new, overbroad federal IP legislation (downhillbattle.org, 2004a). At the same time, alternatives to the existing IP regime that would make space for increased filesharing outside the profit motive are rapidly gaining ground and globalizing. For example, by 2004, Creative Commons licenses had been translated from the United States to Brazil, Finland, Germany, Japan, and the Netherlands, with additional translations underway for 15 more countries (Creative Commons, 2004).

The WIPO wrings its hands at the multibillion dollar "loss" in pirated intellectual property each year. Such figures make the imposition and enforcement of U.S.–style intellectual property law one of the most important planks in U.S. trade policy. However, grassroots resistance to the attempts by capital to impose global "harmonization" of intellectual property rights, especially through the World Trade Organization's Agreement on Trade Related Aspects of Intellectual Property Rights (TRIPS), has mounted steadily to the point where, in 2003, those attempts were temporarily blocked by the collapse of WTO and FTAA trade negotiations.[6] These victories did not proceed, of course, from disorganized filesharers, but from mass movements of the base.

Mass Movements: Globalized opposition to TRIPS

Second, there is significant deepening of the links between mass movements of the base that resist the enclosure of the knowledge commons.

Although it receives the lion's share of popular press in the North, music sharing is far from the only, or the most important, form of resistance to the imposition of IPR regimes. In the global South, strong resistance to IPR has been around for decades. This resistance has come from mass-based peasant and small farmer movements that battle against the privatization of seed genes by the agribusiness and biotech industries, AIDS activists who fight big Pharma for access to generic versions of patented drugs, and demands from Africa for a moratorium on all patents on life. Unlike music sharing, these life-and-death battles against IPR have long been politically organized. In addition, in many cases these movements have shared unlikely common cause with national elites who oppose the imposition of U.S.–style patent protections, which limit the possibilities for technology transfer essential to nationalist "development" aspirations.

Globalized Opposition to TRIPS

These movements of the base that have fought so fiercely against TRIPS, composed largely of poor peasants, farmers, and the landless, are often themselves engaged in the appropriation of ICTs for internal communication and for articulation with solidarity networks that span the globe. For example, the Brazilian MST (Landless Movement) has vigorously embraced F/LOSS and has constructed a nationwide communications infrastructure and training program through its system of free schools (Ortellado, 2003). ICTs have played a key role in linking poor people's movements against TRIPS, seed patents, biotech, and AIDS drug patents within transnational advocacy networks of NGOs and solidarity supporters in the North. These movements have gained such strength and global coordination that they have forced national elites to shift position in recent rounds of global trade talks, contributing greatly to the stalemates in WTO and FTAA negotiations in 2003 (Eleusa and Sean, 2003; Khor, 2003; Wallach, 2003).

One key to resistance to capitalist communication is the link between these forms of organized struggle against IPR, based in farmer, peasant, and other communities, and the unorganized waves of filesharing. This link has been made by some media activists and radical thinkers, and to some degree in the development of an alternative legal regime under GPL and Creative Commons licenses; however, it has not yet been widely popularized (but see Mute magazine, www.metamute.com). Instead, the overwhelming discussion around cultural production remains reformist, as evidenced by the constant talk of "balancing" IPRs with fair use, or the "rights of the creator" with the "rights of the user." There is also every possibility that music sharing, for example, will be recuperated in part via schemes such as Apple's iTunes, which attempts to capitalize on the cultural chic of filesharing. iTunes winks at piracy and attempts to convince people (as consumers) that the process of downloading is "resistant" or "edgy" in and of itself, while continuing to extract profit from false scarcity (see downhillbattle.org, 2004b). Against reformist and recuperative strategies by capital, we need to link mass unorganized rejection of IPR directly to the life-and-death struggles over food sovereignty and biomedicine waged by peasants, farmers, AIDS activists, and other people the world over.

Communication/Knowledge/
Cultural Workers: UNI–MEI

Third, workers and unions in the knowledge, culture, and communications industries are adopting a more progressive internationalist stance.

Although organized labor in all sectors faces severe pressure everywhere under neoliberalism, a few have been marked by increasingly visible organizing campaigns. In the late 1990s and early 2000s in the United States, this has been the case especially for service workers, for example, the highly visible Justice for Janitors campaign (Bacon, 1999). There has also arguably been increased organizing among knowledge workers, in the cultural industries, and among the "creative class." For example, there are mounting drives to unionize graduate students, call center workers, graphic designers, and software workers (Communications Workers of America, 2003; Mosher, 2004). Pressure on these workers to organize builds as communication/knowledge/cultural work, supposedly their "reward" for supporting the new international division of labor, in the form of higher pay, less stressful, more skilled, more creative jobs that replace outsourced industrial production and automated agricultural production, also becomes automated, segmented, deskilled, and outsourced from the "First World" to sites of cheaper labor. This trend is marked, for example, in the call center sector, increasingly outsourced to information sweatshops in "Free Trade Zones," to the informal economy on the margins of global cities, to prisons and Native American reservations in the United States, and to other kinds of information sweatshops (Breathnach, 2002; Costanza-Chock, 2003c; Gurumurthy, 2004; Skinner, 1998). There is mounting pressure for software workers to organize, as higher-skill information jobs flee to the lowest bidder both internationally—as in IBM's 2004 decision to shift several thousand programming jobs to India and China over the next year, and within countries, as in Indian giant Infosys' plan to shift jobs from Bangalore to lower-wage sites in Kerala and Tamil Nadu State (CNN/Money, 2004; World-Information, org, 2005). Of course, it is true that these developments are often met first by nationalist protectionism, and that organized labor has played on white collar workers' nationalism, xenophobia, and racism in shortsighted attempts to organize workers behind simplistic protectionist responses. It is an open question whether this approach can be overcome by more sophisticated strategies that seek not to "stop outsourcing," but to organize information workers across borders. Recent decisions by some of the largest communications and media labor organizations provide reason to hope that this is the case.

UNI MEI

Several of the resolutions passed by the 2003 general assembly of the Union Network International-Media and Entertainment Industries (UNI MEI) are quite radical and global in their focus, especially the decision to actively organize part-time, temporary, and outsourced or intermittent media workers, rather than fight to exclude them from the production process. UNI MEI also is taking the lead among creative workers by recognizing the importance of the trade regime as a primary site of power in the cultural sector and the potentially devastating impacts on workers in the cultural sector if audiovisual services are brought fully into the WTO/GATS. Accordingly, they passed a resolution supporting the Convention on Cultural Diversity, or CCD (UNI MEI, 2003). Although it may not be possible to make broad generalizations across the sector, it is clear that at least some networks of already organized creative workers are internationalizing their perspectives.

There are of course serious questions as to whether the majority of software workers, increasingly outsourced, will continue to accept the decimation of jobs or will begin to organize en masse. It is also true that deskilling produces multitiered infoworkers who don't necessarily identify with each other, as in the gulf between infosweat work, primarily performed by Third and Fourth World women, and professionalized infowork primarily performed by men (International Labor Organization, 2001). Infosweat work is often performed in environments least conducive to organizing, whereas within the "top" tiers of infowork, class consciousness is minimal and programmers are more likely to belong to professional organizations than to identify as workers. Still, some of these organizations take quite progressive stands. For example, Computer Professionals for Social Responsibility (CPSR) has recently played a key role in organizing to pressure for more nongovernmental, noncorporate participation in global communication governance bodies such as ICANN and the ITU. This takes us to the fourth tendency.

Reformers: Media Monitors, Policy Advocates, WSIS, CCD

Fourth, reformist initiatives that aim to change state or corporate communications practice or policy are forging stronger international ties.

The fourth globalizing tendency within the movement against capitalist communication is the forging of strong international ties among progressive media reform organizations and networks. By reformers, I include all those groups that attempt to hold corporate or state media accountable for isolated instances of bias, or to alter state, corporate, or multilateral communications policy primarily through legislation. Both media monitor organizations that observe, critique, and pressure media corporations into providing more "balanced" coverage and policy advocacy organizations that attempt to gain small concessions from capital by carving out government approval for a noncommercial niche, should be understood as reformist. This is not meant in a pejorative sense, but as an analytical category. What reformist groups share is that their demands address current power holders: the (neoliberal) state on the one hand and the corporate media on the other (though it may be more appropriate to describe these as two fingers of the same hand). In the context of this chapter, what is most relevant is that some reformists are also beginning to turn attention to global media governance institutions.

Media Monitors

Media monitors attempt primarily to pressure communication conglomerates into altering their coverage of particular events or issues. Actually, in the U.S. context, the most powerful monitor groups may be those aligned with the center and religious right, who organize mass complaints about levels of violence, sexual content, and threats to heteronormative, patriarchal "family values." Most recently, they organized pressure on the FCC to censure CBS for the broadcast of Janet Jackson's left breast, exposed in a "wardrobe malfunction" during the Superbowl halftime show (NOW with Bill Moyers, 2004a). Occasionally, progressive monitor organizations turn their attention from content to industry hiring practices, for example, to create pressure on media firms to employ more journalists of color, women, or LGBTQ people. Some of the most prominent left media monitors in the United States include Fairness and Accuracy in Reporting (FAIR), Columbia Journalism Review, and Mediachannel.org, just to name a few. The development of the MoveOn.org media corps mailing list, with tens of thousands of subscribers, links the monitor function with a version of citizen "activism" in which large numbers of e-mails and phone calls are occasionally able to influence coverage of a given event.

It may seem at first glance that monitor organizations are little inclined towards the development of global networks. However, this is not entirely the case. For example, some momentum has developed toward the elaboration of an international network of monitor organizations through the World Social Forum process, where Inter Press Service founder Roberto Savio has launched a "Media Watch" initiative that now, after three years, counts ten chapters in Europe, Africa, Latin America, and Asia (Miller, 2004). Media Watch functions according to the classic monitor model, with groups of volunteers observing media content, tallying evidence of biased coverage, and writing letters to corporate media editorial staff.

Policy Advocates

Policy advocates attempt to thwart particularly dangerous attempts at reregulation in the corporate interest, and in some cases introduce new legislation or amendments to existing legislation, by pressuring regulatory bodies and elected representatives. The globalization of policy advocacy operates in at least two ways: increased links between organizations focused on policy reform at the national level, and, at the same time, increased focus on reforming the institutions of global media governance. In the past two years, one focal point for these linked processes has been the World Summit on the Information Society (WSIS).

World Summit on the Information Society (WSIS)

The WSIS, convened as a UN summit under the auspices of the ITU, is intended to bring together governments, the private sector, and nongovernmental organizations to formulate a "common vision" regarding information and communication policy around the world. The summit was designed to take place in two phases: during the first phase, which culminated in Geneva in December of 2003, all participants were meant to create a common Declaration and Plan of Action. During the second phase, in Tunis in 2005, there was meant to be assessment and follow-up on commitments made during the first phase. After a two-year series of regional consultations during which it became clear that "civil society participation" was primarily a token designed to legitimate a process subordinate to the interests of neoliberalism, governments and the private sector succeeded in drafting a common Declaration and Action Plan, predictably watered down to the lowest common denominator and couched in the language of "Public Private Partnerships" to "bridge the Digital Divide."

By contrast, the Civil Society Plenary, a self-organized structure for participation created largely through the efforts of progressive NGOs that engaged with the WSIS process from the start, released their own Declaration, a strong consensus document that should serve as a touchstone in the development of a people-centered "information society." Concretely, WSIS phase I also agreed to set up a high-level committee to investigate the possibility of shifting responsibility for internet governance from the U.S.–based Internet Corporation for Assigned Names and Numbers (ICANN) to a UN body,[7] and another committee to evaluate a proposed Digital Solidarity Fund to subsidize internet infrastructure in the developing world. Most important in the context of the current discussion is not the outcome of the formal WSIS process but the emergence of strong NGO networks targeting global media governance processes and institutions, for example, the international CRIS (Communication Rights in the Information Society) campaign. It is possible that the CRIS campaign, and other networks created around WSIS, will move on to organize for increased transparency and accountability in various global media governance bodies including the ITU, ICANN (or its UN successor), and the WIPO, as well as against further incorporation of communication sectors into the "free trade" regime of the WTO, FTAA, and other regional and bilateral deals.

Convention on Cultural Diversity (CCD)

These same networks may also play a key role in the current battle to establish a new international Convention on Cultural Diversity (CCD). The

CCD, backed by an increasing number of states, would be a binding international legal instrument that would allow each country to exclude its cultural sector from forced liberalization or privatization under the WTO/GATS or other so-called "free trade" deals. The CCD has emerged as a potential buffer against the persistent attempts of the United States Trade Representative (USTR) to fully incorporate audiovisual services into GATS. It has also served as an organizing focus for a global advocacy network that includes cultural ministers of over 80 countries (the International Network on Cultural Policy), the NGO International Network for Cultural Diversity, and the Coalition for Cultural Diversity, with chapters in a dozen countries and growing (Coalitions for Cultural Diversity, 2004). These networks, and the CCD itself, are explicitly designed to counter the reduction of culture to the status of commodity and the further consolidation of cultural industries in the hands of ever fewer media conglomerates. They have drawn from the environmental movement and the concept of biodiversity to articulate a plan to insulate cultural production from the market, and to guard cultural and media policy, including local content quotas, public broadcasting, and limits on foreign ownership, from attack via the WTO/GATS regime (Bernier, 2003). In October 2003 a, proposal to draft the CCD was approved by the General Assembly of UNESCO, and in 2005 the treaty was adopted with overwhelming support despite attempts by the U.S. delegation to shut it down. It remains to be seen whether U.S. attempts to keep countries from signing the treaty will be successful; however, the treaty has already encouraged some countries to exempt their cultural sectors from trade policy (Coalition, 2004).

It is true that the CCD can be seen as, in large part, internecine warfare between different sectors of capital in the cultural industries: on the one side, the largest media behemoths based in the United States; on the other, second- or third-tier national cultural industries of France, Brazil, Canada, and others. The defense of small cultural producers, cultural workers, community media and horizontal communication is not the primary aim of the CCD. Thus, in Argentina, for example, we find the analysis put forward by the artist and cultural workers' collective LuchArte, allied with the workers' movement *Polo Obrero:*

> Not with "forums," "cultural industries," or "media protection laws" will we defend our popular culture, but rather by making ourselves conscious that the only ones who can defend it is those who produce it daily: artists and cultural workers. This is why we propose: "Place the cultural programs and budget under control of the workers and their organizations of struggle," and in this way "nationalize the mass media under workers' control." (LuchArte, 2002)

LuchArte's proposal takes us beyond the simplistic idea that neoliberalism merely erodes state intervention in the cultural industries. Rather, as in other sectors, those states with powerful cultural industries continue to subsidize them for export while simultaneously deploying the instruments of "free trade" and structural adjustment to eliminate cultural/media subsidies by less powerful states, in order to force open smaller cultural markets to unimpeded penetration by their own media services and products. Indeed, the USTR is so keen on liberalizing the cultural sector because cultural "goods and services" is now the second largest U.S. export sector (after aerospace). At the same time, U.S. media conglomerates continue to receive massive state subsidies in the form of free access to public airwaves, tax breaks, and countless other sleights-of-hand (McChesney and Schiller, 2002). This hypocrisy behind the free-trade rhetoric has not yet been laid bare in the cultural sector as it has, for example, in agriculture, where the Group of 20-plus developing countries, led by China, Brazil, and India, called the United States' bluff during the Cancun WTO ministerial.

The point here is that, as in other sectors, neoliberalism in the cultural sphere does not operate on "the state" in the interests of "capital" in the abstract. Rather, neoliberal tools are deployed by the most powerful (mostly) U.S.–based media conglomerates in order to most effectively pursue expanded markets, which includes sweeping aside state protection of national cultural industries. This process is opposed both by powerful sectors of capital, including national communication industries and lower-tier media firms, and by smaller cultural producers, cultural workers, and policy lobbyists. Still, it is possible to recognize these motivations behind the CCD but continue to support the convention on the grounds that the national space it would protect remains, for the most part, more accountable and amenable to pressure from below than the alternative: unchecked domination by U.S.–based conglomerates.

Autonomous Media Networks: Indymedia, Hurakán Cancun, F/LOSS

Fifth, local autonomous media production is increasingly linked in global networks.

The final tendency in the globalization of the battle over communication is perhaps the most vibrant: the increasing articulation of local autonomous media production within global networks. Here, radical alternatives are daily put into practice. It must be said that the terms autonomous, horizontal, independent, alternative, community, and citizen's media, as well as underground, samizdat, or guerrilla communication, might all apply to this category; each of these terms has its own meaning and its own history, and I do not have space to delve into each. For the purposes of this discussion, by "autonomous media" I embrace a loose inclusive definition of communication practices, groups, sites, and networks of production and distribution that are at base dependent on neither the market nor the state. Autonomous media are not supported by advertising and are not subsidized by corporations or political parties. They are the realm where "actually existing communication commons" are developed, put into practice, and extended.

There are so many beautiful autonomous communications projects, events, groups, and networks that there is no way to do justice to them here. In 2003 the bottom-up globalization of autonomous media manifested in a dizzying array of convergence spaces such as (just to name a few) Hurakán Cancun against the WTO ministerial and We Seize! against the WSIS; media workshops within Enero Autonomo and the World Social Forum; distributed projects such as the Free Radio Area of the Americas; the extension of global networks such as Indymedia; articulations between autonomist media and labor unions such as Jinbonet; the list could go on and on. Rather than fill the remaining pages with a list, I'll elaborate slightly on just a few of these.

Indymedia

One undeniable instance of the globalization of autonomist communication is the explosive growth of the Independent Media Center (IMC) network since its birth in 1999, drenched in tear gas and rubber bullets, in the streets of Seattle. I could not repeat the history and analysis of Indymedia that has been written by Dorothy Kidd, Dee Dee Halleck, Sheri Herndon, and many others, often members of IMC collectives themselves—in fact, the IMC network itself has developed a participatory documentation project that will prove a goldmine for future IMCistas and scholars of all kinds (see docs.indymedia.org). Rather than tell that history again, I point here to Indymedia as a living example of autonomous counterweight to corporate global communication control in several key facets: Indymedia was created and continues to develop through self-valorized labor; it is opposed to corporate control both in content and process; it operates according to the system of open publishing, which means that anyone with Net access can publish. Editorial control is exercised by collectives open to anyone with the time to participate and the amount of control is explicitly limited. Perhaps most important in the context of the current discussion, Indymedia provides a model for the articulation of local with global that demonstrates the possibility of communication practices grounded in local specificity, language, struggles, and issues of importance, at the same time amplified and projected across the world. This happens both on a technical level, through content syndication, and in the social networks that have emerged around the IMCs: Indymedia is not only a media organization but also provides a substrate for the circulation of struggles, as well as for the physical movement of radical communicators.

The IMC network has its problems, including hidden and not-so-hidden hierarchies of technical knowledge, gender, race, and class. Indymedia has been critiqued for its overwhelming emphasis on the internet, often to the exclusion of more accessible forms of communication. It was born and continues to be dominated by those located in the North and in cities. There are also the difficulties of balancing open publishing with "good" content (regardless of the measuring stick). All of these are the subject of often fierce debate within the IMC network itself. None of them eliminate the power of the IMC as an actually existing example of global, horizontal linkage between local autonomist communication.

Hurakán Cancún

The globalization of autonomous communication also operates in ways that mirror corporate globalization: in parallel and against the summits of the powerful, independent media convergence spaces form temporary autonomous zones where communication activists gather not only to respond to capital but share concrete alternatives, skills, software tools, social technologies, and collaborate on independent journalism and cultural production. In 2003, the Hurakán Cancún alternative media convergence marked a model for broadening and strengthening the radical communications networks, as an international space of encounter for trainings, workshops, and skillshares that then fed into comprehensive, in-depth coverage of the successful mass mobilization against the WTO Ministerial (see cancun.mediosindependientes.org). Hurakán Cancún was also a space where older community media networks such as the World Association of Community Radio (AMARC), media makers aligned with supposedly anti -capitalist but structurally hierarchical organizations such as the Italian Disobedienti (Global Project), and more "professionalized" alternative media organizations (such as Free Speech TV) physically worked side by side within a space predominantly defined by autonomist communicators from the Indymedia network (Ruiz and Coyer, 2003). In terms of the articulation between the local and the global, Hurakán Cancún was also noteworthy for the attention its organizers paid to information distribution via channels not accessible to those without access to internet. For example, a daily broadsheet called La Boca del Hurakán (The Mouth of the Hurricane), based on articles drawn from the open publishing space of the IMC Cancún newswire, was printed and distributed throughout the city. This radical communication apparatus stumbled across a new articulation with reappropriated transportation service sector labor, as taxi drivers requested multiple copies to hand out to their fares throughout the city.

Free/Libre Open Source Software (F/LOSS)

Indymedia and Hurakán Cancún, of course, would not be possible without the existence of what is actually another one of the most powerful examples of the global circulation of autonomous communication practice: the Free/Libre Open Source Software (F/LOSS) movement. The distributed, self-valorized labor of thousands of programmers has resulted in the most dynamic, flexible, scalable, software development process on Earth—all for free, in fact antiproprietary; a living refusal of the logic of capital. Not only that, this process has developed useful tools and systems that extend far beyond the persistent "demo mode" that arguably constrains many autonomous media projects. F/LOSS has crossed the threshold from geeky periphery to, in some cases, adoption by entire educational systems or state institutions. The widespread adoption of F/LOSS poses a material threat to the multibillion-dollar proprietary software industry, to the point that internal memos reveal worried hand-wringing in the depths of Microsoft's corporate offices (Weber, 2000). Not only that, but as a model of collective, self-valorized production, F/LOSS threatens informational capital in parallel to the way that autonomous worker-owned factories in Argentina threaten industrial capital, or collective land ownership by Movimento Sem Terra (MST) in Brazil threatens agricultural capital. Not surprisingly, the links are increasingly explicit: in 2003, MST strengthened the communications network it has created between its own autonomous schools, built with donated, retooled computers and F/LOSS software. At the World Social Forum in 2003, MST activists entered computer labs and replaced Microsoft operating systems with Linux, then remained in the space to train all those who needed help (Ortellado, 2003). What's more, the already internationalized F/LOSS movement is increasingly finding it necessary to take action offline as well as on. In the European Union, for example, there was organized opposition against the EU Copyright Directive, with programmers demonstrating in the streets from Brussels to Budapest (Varady, 2004).

Microsoft is fighting back, of course. In 2003, the software giant attempted to consolidate its hold in the developing world with "donations" of billions of dollars of software and hardware. Within international treaties, and even discussion venues such as WSIS, Microsoft lobbies hard to delete even *references* to F/LOSS (Barr, 2004). Microsoft is now actively attempting to use the language and institutions of the development establishment to establish hegemony in the South. For example, in 2003 Microsoft announced a new partnership with the United Nations (UNESCO, 2004); at the same time, the software giant put heavy pressure on WIPO to abandon a planned meeting to simply discuss the possible benefits of F/LOSS (Krim, 2003). Adoption of Microsoft OS and software in educational systems throughout the South is designed to ensure the future hegemony of the software behemoth, based on the difficulty of retraining and retooling entrenched software systems and skills. Yet already national and municipal governments in countries including Brazil, China, England, France, Germany, Israel, Japan, and South Korea have passed laws requiring the adoption of Open Source or F/LOSS software by publicly funded agencies (Schenker, 2003; Veloso et. al., 2003). Government adoption of F/LOSS ushers us into the discussion of articulations between the various tendencies in the movement for control of communication.

CONCLUSION: ARTICULATIONS

Intense pressure, both external and internal, generated by the state, the corporate sector, multilateral institutions, funders, and even from NGOs and movement organizations themselves, militates towards a split between the tendencies I have just described, especially between autonomists and reformists. When pressed, power, as always, responds by offering seats at the table to a select few who promise to behave. This process took place with the "at-large" membership of ICANN, over time whittled down to fewer and fewer seats with less and less input. It has taken place with the "opening" of the ITU to NGOs that can pay huge fees. It has taken place in the supposed "participatory" process of WSIS, where "civil society" has been allowed entrance, along with the private sector, to a forum where the dominant discourse holds that universal access to ICTs will magically appear through a process of privatization and "public-private partnerships." At the same time, capital offers repression if you get uppity: witness the brutal attacks on independent communicators during the G8 protests in Genoa; the attacks and arrests of "nonembedded" reporters in Miami during FTAA protests; the killing of "nonembedded" journalists in Iraq (Independent Media Center, 2001; International Federation of Journalists, 2003; Hogue and Reinsborough, 2003). However, it is not my purpose to paint a pessimistic picture or to indicate that the movement to wrest control of communication from capital is stillborn, hopelessly fragmented, always at cross-purposes, or subject to immediate defeat, dilution, appropriation or incorporation by capital. If we look more closely, we find numerous instances of cooperation, coalition building, and resource, tool, and skill sharing, producing concrete impacts at multiple levels. It is these types of articulation between tendencies that feed the growth of the movement.

For one, reformist policy initiatives to curb the worst excesses of corporate communication control can be and often are supported tactically by groups that ultimately aim to establish fully autonomous communication. For example, groups affiliated with Indymedia have provided extensive organizing support and coverage of the ongoing FCC battle. Indeed, autonomist groups often pioneer strategy to force policy changes; for example, the Prometheus Radio Project, originally founded by pirate radio enthusiasts, was instrumental in winning Low Power FM licenses across the United States (Huron and Tridish, 2003). Horizontal communication networks, or at least instances of horizontal communication, can be embedded within "vertical" structures such as organized labor, political parties, or membership-based liberal advocacy organizations: examples include Jinbonet, a radical media network linked tightly to the progressive arm of Korean organized labor; the incorporation of blogs into the Howard Dean campaign strategy; and the use of e-voting tools by MoveOn.org to devolve some decision making to its membership. In some instances, national governments support attempts by community media to link with global networks; this may be the case with the Chavez government's support of aporrea.org, a portal that nationally syndicates what is purportedly community-based news. It remains to be seen whether, in Venezuela, the devolution of government funds to local control via the Bolivarian Circles will lead to a new kind of relationship between horizontal communication and the state, or whether the state is simply interested in a strategy of reappropriation of horizontal communication. Indeed, the state stance towards horizontal communication can serve as an indicator of the "true" limits of social democratic party politics. The Lula administration in Brazil, swept to power on a populist platform that included promises to resist neoliberalism and neoliberalism and the machinations of the international financial organizations, has with one arm supported free software and fought across international venues including UNESCO, WIPO, and the FTAA against the imposition of U.S.-style copyright and patent law. Yet, with the other arm, the Lula administration has increased funding for enforcement of the so-called "Community Radio Law" passed by the previous administration. Under that law, close to 13,000 Brazilian community radio stations have now been shut down (Milan, 2004).

These examples point to the difficulty for movements of engaging with state media policy: on the one hand, movements must attempt to work with the state in order to check the rise of corporate conglomerate control, while at the same time they must fight the tendency of the state to centralize media control in its own hands. There is a need for new models and mechanisms of state-supported, or at least enabled, horizontal communication practices. For example, concretely: the state can take action to retake the commons of the electromagnetic spectrum, by forcing corporate users to pay rent that can then be devolved to support local communications, or by mandating swaths of "free spectrum" for use by the public. If there can be a system of public parks, highways, and waterways, there is no reason why we can't imagine systems of public spectrum. In a similar vein, we can easily imagine, and in fact we see in at least a few cases, the nation, state, or city putting resources into ensuring free ubiquitous high-speed wireless, as a public service akin to water or roads. The state can, and as we have seen some have begun to, mandate the adoption of Free/Libre Open Source Software by all state offices and agencies, including the education system.

There are many other ways in which movements can pressure states into rolling back the IPR regime, blocking the further enclosure of the knowledge commons, and laying a fertile field for the growth of public knowledge and culture. Movements must continue to encourage states to resist arm-twisting towards the criminalization of filesharing and of so-called "intellectual property theft" via trade instruments such as TRIPS (or "TRIPS plus," as in the FTAA). In fact some states are resisting the IPR regime, most notably Brazil and India over drug patents, but this lays the groundwork for broader resistance in the sphere of cultural production and communication. Increasing numbers of states are taking explicit stands in favor of F/LOSS. From the perspective of policymakers in India, Brazil, and elsewhere, this last may simply be a cost-saving measure, or even a snub to Washington; the result, however, is a greatly expanded field of opportunity for the spread and mainstreaming of the horizontal, participatory, global gift economy project that is F/LOSS. In terms of trade in cultural "products," as I have discussed, there is growing momentum behind the proposed Convention on Cultural Diversity to exempt cultural industries from the trade agreements entirely, allowing countries to protect and invest in local cultural production without threat of economic sanctions.

In another form of articulation between movement tendencies, "alternative" communication channels operating within the framework of the media market system can provide space for the wider dissemination of media content produced by autonomist networks. For example, Free Speech TV regularly runs Indymedia content on the Dish satellite network, and FSTV producers often share footage with Indymedia videographers. In the Miami mobilization against the FTAA, as in many other cases, the Indymedia video working group shared hours of footage with FSTV producers, and vice versa, while in Hurakán Cancún, FSTV and Indymedia worked out of the same physical space (Ruiz and Coyer, 2003). These collaborations do often run afoul; for example, when the FTAA IMC video working group provided footage to Bill Moyers' NOW for a segment on police brutality in Miami, NOW ultimately ran clips from the footage without crediting FTAA IMC, and to add insult to injury, the clip was used in a segment that replicated the classic "good peaceful protesters/bad anarchists" script (NOW with Bill Moyers, 2004b). This took place after debate raged within FTAA IMC over whether and under what terms footage could be shared, sold, or given to producers working on content to be aired on corporate TV networks, including PBS. Still, when such terms are carefully negotiated, autonomist networks are occasionally able to sustain and extend explicitly anticapitalist communication in practice. It is also clear that alternative media networks, including autonomists, are the only media that we can expect to provide good coverage of policy battles over control of communications.[8]

Links also exist between media monitors and policy reformers. Although all media monitor work to some degree provides fodder for those groups aiming at policy change, a few organizations have made the link between the two types of media reform explicit. This is the case with Calandria, a Peruvian NGO that combines media watch, policy advocacy, and development of participatory democracy. In 2003 Calandria gathered the requisite number of signatures (45,000) to introduce a referendum to reform the Peruvian media system. The initiative currently faces a stonewall by legislators but, significantly, was successful at denaturalizing the commercial media system and creating widespread awareness and action towards structural media reform (Alfaro, 2003).

A few networks, for example, the CRIS campaign and OURmedia/ NUESTR@Smedios internationally, the Medios Libres group in Mexico, and the N/Euro meeting in Europe, have recently emerged as spaces devoted explicitly to developing and strengthening links between the various tendencies. Other spaces for dialog between movements, for example, the World Social Forum and various regional Social Forums, have increasingly included communications in their analysis and groups focused on communication among their attendees.

Finally, as problematic as "civil society" inclusion in global governance mechanisms may be, the slight opening of global media governance institutions also provides unprecedented opportunities for the growth and strengthening of grassroots media networks. Funds and face-to-face meetings cluster around official "inclusion" processes, which may be quite important not for the stated reasons (inclusion is largely token), but as venues where groundwork is laid to strengthen the emergence of a global movement for people-centered communication on a scale similar to other transnational movements.

These developments all take place alongside growing awareness by independent media makers, media policy activists, and trade justice activists that the struggle over control of communications must link more tightly with other arms of the global justice movement. Corporate communication conglomerates, faced with a new wave of dissatisfaction and mobilization in national contexts, are shifting communications policymaking to even less democratic venues. Even modest national level policy victories will evaporate in the face of trade sanctions and other enforcement mechanisms unless the battle is joined at the institutions of global media governance. The various tendencies within the growing global movement for control of communications must guard against mounting pressures to succumb to "in/out" dichotomies and seek out articulations, links, and common areas of mobilization. These articulations are indeed taking place, while the movement builds strength in global, national, and local policymaking arenas and continues to construct radical alternative communication practices on the ground.

NOTES

1. Although I cannot do justice to any of them in this brief space, several other elements deserve mention. These include the backlash against surveillance of public and virtual space; culture jamming, including billboard defacement and detournement; and the emergence of cross-cutting coalitions like the Media Justice network, which introduce race and class analysis simultaneously into the largely liberal democratic framework of the media democracy movement and into the largely white anarchist framework of autonomist media networks.
2. Activists projected *Gimme the Mermaid*, a film made entirely from sampled Disney cartoons and the voices of record company lawyers, on the walls of the WIPO, while handing out Free/Libre Open Source Software (F/LOSS) CDs and press statements denouncing the IPR regime for its impacts on health, biodiversity, food sovereignty, cultural production, public knowledge, and creativity (geneva03, 2003).
3. For an interesting application of collaborative Web publishing in the service of documenting autonomous media activism, see the Indymedia documentation wiki pages at docs.indymedia.org.
4. For a brilliant, classic example, see Frantz Fanon's analysis of the appropriation of radio, originally spread throughout Algeria by the French colonial administration in order to coordinate state repression, by the Algerian liberation movement (Fanon, 1965).
5. The degree to which the Net can be conceived not only as infrastructure for free information flow but also as surveillance apparatus is also indicated, for example, by reports on state surveillance, corporate data-mining, and countermovement surveillance (for example see Costanza-Chock, 2004; Gandy, 2002; Lyon and Hier, 2004).
6. Of course, those negotiations collapsed primarily due to disagreements over agricultural subsidies in the wealthy countries. Also, although the collapse has meant a set back for IPR industries, they have continued to successfully lobby for bilateral trade negotiations to impose "TRIPS+" obligations on developing countries. See http://www.bilaterals.org for ongoing developments in bilateral trade negotiations.

7. Battles over internet governance continue, with the US. Government maintaining that it will retain root server control despite the UN Working Group on Internet Governance report recommending decentralized control. See http://worldsummit2005.de for detailed reports.

8. A search of *The New York Times* online for articles on the FCC since 1996 finds 351 results. By contrast, a search of www.indymedia.org for FCC news finds 8,670 articles.

REFERENCES

Alfaro, Rosa Maria (2003) Personal communication.

Association for Progressive Communication (1997) *Global Networking for Change: Experiences from the APC Women's Programme.* London: APC.

Bacon, David (1999) "Organizing Silicon Valley's high tech workers." http://dbacon.igc.org/Unions/04hitec1.htm

Banks, Karen, Sally Burch, Irene Leon, Sonja Boezak, and Liz Probert (2000) "Women in sync: Networking for change: The APCWNSP's first 8 years." http://www.apcwomen.org/netsupport/sync/sync2.html.

Barr, Joe (2004) "Why UN's information society summit is doomed to fail." *NewsForge,* 17 February.

BBC (2003) "Music firm targets 12-year-old." BBC, 10 September. http://news.bbc.co.uk/1/hi/entertainment/music/3096340.stm

Bernier, Ivan (2003) "On the relation of a future international convention on cultural diversity to other conventions." Korean Coalition for Diversity in Moving Images.

Breathnach, Proinnsias (2002) "Information technology, gender segmentation and the relocation of back office employment: The growth of the teleservices sector in Ireland." *Information, Communication, and Society* 5(3): 320-355.

CNN/Money (2004) "IBM giveth, IBM taketh away." CNN/Money, 19 January.

Coalitions for Cultural Diversity (2004) Coalition Currents, v22.

Communications Workers of America (2003) "Update on CWA contract negotiations at Verizon." *Wireless Worker.*

Costanza-Chock, Sasha (2003a) "Our media are not for sale." Free Press Global Communication Project.

Costanza-Chock, Sasha (2003b) "Mapping the repertoire of electronic contention." In Andrew Opel and Donnalyn Pompper (Eds.), *Representing Resistance: Media, Civil Disobedience and the Global Justice Movement.* Westport, CT: Greenwood.

Costanza-Chock, Sasha (2003c) "Data slaves." MA Thesis, Annenberg School for Communication, University of Pennsylvania.

Costanza-Chock, Sasha (2004) "The whole world is watching: Online surveillance of social movement organizations." In Thomas Pradip and Nain Zaharom (Eds.), *Who Owns the Media? Global Trends and Local Resistance.* London: WACC & Southbound.

Creative Commons (2004) "International commons." http://creativecommons.org/projects/international/

Di Martino, Vittorio (2001) "The high road to teleworking." International Labor Organization.

Downhillbattle.org (2004a) "Save Betamax." http://www.savebetamax.org.

Downhillbattle.org (2004b) "iTunes music store: Facelift for a corrupt industry."

Dyer-Witheford, Nick (1999) *Cyber-Marx: Cycles and Circuits of Struggle in High-Technology Capitalism.* Urbana and Chicago: University of Illinois Press.

Eleusa and Sean (2003) "Two weeks against the WTO." *Indymedia Cancún*, 17 September.

Fanon, Frantz (1965) *"This Is the Voice of Algeria." A Dying Colonialism.* New York: Grove Press.

Gandy, Oscar H. (2002) "Data mining and surveillance in the post-9.11 environment." Presentation to IAMCR, Barcelona, July.

Geneva03 collective (2003) "Wipe Out WIPO!" www.hubproject.org. http://hubproject.org/archives/display_by_id.php?feature_id=27.

Gurumurthy, Anita (2004) "Unpacking the knowledge economy." http://itforchange.net/resources/Unpacking.pdf

Halleck, Dee Dee (2002) *Hand Held Visions: The Impossible Possibilities of Community Media.* New York: Fordham University Press.

Halleck, Dee Dee (2003) "Indymedia: Building an international activist internet network." *Media Development.* http://www.wacc.org.uk/modules.php?name=News&file=article&sid=240

Hogue, Ilyse and Patrick Reinsborough (2003) "Information warfare in Miami." *AlterNet.* 1 December. http://www.alternet.org/story/17293

Huron, Amanda and Pete Tridish (2003) "The Fight is On." Free Press Media Reform Network. http://www.freepress.net/lpfm/essay.php

Independent Media Center, Ad hoc Genoa Solidarity Committee (2001) "Response to police raid on Genoa social forum and IMC Italia offices." 23 June. http://amsterdam.nettime.org/Lists-Archives/nettime-bold-0107/msg 00525.html

Indymedia Documentation Project (2004) "Indymedia debate at next five minutes." http://docs.indymedia.org/view/Global/NextFiveMinutes

Indymedia UK (2003) "For free movement and free communication." indymedia.org.uk; http://www.indymedia.org.uk/en/2003/05/108951.html

International Federation of Journalists (2003) "Justice denied on the road to Baghdad: Safety of journalists and killing of media staff during the Iraq War." International Federation of Journalists. http://www.ifj.org/pdfs/iraqreport2003.pdf

International Intellectual Property Association (2004) "IIPA's 2004 'Special 301' Recommendations, including preliminary trade loss estimates and piracy levels for 2002-2003." http://www.iipa.com/pdf/2004_April_08_losses_full.pdf

International Labor Organization (2001) "The information technology revolution: Widening or bridging gender gaps?" ILO Communication, 10 January.

Keck, Margaret E. and Kathryn Sikkink (1998) *Activists Beyond Borders: Advocacy Networks in International Politics.* Ithaca, NY: Cornell University Press.

Khor, Martin (2003) "Statement by the third world network on the events of the final day of the Cancun Conference." Third World Network. http://twnafrica.org/news_detail.asp?twnID=523.

Kidd, Dorothy (2002) "Which would you rather: Seattle or Porto Alegre?" Presentation for OURMedia/NUESTR@SMedios, Barcelona, July. http://www.ourmedianet.org/papers/om2002/Kidd.om2002.pdf

Kidd, Dorothy (2003) "The independent media center: A new model." *Media Development* 4. http://www.wacc.org.uk/modules.php?name=News&file=article&sid=239.

Krim, Jonathan (2003) "The quiet war over open-source." *The Washington Post.* 21 August: E01.

León, Osvaldo, Sally Burch, and Eduardo Tamanyo (2001) *Social Movements on the Net.* Quito: ALAI.

Lessig, Lawrence (1999) *Code and Other Laws of Cyberspace.* New York: Basic Books.

LuchArte (2002) "Por un Argentinazo cultural: Que se vayan todos." 24 June. (Trans. Sasha Costanza-Chock, 2004). http://www.lucharte.com.ar/ArgentinazoCultural.htm

Lyon, D. and Sean P. Hier (2004) "Globalizing surveillance." *International Sociology* 19(2): 135-149.

Martin, Brian (1998) "Against intellectual property." Information Liberation, Challenging the Corruptions of Information Power. Freedom Press: London.

McChesney, Robert W. and Dan Schiller (2002) "The political economy of international communications: Foundations for the emerging global debate over media ownership and regulation." UNRISD Program on Information Technologies and Social Development. http://www.unrisd.org/80256B3C005BCCF9/httpNetITFrame?ReadForm&parentunid=C9DCBA6C7DB78C2AC1256BDF0049A774&parentdoctype=paper&netitpath=http://www.unrisd.org/unpublished_/tbs_/chesney/content.htm

Milan, Stefania (2004) "Brazil: Community Radio Muzzled." *Inter Press Service*, 8 August. http://www.ipsnews.net/interna.asp?idnews=24991

Milberry, Kate (2003) "Indymedia as a social movement? Theorizing the new global justice movements." University of Windsor, Windsor, Ontario. http://docs.indymedia.org/twiki/pub/Global/ImcEssayCollection/Indymediaasasocialmov.pdf

Miller, Dionne Jackson (2004) "Landscape worsening but . . . media watch makes progress." Terra Viva Mumbai. 16-21 January. http://www.ipsnews.net/focus/tv_mumbai/viewstory.asp?idn=248

Mosco, Vincent (1996) *The political economy of communication: Rethinking and renewal.* London/Thousand Oaks/New Delhi: Sage.

Mosher, Mike (2004) "Unionizing Silicon Valley: Victories and cultural strategies." *Bad Subjects* 65, January 2004. http://eserver.org/bs/65/mosher.html

Neil, Garry (2003) "Cultural diversity and the WTO Doha development agenda: Report from the Cancún ministerial meeting." International Network for Cultural Diversity. http://www.incd.net/docs/CancunReport_GN2.htm

Noronha, Frederick (2004) "Going beyond the digital divide orthodoxy." Third World Network Features. http://www.wacc.org.uk/modules.php?name=News&file=article&sid=1460

NOW with Bill Moyers (2004a) "Defining decency: FCC and congress face-to-face." PBS. http://www.pbs.org/now/politics/indecency.html

NOW with Bill Moyers (2004b) "Transcript: February 27, 2004." PBS.

Ortellado, Pablo (2003) "MST wiping windows, Leaving linux." Personal communication.

Ó Siochrú, Seán with Sasha Costanza-Chock (2003) "Global governance of information and communication technologies: Implications for transnational civil society networking." Information Technology and International Cooperation program, Social Science Research Council. http://www.ssrc.org/ programs/itic/.

Rodriguez, Clemencia (2001) Fissures in the Mediascape: An International Study of Citizens' Media. Cresskill, NJ: Hampton Press.

Ronfeldt, David and John Arquilla (2001) "Emergence and influence of the Zapatista social netwar." In John Arquilla and David Ronfeldt (Eds.), Networks and Netwars: The Future of Terror, Crime, and Militancy (pp. 171-199). Santa Monica, CA: RAND.

Ruiz, Luz and Kate Coyer (2003) "Tidal wave Cancún." Presentation to OURmedia/NUESTR@Smedios conference, Colombia, July. http://www.our-medianet.org/reports/Coyer_Ruiz.TidalWave_2003.pdf

Schenker, Jennifer (2003) "Open-source software gets boost at UN." IHT, 11 December.

Skinner, Ewart (1998) "The Caribbean data processors." In Gerald Sussman and John Lent (Eds.), Global Productions: Labor in the Making of the Information Society. Cresskill, NJ: Hampton Press.

Smith, Jackie (2001) "Globalizing resistance: The battle of Seattle and the future of social movements." Mobilization 6(1): 1-19.

Surman, Mark and Katherine Reilly (2003) "Appropriating the internet for change: Strategic uses of networked technologies by transnational civil society organizations." New York: Social Science Research Council. http://www.ssrc.org/programs/itic/civ_soc_report/

UNESCO (2004) "UNESCO and Microsoft plan to strengthen cooperation." UNESCO, 28 January. http://portal.unesco.org/ci/ev.php?URL_ID=1 4202&URL_DO=DO_TOPIC&URL_SECTION=201&reload=1075339322 &PHPSESSID=db102dc7981a5ab670bf3f34dd5d139b

UNI MEI (2003) "List of resolutions adopted." 4th UNI-MEI World General Assembly, Los Angeles, 1-3 October. http://www.unionnetwork.org/ unimei.nsf/c642ee014caad5a6c12568110025fa6a/f185539226781edbc1256df000 3a1eb7/$FILE/ResolutionsAdopted.pdf

Varady, Zoltan (2004) "Hungarian demos against EU copyright directive." Communication to Global Governance Project mailing list. http://swpat.fsf.hu

Veloso, Francisco, Antonio Junqueira Botelho, Ted Tschang and Alice Amsden (2003) "Slicing the knowledge-based economy in Brazil, China, and India: A tale of 3 software industries." MIT & SOFTEX. http://www.softex.br/media /MIT_final_ing.pdf

Wallach, Lori (2003) "The beginning of the end of the FTAA." Statement by Public Citizens' Global Trade Watch. http://www.citizen.org/pressroom/release. cfm?ID=1594

Weber, Steven (2000) "The political economy of open source software." Berkeley Roundtable on the International Economy. Paper BRIEWP140. http://repositories.cdlib.org/brie/BRIEWP140

Werde, Bill (2004) "Defiant downloads rise from underground." *The New York Times*, 25 February.

Whitney, Jennifer (2005) "Make media, make real trouble: What's wrong (and right) with Indymedia." *LiP Magazine*, Summer 2005. http://www.lipmagazine.org.

Williams, Bob and Morgan Jindrich (2004) "On the road again—and again: FCC officials rack up $2.8 million travel tab with industries they regulate." The Center for Public Integrity. http://www.publicintegrity.org/telecom/report. aspx?aid=15

Wilson, Mark (1998) "Information networks: The global offshore labor force." In Gerald Sussman and John A. Lent (Eds.), *Global Productions: Labor in the Making of the Information Society*. Cresskill, NJ: Hampton Press.

World-Information.org (2005) "Urban futures: Global Bangalores." http://world-information.org/wio/readme/992021819/1112363129

WSIS (2003) "Declaration and action plan." Geneva: WSIS.

AUTHOR INDEX

SUBJECT INDEX

Printed in the United States
131020LV00002B/30/A

9 781572 737310